ar on Drugs
anzania

The War on Drugs in Tanzania

Prohibition and Punishment

Dane Degenstein

LEXINGTON BOOKS
Lanham • Boulder • New York • London

Published by Lexington Books
An imprint of The Rowman & Littlefield Publishing Group, Inc.
4501 Forbes Boulevard, Suite 200, Lanham, Maryland 20706
www.rowman.com

86-90 Paul Street, London EC2A 4NE

Quoted interviews from the author's fieldwork are anonymous to protect the interviewees' identities.

British Library Cataloguing in Publication information available

Library of Congress Cataloging-in-Publication Data

Names: Degenstein, Dane, 1986- author.
Title: The war on drugs in Tanzania : prohibition and punishment / Dane Degenstein.
Description: Lanham : Lexington Books, 2022. | Includes bibliographical references and index.
Identifiers: LCCN 2022003060 (print) | LCCN 2022003061 (ebook) | ISBN 9781793654199 (hardcover) | ISBN 9781793654205 (epub)
Subjects: LCSH: Drug control—Tanzania. | Drug abuse—Government policy—Tanzania. | Drug abusers—Services for—Tanzania. | Harm reduction—Tanzania. | Tanzania—Social conditions—21st century.
Classification: LCC HV5840.T34 D445 2022 (print) | LCC HV5840.T34 (ebook) | DDC 362.2909678—dc23/eng/20220121
LC record available at https://lccn.loc.gov/2022003060
LC ebook record available at https://lccn.loc.gov/2022003061

Narcotic addiction is a major contributor to crime. Untreated narcotic addicts do not ordinarily hold jobs. Instead, they often turn to shoplifting, mugging, burglary, armed robbery, and so on. They also support themselves by starting other people—young people—on drugs.

We are not without some understanding in this matter, however. And we are not without the will to deal with this matter. We have the moral resources to do the job. Now we need the authority and the funds to match our moral resources.

The final issue is not whether we will conquer drug abuse, but how soon.

—President of the United States
Richard Nixon, June 1971

Africa has recently become a focus of drug trafficking and illicit use, posing a new challenge to international counter-narcotic efforts. Drug trade generates organized crimes, including human trafficking, terrorism, money laundering, dissemination of weapons and cybercrimes. On the other hand, combating drugs will have a huge impact not only in the fight against drugs but also reduction in other organized crimes.

—Tanzanian Prime Minister Kassim
Majaliwa, September 2018

Contents

Acknowledgments

This book is the result of many years of work and the support of a great many people. The work presented here does not represent my efforts but rather the work of so many who supported it in every way and at every step, even when I didn't believe in it.

Stephen Brown is, and has been, a remarkable support. He trusted that I would actually finish the project that became this book and provided more than a little intellectual support. He read drafts, both good and bad, and graciously provided input and comment, making me a much better writer. I am immensely grateful for his support and guidance throughout.

I am very grateful to the many people who provided input, ideas, and support as this book came to fruition. Professor Cedric Jourde, Professor Rita Abrahamsen, Dr. Gernot Klantschnig, and Professor Philippe Frowd all provided incredible comments and support on this project. I am also indebted to a great many scholars who are featured in this book and provided the basis for my fieldwork and findings. Thank you as well to the team at Lexington Books. Having never published a book before, I had many, many questions. Every step of the way, the editorial staff was there to guide me through next steps and provide support. Thanks to Trevor, Shelby, and Sydney!

As with any study completed by a foreigner in Africa, the contribution of local supporters is immeasurable. While the bulk of studies on Africa continue to be undertaken by those not from there, the difference is not in intelligence or talent but in opportunity. Gasto Mgomoka is an accomplished and passionate worker for development in Tanzania, and without him, and many like him I would not have had the connections, the knowledge or the ability to complete this work. Kwame Juma provided extensive support and guidance in Dar es Salaam. His work on behalf of people who use drugs is truly remarkable. To all the other amazing people I met and talked to in

Tanzania who are tireless advocates for people who use drugs and vulnerable populations, I thank you all for talking to me. I don't name everyone here for anonymity, but it is all of your work that drives progress forward. The world needs to better support those who use drugs and the people who advocate for them, keeping up the fight for human rights and dignity even in the face of almost impossible odds. I want to recognize those who do not have equitable opportunities to write about and discuss their own politics, their own country, and their own way forward.

This book also would have been impossible without the support of family. To Bob and Jeanne, who allowed me to live with them during parts of my studies and gave me continued support throughout, I cannot thank you enough. To my Mom, the help you have given financially, morally and just through believing in me over the course of an extended academic career, allowed me to continue this work. To my sister, thank you for showing me the way in pursuing scholarly work, even if it meant sacrifice and risk.

Upon completion of my master's degree, my father passed away suddenly. This event significantly impacted how I felt about going forward with my studies. His memory has accompanied me throughout my work, and completing this makes me wish he was here to celebrate over a beer.

Finally, to my wife Lisa. Without your understanding and patience I would have quit long ago. Lisa has put up with absences, long distance, my stress and complaints. Throughout, she provided me with love and understanding. I am very lucky and thankful to have a partner in life who is supportive and compassionate, and who also shares the important values that guided this work.

This book is dedicated to people who use drugs, in Tanzania and elsewhere. You have all deserved far better for far too long. Tupo Pamoja.

Introduction

INTRODUCING THE WAR ON DRUGS IN TANZANIA

In early 2017, Tanzanian President John Magufuli declared a war on drugs, marking the beginning of a crackdown on drug users that would result in close to 10,000 arrests. The public rhetoric and crackdowns were accompanied by work behind the scenes to reverse some of the harm reduction[1] practices established in the country. When President Magufuli was elected, Tanzania, despite having a limited health-care system, had a growing methadone program with outreach services, needle exchanges, and drop-in centers supporting people using heroin. These services were almost entirely funded by foreign organizations, and were developed in response to the staggering HIV/AIDS rates among injection drug users mainly in the country's most populous city, Dar es Salaam.

When I arrived in Tanzania in 2018, the foreign-funded methadone clinics still existed, but the crackdowns on drug use had clear impacts on the daily lives of people who use drugs, raising costs and making use riskier. The attacks on harm reduction had also resulted in an environment where methadone clinics appeared to be the only option for heroin users. The Tanzanian government allowed these clinics to continue while committing human-rights abuses against drug users and spouting rhetoric demonizing drug use. In essence, the government was doing what so many other states across the globe do to drug users—providing a bare minimum of top-down services for drug users while maintaining the legal, social, and economic restrictions that make their lives incredibly difficult.

Criminalizing drug use makes those who use drugs illegal and their existence a crime to be punished. In Tanzania, drug use is not only illegal, the possession of syringes and paraphernalia is illegal as well. During my fieldwork, I noticed the efforts to marginalize a population who did not fit in with the Tanzanian government's vision for a moralistic state. The reality on the ground contrasted with the international reports on drugs and harm reduction where Tanzania is lauded as a strong fighter against drug trafficking and one of the few sub-Saharan African countries to possess harm reduction services.

In this book, I explore the realities of the Tanzanian war on drugs, considering how drug policy is shaped and created in an African country where heroin use and the services available to the people who use drugs is not widely studied. Illicit drugs in Africa are a growing topic of study, yet much of what is covered can be sensationalist, raising the specter of drugs as a source of chaos and violence, while other studies are mainly medical or clinical, without the necessary political, social, and economic context. As progressive work on drug policy in the West increasingly moves to deconstruct addiction and the war on drugs and rightfully place drug use in the context of systemic racism, colonialism and socioeconomic disparity, few African countries have been subject to similar analysis.

Instead, African drug use is situated within fantastic tropes of corruption, violence and terrorism, devoid of any agency or background. In these narratives, African governments working to shape their own drug policies do not have a place nor do the many activists and people who use drugs fighting for harm reduction and basic rights. Furthermore, the diverse array of actors, from local activists to foreign nonprofit workers, are also not considered as part of the ongoing formation of policies that govern drug use in African countries. In many ways, the small amount of literature on drug use in Africa, mirrors how drug policy itself is crafted—leaving out the voices and concerns of people who use drugs themselves.

This book is about drug policy in Tanzania, specifically the services that are provided to people using heroin primarily in Dar es Salaam. Over the course of several months in 2018, I discussed the realities on the ground for people who use drugs, how they have been impacted by policy change and crackdowns and how top-down interventions meet, or more accurately do not meet, their needs. I found Tanzania to be similar to other countries with harm reduction programs. The only reason these programs exist, even in their imperfect form, is due to years of tireless activism by drug users themselves. The Tanzanian government prior to 2015 seemed open to these activists' concerns, allowing services such as needle exchanges to develop, leading the way in East Africa and spurring Kenyan and South African nonprofits to learn from the Tanzanian model. As I lay out in the coming chapters, however, the positive collaboration between international groups and local activists became a key focus of the Magufuli regime, despite posing little threat to his party or to others.

Arriving in 2018, I was able to observe an important era in Tanzanian politics during which the Tanzanian government tried to reverse the nascent harm reduction model, establishing instead a depressingly familiar war on drugs in the country. A new, harsh leader had emerged willing to speak difficult truths to Tanzanians, actively calling out and shaming drug users and turning the government's attention toward vulnerable Tanzanians to ensure drug use was eradicated and harm reduction policies curtailed. While President Magufuli passed away shortly into his second term, his government's turn toward those who use drugs slowed the advance of more humane policies, led to the mass arrests of people who use drugs and ensured needed supports were interrupted and delayed.

FIGHTING DRUGS: AN INTERNATIONAL CONSENSUS

In this book, I refer to the war on drugs often as a way of describing a suite of policies, an ideology and an attitude which continues to shape the services and supports available to drug users.[2] While the history of using mind-altering substances is long, the 20th century saw the birth of a global project aimed at limiting the supply of drugs and punishing those who use them. The spread of globalization and capitalism afforded the war on drugs a global reach as a policy framework that has proven remarkably adaptable and useful for governments to score political points and control vulnerable populations.

The dream of a drug-free world, a notion posited by the United Nations and many states pursuing their own drug wars, has been reiterated through numerous policies, agreements, and protocols since American President Richard Nixon famously coined the phrase "the war on drugs" in the early 1970s. Although Nixon and his successors used the war on drugs to punish and discipline African Americans, their governments also helped create and firmly establish the idea of drugs as criminal, threatening and inherently evil, epithets that also came to define those who use drugs.

The epistemic linkage of drugs with criminality, the disaffection of youth, corruption, and poverty make the idea of eliminating drug use a way to create a world without these problems. The idea that war-on-drugs policies are the way to create a better world is still the underlying assumption shaping drug policies in most countries around the world, even though there is evidence of increased drug use and availability despite, or because, of these policies. The focus on the need to eliminate drugs among many governments and at the international level, is so pervasive that there is little thought given to the realities of drug use, and the larger socioeconomic situations that shape the ways in which drugs are perceived and used.

Increased drug use globally is unquestioned as an absolute negative and is used as a reason to continue failed supply-side policy. In poorer countries, the idea of drugs impeding development is now a commonly accepted idea, justifying aggressive measures to ensure supply is reduced. In the Western world, dangerous opioid analogues such as fentanyl are now common and, across the globe, new and different supply routes have appeared for other drugs such as heroin and cocaine. There is well-established evidence that policies such as abstinence, prohibition, incarceration and the militarization of borders have clearly failed, priorities for most countries and the United Nations have not changed and remain resolutely focused on reducing the supply of illicit drugs. The few treatment options available for people who use drugs are implemented in the midst of repressive and costly policies which often significantly reduce access to basic services.

The lasting power of war-on-drugs policy is the construction and distillation, by a number of domestic governments and international organizations, of the disparate threads of prohibition and moral panic into a coherent political agenda transferable across cultural and political contexts. These policies, which conservative American governments initially constructed and put in place internationally in the 1970s and 1980s, are now supported more broadly by a number of international organization and governments, such as China, Russia, and the African Union. While the Western world is facing unprecedented rates of overdose poisoning deaths as the result of decades of failed drug policy, countries previously considered peripheral to the global drug war are also facing their own challenges with increased drug use.

Yet, the continued presentation of drugs as an inherent threat at the international level by numerous countries, for the most part, persists in shaping governmental policy and international agreements. Decades of activism to oppose this idea and present people who use drugs in a more compassionate light and advance limited harm reduction supports continue, but are often hindered by a better resourced and supported campaign to maintain the status quo. The assumptions of a war on drugs ideology, which I show in this book as being promoted and reified by governments and international organizations, serves as the continued basis for domestic drug policies across the globe.

LESSONS FROM THE WAR ON DRUGS IN TANZANIA

This book is based on research undertaken in Dar es Salaam, Tanzania in the fall and winter of 2018. While the topic of heroin in Tanzania was gaining scholarly attention, particularly the methadone program, I wanted to learn more about the realities of drug use on the ground. During the course of 2017, as President John Magufuli and members of his government became increasingly vocal about combatting drugs, I also wanted to see how crackdowns on drug use and policy changes were experienced by people who use drugs and by those who work with them. In 2016/2017 President John Magufuli re-created crisis narratives surrounding drug use by echoing the language of the war on drugs and declaring an all-out "war" on substances, drug traffickers, and users (Apolinairi 2017; *Famagusta Gazette* 2017; *Xinhuanet* 2016). Again, the little media attention this garnered outside of Tanzania made it difficult to understand the impacts, and I became very interested in what Magufuli's drug war meant for people who use drugs primarily, but also for the foreign-funded methadone program and the harm reduction supports being offered by Western NGOs.

Tanzania is not often considered a hot spot for drug use in the way producing countries such as Colombia and Afghanistan, or major transit countries such as Mexico, are. However, Tanzania and East Africa in general have become a major route for heroin trafficking since the 1990s, increasing supply in the region and resulting in significant drug use in coastal towns such as Mombasa and Dar es Salaam (see Figure 0.1). Despite the increase in drug use in East African countries, global war-on-drugs policies and their connections with the developing world, save for producing countries, is relatively under-theorized. The lack of scholarly and political interest in the war on drugs in countries such as Tanzania creates the semblance that these states are not engaged and active in shaping policy and contributing to international arguments about how to deal with drugs.

While some scholarly works pay attention to Africa and drugs, they are not always accurate and comprehensive in describing the realities faced by people who use drugs. As noted by Carrier et al. (2012), war-on-drugs rhetoric in regard to sub-Saharan Africa is alarmist, focusing on societal degradation, corruption of youth, and increasing flows of drugs being used to fund criminality and terror. Scholars are often concentrated more on the security aspects of the growing drug trade in Africa, the control of traffic and the potential violence of this trade, as illicit flows have increased over the past two decades through both East and West African ports on their way to destinations in Europe and North America.

Scholars have done ground-breaking work on injection drug use in an East African context as the practice became more common, especially along the Swahili coast (see Sheryl McCurdy 2013, 2016; Reid 2009; Dimova 2016). However, there are no major studies on drug policy in these countries, nor any studies that consider the international and domestic relationships informing their creation and implementation. This book aims to address some of these gaps, specifically focusing on policies toward drugs users, the perspectives of drug users on these policies, and framing a domestic war on drugs within a larger international context.

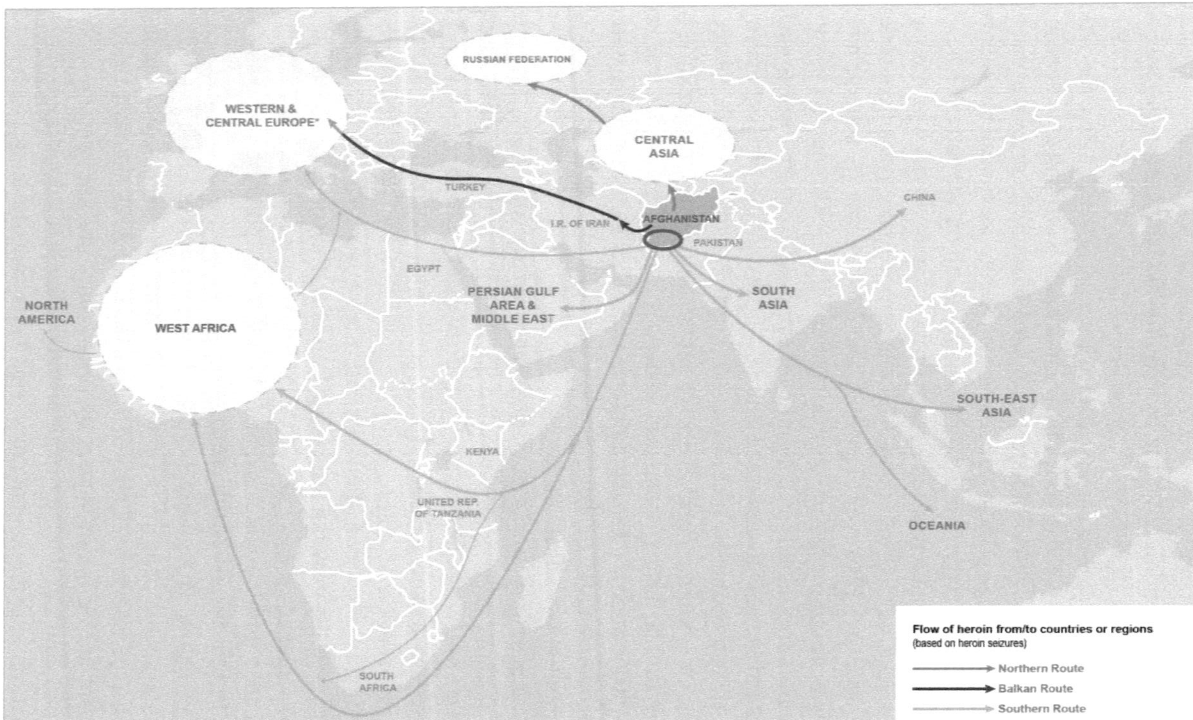

Note: The designations employed and the presentation of material in this map do not imply the expression of any opinion whatsoever on the part of the Secretariat of the United Nations concerning the legal status of any country, territory, city or area or of its authorities, or concerning the delimitation of its frontiers or boundaries. Dashed lines represent undetermined boundaries. The dotted line represents approximately the Line of Control in Jammu and Kashmir agreed upon by India and Pakistan. The final status of Jammu and Kashmir has not yet been agreed upon by the parties. The final boundary between the Sudan and South Sudan has not yet been determined. The trafficking routes represented on the above map should be considered broadly indicative and based on data analysis rather than definitive route outlines. Such analyses are based upon on data related to official drug seizures along the trafficking routes as well as official country report and Annual Response Questionnaires. Routes may deviate to other countries along the routes anc there are numerous secondary flows that may not be represented.

Figure 0.1 Indicative Afghan Heroin Trafficking Routes. *Source*: United Nations Office on Drugs and Crime. (2016). *The Afghan Opiate Trade and Africa—A Baseline Assessment 2016*. Vienna: United Nations Office on Drugs and Crime.

It became clear during my fieldwork that the war on drugs in Tanzania was not simply a short-sighted tactic to gain popularity or appear tough. It was also part of a concerted effort to develop policies and narratives around drug use that erase the larger socioeconomic context underlying addiction and place the blame for societal problems, such as corruption or unproductivity, on drug users themselves. In this book, I explore how the Tanzanian government framed its war on drugs to focus popular anger toward insidious drug use as the agent of the long-standing issues of corruption and poverty, reducing the linkage of these problems to the ruling party. The war on drugs in Tanzania, in the inflammatory language used by the president and the reactionary approach to harm reduction, was outdated, in contrast with the milder language now being used by donor countries and the United Nations Office on Drugs and Crime (UNODC). Repressive language, which justified mass incarceration, police harassment and, in the end, did little to hinder drug supply in the country disappointingly went largely unremarked upon by international and domestic observers, showing how acceptable attacking drug users still is.

Tanzania went from allowing major foreign agencies, such as the Global Fund, space to provide limited supports to people who use drugs through collaboration with local NGOs and activists to outright attacking drug users who posed little threat to the power of the Tanzanian state. As with drug wars pursued by authoritarian leaders elsewhere, I assumed that it was a measure of controlling the populace and a political ploy to instill fear. The small group of local and international NGOs, and the methadone program, seemed largely untouched and it appeared possible that the crackdown on drug use was simply a momentary effort, not seriously aimed at solving issues of drug use and trafficking. What I found surprising, however, was the length and extent the government went to control people who use drugs and reverse the limited advances drug users, in cooperation with International NGOs and donors, had made in accessing basic healthcare and human rights.

This book positions people who use drugs at the center of how drug policy is experienced and examines the impacts of the Tanzanian government's interest in people who use drugs. The Magufuli government's policy changes and repression directly limited access to services for drug users, including those most at risk and living with HIV/AIDS. As a direct result of the Tanzanian government's policy changes and crackdown, drug users faced increased police harassment, were forced into hiding, faced greater difficulties in accessing services and became the target of renewed stigma, systemically and in official rhetoric. While the Tanzanian government did not completely eliminate foreign-funded supports for drug users, it narrowed it to a methadone program and actively hindered any greater social, economic, or harm reduction services for drug users that would improve the lives of drug users.

Many individuals I interviewed heard from clients that they were resorting to riskier drug-use practices, such as needle sharing, were being arrested and harassed by police and had to pay more and go farther to find drugs and access treatment. Despite all of these issues increasing the risks of HIV transmission, and making a population with very high rates of HIV/AIDS harder to reach, organizations with a focus on reaching drug users and supporting them were unable to challenge the government. As I was told during fieldwork, in 2018 drug users still faced harassment, arbitrary detainment, and lacked the outreach and services that are desperately needed.

Another lasting impact of the Tanzanian government's involvement in drug policy is the presentation of methadone as an example of comprehensive treatment and using the program to promote abstinence and cure drug use. This vision for drug treatment goes against the principles of harm reduction and does not meet the needs of many people who use drugs. Seen as a whole—from legal, social, and health-based perspectives—Tanzanian drug policy is a continuation of the war on drugs and is having harmful effects on people who use drugs. In hindering the development of harm reduction supports and eliminating needed services for drug users, the Magufuli regime delayed the development of better supports for people who use drugs. This book will explore how the interventions in the everyday lives of drug users by the government of Tanzania, made life for people who use drugs in Tanzania much worse and contributed to the ongoing normalization of abusing their human dignity and rights.

THE WAR ON DRUGS IN TANZANIA: APPEASEMENT, INTIMIDATION, AND CONTROL

In the coming chapters, I show how the Tanzanian government shifted from allowing evidence-based practices, which reduce the spread of HIV/AIDS and other communicable diseases, toward a harsh, abstinence-based and punitive ideology which has severely restricted services for people who use drugs. The Tanzanian government evaded donor pressure or interference in pursuing this agenda through strategies of appeasement, intimidation, and the exploitation of a neglected policy area. Touting its harm reduction program at the international level to produce a narrative of continued support for drug users to appease donors and foreign agencies the Magufuli regime was, in reality, narrowing the scope of treatment to the detriment of people who use drugs. The government also used intimidation tactics, threatening the work of foreign NGOs working with vulnerable population, which chose to stay and provide limited services rather than risk being kicked out of the country. The Tanzanian government, with limited resources, took advantage of donors' focus on HIV/AIDS and lack of commitment to drug users, to maneuver and achieve a repressive policy agenda without interference.

This book is not just about Tanzania, however. While the war on drugs in that country may appear harsher than a global consensus that is moving toward less punitive policies for people who use drugs, this case study reveals continued global antipathy toward actually listening to drug users and providing the supports they need. Tanzania is contributing to an international consensus that the war on drugs is justified as long as basic treatment is provided. Drug policy in many countries is similar to the Tanzanian approach, of providing the bare minimum of treatment while punishing and imprisoning drug users, forcing abstinence upon them, and leaving many at the mercy of an often poisoned drug supply. In writing this book, I argue for the inclusion of those with lived experiences in changing the repressive drug policies and epistemologies that are being produced by the Tanzanian state and which are shared across the globe.

LOCATING AGENCY IN TANZANIAN DRUG POLICY

This book attempts to explain the Tanzanian government's change in focus, but also will show how the Tanzanian government, despite its seemingly limited involvement in the sector and few resources, was able to impose repressive policies in direct opposition to the foreign-funded services being provided to drug users. While drug policy in Africa is not subject to an extensive literature, there are works in African Studies on a number of areas, such as democratization and securitization, where narratives and policies seemingly imposed on Africa by the West are demonstrated to be produced and constructed by African governments for their own benefit.

Jonathan Fisher sums up the assumptions limiting African agency in the international sphere well:

> African governments arguably have less autonomy over their domestic policy agendas than any other group of state actors in the international system. Dependence on international aid flows, in particular, has historically provided many African regimes with limited room for maneuver in the design and implementation of national policies, given the frequent attachment by donors of highly prescriptive economic and political conditionalities to their much-needed aid disbursements since the 1980s. (Fisher 2013: 97)

As Brown and Harman note, African countries are often viewed as marginalized and inactive in international relations, "victimised, chaotic, violent and poor" (Brown and Harman 2013: 2). I follow their approach by placing an African government at the fore and "focus on interaction, rather than one-way domination" (Brown and Harman 2013: 2). Utilizing such a framework flips the script that I found in academic and policy works on drugs and development. It also allows exploration, not of the Tanzanian government having undue influence in the international sphere, but of how they [the Tanzanian government] operate and act within it, and "what might be done with room for maneuver" (Brown and Harman 2013: 3). By analyzing Tanzania and the war on drugs, I intend to provide another case of African agency in shaping policy and contributing to narratives on development, drug use, and prohibition.

In this book, I describe the material and epistemic roots of the war on drugs, and focus on the dominant war-on-drugs narratives often applied to African countries in academic and policy literature—drugs as a hindrance to development, drugs as a security threat to be eradicated and drug users as a vector of disease, causing health crises. I illustrate that these narratives are being influenced and shaped by Tanzania and are, subsequently, contributing to the continued ideology that drug users still deserve punishment, harassment, and limited access to needed services. In this ideological framework, treatment is a top-down option that does not reflect the perspectives of drug users themselves, harsh measures are justified to limit the supply of drugs in the country, regardless of whether human rights are respected, and incarceration and police harassment are needed to end the corruption drug use causes.

As with other areas where African governments have been shown to be contributing to agendas for their own benefit, such as the securitization of development, in the less prioritized area of drug policy, the Tanzanian government is shaping and determining policies aimed at reducing donor influence and denying human rights to people who use drugs. As I show in later chapters, treatment in Tanzania is not comprehensive and, when coupled with the crackdown on drug users and the elimination of harm reduction services such as drop-in centers, is a model that does not support the needs of people who use drugs.

Contrary to the idea that African governments do not have agency in shaping domestic policy, and influencing international policy norms, this book provides an example that supports the theory of African agency, showing how an African government is able to shape policy despite limited access to resources. As Jonathan Fisher notes, "agency can be carved out by even the most aid-dependent African states" (Fisher 2013: 97). I apply this idea to a highly aid-dependent state, Tanzania, and to the war on drugs, to provide an example of how the Tanzanian government "carved out agency" in driving the development of policies and beliefs that surround drug use, as opposed to the foreign actors working with drug users in the country driving a more progressive agenda.

BROADER IMPLICATIONS

Few studies look at the formation of domestic drug policies and how these interact with global policy debates and norms. Studies on war-on-drugs policies, as they are practiced in many unique contexts, have not fully engaged with countries such as Tanzania, the domestic and international aspects of policy formation, and how unique historical and cultural contexts, as well as unique political moments, impact drug policy change. Questions remain as to why such a suite of defective policies are put in place by governments across the globe, yet few studies have sought to examine their implementation at the domestic level, their effects, and how international influence plays a role. Even fewer studies use the example of a country not considered relevant or important in such policy debates.

In the case of the war on drugs, Tanzanian policy interacts discursively with an evolving discourse on drug use which is adapting to calls for more progressive policy. This adaptation increasingly looks like the Tanzanian war on drugs—concessions to allow very basic treatment for people who use drugs, while continuing to limit access to services and deny the human rights of this population. The fact that Tanzanian government officials have spoken in support of harm reduction abroad while at home, politicians use inflammatory language and the government imprisons and harasses people who use drugs, challenges simple understandings of complex policy issues. Instead of substantive and meaningful change, change which would reverse decades of epistemic assumptions around drug use, war-on-drugs policies are being adapted and changed by government and international institutions. Harm reduction is increasingly integrated into a comprehensive drug control framework, which still includes the failed policies of the past.

Considering the context of Tanzanian politics and history, and the long relationship with donors and NGOs entering the country from outside, I also wanted to illustrate how policy and rhetoric were influenced by these international actors. Tanzania itself has long been donor-dependent and while this dependency is decreasing, health care, and more specifically funding for HIV/AIDS interventions, remain largely funded by donors. The evidence I found of how the war on drugs impacts people who use drugs and how policy is implemented for these people shows that, despite the large number of foreign actors involved in this sector, these actors have done little to challenge the punitive policies of the Tanzanian government.

The Tanzanian war on drugs was not just an attempt to consolidate power, but was genuinely intended to discipline and order society along a strict moralistic vision. Magufuli's challenges to donors were answered at times with threats of removing funding. For the most part, however, donors continue to be along for the ride, supporting top-down and centralized government control in Tanzania, just as they did during the years of one-party rule. The moral nationalism and state power promoted Magufuli was a vision well suited to incorporate war-on-drugs ideology, which always excludes people who use drugs. The war on drugs is an ideology rooted in decades of creating and re-creating the notion of people who use drugs as criminal, weak-willed, and a vector for disease.

A final, but important point underlying my approach is that new policies and epistemologies are needed to support drug users. While the war on drugs has already attracted a number of critiques that I review in the next chapter, few studies consider the deep roots of why these policies are trapped within an epistemic framework that pervades even progressive approaches to drug use such as harm reduction. A new approach that considers the inherent human rights of drug users, their needs, and the systemic factors that prevent them from getting the supports they need is important and this study is intended as just one of a growing number of works that advances a new approach. This book takes drug policy in an African country seriously in how it may shape narratives and influence global policy debates, while also showing how countries with few resources can manipulate and shape a global policy framework. Furthermore, people who use drugs and their perspectives are at the heart of this study and reveal important gaps in how drug policy is currently developed.

PLAN OF THE BOOK

The book is broken down into three sections, the first focusing on an overview of the international war on drugs and harm reduction, the second providing an in-depth case study of the Tanzanian war on drugs, and the final section bringing these two areas together to analyze the war on drugs in Tanzania within a broader context.

The following chapters in the first section focus on both the ideology and institutional structure underlying the war-on-drugs policy framework. Chapter 1 considers the ideological underpinnings of the war on drugs and how, despite its well-documented failures, it remains the epistemic basis of drug policy worldwide. This chapter also explores how harm reduction practices, and the recognition of drug users as individuals deserving of human rights, have faced difficulty in overcoming the strong assumptions associated with addiction, abstinence, and prohibition. Chapter 2 provides the structural basis for the continued war on drugs, examining the international consensus around prohibition, criminalization and control, before situating African states and Tanzania within this global policy framework.

The second section of this book dives deep into the war on drugs that was undertaken in Tanzania from 2016 to 2018 under late President John

Magufuli. In alignment with my research approach, which requires drug policy and use to be understood in a broader social and political context, chapter 3 provides background on the political situation in Tanzania with a focus on some of the major aspects of Tanzanian politics that shaped how drug policy developed in the country. Chapters 4–6 describe the services available to people who use drugs prior to 2015, the strategies and efforts undertaken by the Tanzanian government to pursue a war on drugs after the election of John Magufuli, and the aftermath and outcomes for people who use drugs on the ground.

The final section considers international involvement in providing services to people who use drugs in Tanzania, how the crackdowns were experienced by NGOs, and how the Tanzanian government drove a strategic approach to drug policy that undermined harm reduction, marginalized people who use drugs, and reduced access to needed services. I look at the Tanzanian government's practical efforts to reduce services to drug users, such as delaying harm reduction NGOs from operating in the country. I also analyze three key war-on-drugs narratives, often applied to drug policy in African states—drugs as a cause of corruption, a security threat, and a health crisis—and discuss how Tanzania adopted and reproduced these ideas to suit their repressive approach to drug policy. This section concludes with a reflection on how Tanzania is part of an international system that still prioritizes prohibition, criminalization and anti-human-rights based efforts to limit drug supply, contrary to the informed and humane approaches favored by people who use drugs themselves.

NOTES

1. Harm reduction aims at treatment of addicts rather than punishment, focused on reducing harms associated with drug misuse and not necessarily forcing abstinence. This practice is controversial, with policies such as needle exchanges, safe injection sites, provision of clean drug paraphernalia and Opioid Replacement Therapy (ORT), being seen by proponents of the war on drugs as encouraging drug use (HRI 2016).

2. The war on drugs is a term associated with policies of criminalization and prohibition, with the aim of creating a drug-free world. Policies associated with this approach are often referred to as supply-side interventions which focus on eliminating drugs or limiting their availability through policies including increased border control and policing, harsh punishments for users and traffickers, treating drug use as a criminal issue and raising fears, real and false, as to the realities of drug use (Herschinger 2011).

Part I

INTRODUCING THE WAR ON DRUGS

Chapter 1

An Unwinnable War and an Enduring Global Threat

The War on Drugs

The war on drugs, as a policy framework and ideology, appears to be an inescapable reality in the modern world. The ideas of eliminating drug supply and punishing and stigmatizing those who use drugs are pervasive, forming an epistemology that is rarely questioned. The fact that families and individuals across the world often have first-hand experience with drug misuse has not resulted in empathetic drug policy. Rather, drug policy in most countries remains wedded to criminalization and abstinence, a world where people who use drugs have only two options—punishment or redemption. Basic human rights have not been offered to drug users who are still considered appropriate targets for incarceration, punishment, and enhanced control despite the fact that their vulnerability is produced by the state and illicit drug policy.

Drugs as a substance are vested with incredible moral, economic, and political power. Their very existence is considered a threat to society, prompting the unending desire to erase drugs, and those who use them, from the social landscape. Those who use drugs are likewise considered as threats and failures, unable to contribute to development or be constructive members of society unless they have achieved and maintained sobriety. Furthermore, people who use drugs are often constructed as individuals living in a world free of socioeconomic and historical context, solely responsible for their plight, even as drug policy actively produces endless obstacles and barriers to their survival.

When the war on drugs is positioned appropriately in its socioeconomic and historical context, however, assumptions surrounding drug use can be easily deconstructed and seen for what they are: not evidence-based positions but rather purely ideological beliefs constructed and promoted over the past several decades. The result of the hard ideological lines of the drug war is that harm reduction or alternative approaches do not receive necessary support, while top-down policies based on false narratives trap society in an endless drive to end drug use and harass drug users.

A constructivist approach aims to disentangle the realities of drug policy from the epistemology of the drug war. While acknowledging the materialism of the drug and economies and practices surrounding drug use, constructivism lends more emphasis to the social construction of the material as a threat, how the drug itself, and reactions to it, are shaped socially. This approach deconstructs casual theoretical assumptions such as drugs being a threat to development, drugs corrupting youth and drugs causing criminality, all ideas I argue against in this book. The evidence-based ideas behind harm reduction have challenged the war on drugs yet the seemingly obvious health and economic benefits of this approach have not translated into better policy decisions. The inability to promote harm reduction which, at its most basic form, recognizes people who use drugs as deserving of support, reveals a deep commitment to a war-on-drugs epistemology. At the international level, as Emily Crick states, "the global drug prohibition regime continues to remain pre-eminent despite the wealth of unintended consequences it causes" (Crick 2012: 407). In this chapter I review how, despite its constant and well-documented failures, the war on drugs has remarkable staying power and is being constantly adapted and renewed.

THE RISE OF THE DRUG WARRIORS

The development of international cooperation in combatting illicit drugs has reflected, and subsequently been shaped by, dominant cultural and political attitudes around drug use. The global war on drugs is the evolution of a US-led prohibition and punishment approach toward drug users formalized at the international level through the United Nations over the course of several decades (Paoli et al. 2012). Bryan Roberts and Yu Chen provide a good overview on this war and its major failures, effectively showing the general moral underpinnings (initially emanating from the United States) and assumptions that promote prohibition, mainly viewing drug users as threatening, criminal, and failed elements of society (Roberts and Chen 2013). Works by Barrett (2014) and Wodak (2014) similarly show how the development of a drug-control regime was linked to the post–World War II international order, based on the heavily US-influenced Bretton Woods Institutions. This global regime was formalized through a succession of drug-related protocols passed by the United Nations in 1961, 1971, and 1988 which remain in place today—all focused on the absolute eradication of drugs and the punishment of drug users (Barrett 2014).

The international consensus on drug control is clearly connected to prohibition and supply-side controls. While Collins (2018: 113) writes that this international system "was a reflection of these [cultural] norms, not a determinant," the system is more of a discursive space, shaped by states but also providing a set of policies that could be utilized and followed in domestic spaces. The war on drugs produces crisis narratives, which both create the problem of the drug user and establish a set of punitive policies to deal with them. While the American war on drugs initially appeared as a domestic fight with specific, racialized targets, the assumptions became widespread globally in the 1970s and 1980s. The global consensus on drug prohibition is a result of the deep and long-standing construction of a threat to society and the use of this construction for political purposes.

The term "war on drugs" was coined by Richard Nixon in 1971, formalizing a post–World War II American agenda of limiting the global supply of illicit substances. As has been the case since its declaration, the war on drugs has had implicit racial and class connotations. In seeking election, Richard Nixon courted the silent majority, a group of older, mainly white voters, who feared a perceived rise in crime and the use of substances as a target allowed a population advocating for greater political power, African Americans, to be targeted without being named explicitly (LoBianco 2016). Ronald Reagan continued the fight in the 1980s, increasing punishments and legal restrictions on possession and further entrenching discrimination in the United States.

At the height of the HIV/AIDS crisis in the United States, along with increased criminal penalties for drug possession, Reagan also systematically removed supports for mental health, addiction, and social programming (Cummings 2012). When Reagan announced his war on drugs in 1982, "less than 2 percent of the American public viewed drugs as the most important issue facing the nation" (Alexander 2011: 49). Reagan framed the issue, created a crisis and, with the passing of his Anti-Drug Law of 1986, "effectively criminalized addiction" (Cummings 2012: 418). One of the most cited examples of how this law acted discriminatorily was the difference in penalties for possession of crack-cocaine, primarily used by marginalized African Americans, versus lesser penalties for cocaine possession, used more often by wealthier, white Americans (Cummings 2012). In the early 1980s, "FBI antidrug spending increased from $8 million to $95 million" and "DEA [Drug Enforcement Agency] antidrug spending grew from $86 to $1,026 million" (Alexander 2011: 49). As is clear today, the war on drugs did not eliminate drug use, but it helped produce massive inequality and a prison industrial complex mainly designed to destroy the lives of young, African American men. Alexander (2011) compares this outcome to the Jim Crow era, given its clear similarity to the control and punishment of African Americans following the American Civil War. In the United States in 2006, the war on drugs was a major factor in the rates of incarceration for black men being 1 in 14, compared to 1 in 106 white men (Alexander 2011: 98). These remarkable inequities do not include even more onerous challenges faced once out of prison such as stigma, probation, and legal costs.

Prohibition and moral panics against illicit drugs existed and played out for political ends in other countries over the 20th century, but it was the war on drugs, initiated by the Nixon Administration for "short-term domestic political reasons," that left its footprint in the design of many other prohibitionist pushes throughout the globe (Wodak 2004: 800). Salvador Santino Regilme argues that the Uribe and Duterte regimes, in Colombia and the Philippines respectively, "deployed the notion of peace as a justificatory discourse for increased state repression, intensified criminalization of the drug problem, and the reluctance of the state in embracing a public health approach to the proliferation of illegal drugs" (Regilme 2020: 1). The resilience of the American-style war on drugs can be seen in these countries, and in a number of states pursuing increased control and power. Most efforts to control drugs still follow the same model and have the same effects: criminalizing marginalized groups, stripping the social and cultural context away from drug use, increasing violence and vulnerability among drug users, and stigmatizing specific substances and the people that use them. Despite its cost and ineffectiveness, the approach remains a hallmark of repressive regimes who have grasped the political power of the war on drugs.

Internationally, the 1988 UN Convention Against Illicit Traffic in Narcotic Drugs and Psychotropic Substances, encouraged the approach of criminalizing drug use while weakening social and health supports for people who use drugs. This convention was perhaps the clearest distillation of war-on-drugs policies at the international level, as it encouraged criminalization and punishment, reflecting the growing social anxieties around widespread drug use and the Reagan-era tough-on-crime agenda. Meetings to continue the approach established through UN conventions now take place under the guise of the UNODC and are enforced by the International Narcotics Control Board (INCB). Therefore, this drug-control regime which I refer to as a global war on drugs (also referred to as the "Vienna consensus"[1]) in the last century can now be seen as a general international agreement, reaffirming a "zero-tolerance" approach to drugs practiced by a majority of states across the globe (Boister 2016).

The failures of this widespread approach are well documented, as are the negative impacts of the war on drugs. As Alex Wodak argues, not only has drug prohibition not addressed the problems it was aimed to solve, namely reduction in "drug production, drug consumption, or drug related harms," it has resulted in unforeseen consequences such as "a rise in organized crime, corruption, high social and healthcare costs, and the deaths and incarceration of thousands of drug users" (Wodak 2014: 191, 193–195). Even drugs considered mild, and with long histories of cultural use and value such as Khat, are targeted resulting in unforeseen consequences both economic and social. As Gezon (2012) points out Khat, a stimulant milder than coffee yet illegal in many Western countries, became the focus of alternative crop programs which unfairly painted Khat farmers as lazy and the drug itself as the cause of food insecurity. In reality, Khat farmers simply supplemented their existing crops with a profitable one, using areas that did not impact their output of edible crops (Gezon 2012). As with alternative crop programs elsewhere, the programs do not work nor do they recognize the context and reasons for producing the drug in the first place—reasons that can range from deep cultural significance to profits which are largely driven by the war on drugs itself.

In many ways, the war on drugs, and those it leaves as victims in its wake, are a reflection of modern capitalism and neoliberalism. As Seddon (2010) argues, it is impossible to discuss drug use and control without considering global systems and modern liberalism with its focus on choice and free will. Dominic Corva, in discussing the spread of the war on drugs in the Americas, sees this war as inseparable from neoliberalism and illiberal governance, with the "economic vulnerability" produced by neoliberalism creating the conditions for the punitive war on drugs and prison industrial complex targeting victims of this neoliberal order (Corva 2008: 181).

The war on drugs is analogous to neoliberal capitalism, in which free markets ensure an unrestricted flow of drugs, and a corresponding system of punishment and control that allows for the politicization of drug use and the criminalization of poverty. The epistemic basis of drug use in this system is similar to neoliberal capitalist ideology, where race, stigma, discrimination, and systemic poverty are erased as factors in drug use, just as they are erased in why certain segments of society are more prone to poverty and poor health outcomes. The war on drugs paints drug use as an individual failure, rather than one linked to numerous socioeconomic factors. Dominic Corva goes as far as to call this "the penalization of poverty," stating "poverty is criminalized, de facto, but it would be more accurate to say that narco-delinquency tends to produce excluded populations, and the spaces they inhabit, as criminal" (Corva 2008: 191).

The ongoing failures of the policies enforced internationally have resulted in more space for alternative discourses. However, the major UN positions enshrined in 1961, 1971, 1972 and 1988 remain the basis of response to global drug control (UNGASS 2016 Draft Outcome Document). The 1961 Convention on drug control, which remains in place today, "provided the international law basis for the 'war on drugs'" allowing "a stricter and wider ranging multilateral framework that became more prohibitive in focus . . . [introducing] widely accepted penal obligations for states to criminalize, under their domestic law, unlicensed production and trade and extended the pre-existing control regime to the cultivation of opium poppy, coca and cannabis" (Bewley-Taylor 2011: 16).

In understanding the international drug control system, it should be considered "a complex global governance phenomenon rather than simply as a matter of international relations in which the sovereign nation-state is the basic unit of analysis" (Seddon 2010: 116). In this complex international space, most authors (Seddon 2010; Wodak 2014, 2017; Roberts and Chen 2013) agree that prohibition and the moral judgment of drugs users has had a disproportionate influence in shaping drug policy. The most recent gathering, UNGASS 2016, revised prohibitionist language of a society free of drugs to "a society free of drug abuse," with major prevention and treatment options recognized (UNGASS 2016 Draft Outcome Document). Harm reduction is still not mentioned. The main concerns with limiting drug use internationally are overwhelmingly connected to reducing criminality and the spread of HIV/AIDS. It is the latter concern that has attracted the most funding in sub-Saharan Africa, rather than supporting interventions shaped and requested by people who use drugs themselves.

Along with the domestic political benefits of executing a war on drugs, the expansion of international control and power into other countries allowed for an extension of US soft power, coinciding with the rise of a powerful global security apparatus (Pembleton 2016: 30–31). While the United States does not always have a positive relationship with the United Nations, the United Nations has been a partner in supporting the execution of this soft power throughout the globe. This support comes not only through the chairing and holding of meetings that reiterated the prohibitionist message of conservative American presidents, but through the creation of an office, the UNODC, dedicated to prosecuting the war on drugs in partnership with member states.

Illicit drugs are depicted as a source of crime, corruption, and waste so often that they are an easy political target across wide spectrums of society. People impacted by drugs want the scourge to end and many less impacted by drug use want their families and children to be safe. The connection of drugs to vulnerable populations also allows an appeal to a majority with less understanding of the complex socioeconomic dynamics that produce severe addiction. Ending the war on drugs and reversing these ideas requires much greater resources and attention than most governments are willing to give. Thus, the war on drugs remains in place in various assemblages throughout the world today.

THE COST OF PURSUING A DRUG-FREE WORLD

Despite efforts toward prohibition over past decades, there has been little change in the production and trade of illicit drugs such as heroin. On the contrary, riskier uses such as injection drug use have spread. Drug use and availability are more prevalent than ever. In 2011, the UNODC estimated between 149 and 271 million people between 15 and 64 years old had used an illicit drug at least once (Degenhardt 2012: 56). Global opioid users were estimated to number approximately 12 and 21 million and, in 2007, the number of people who inject drugs (PWID) was estimated to be between 11 and 21 million people (Degenhardt 2012: 56–57). In 2017, UNODC reported the range of people who have used drugs at least once in the previous year to be between 201 to 341 million (UNODC 2019). Of this sample, 53.4 million people used opioids (UNODC 2019). Overall, UNODC estimates that global drug use has increased by 30% since 2009 (UNODC 2019).

These numbers continue to be difficult to estimate, but they have risen. The 2019 drug report I am citing utilized more in-depth studies in Nigeria and India, where data has been difficult to access, to show that the numbers of opioid users and people with drug-use disorders is much higher than previously estimated (UNODC 2019). The problem seems to be growing, yet harm reduction language continues to be limited, and is not mentioned at all in this report. While references to health and treatment are many, this is only in regard to dealing with the spread of diseases such as HIV and hepatitis C.

Furthermore, even though the war-on-drugs approach has apparently been slowing, higher use now also includes use of harsher drugs such as fentanyl and rising opium and cocaine use in countries with previously lower levels. The emergence of more potent drugs and their prevalence reflect a global market in which more potent formulas are more profitable. Small amounts of fentanyl are easier to mail or smuggle and produce much more profit than larger quantities of heroin. The increase in the use of more potent drugs is directly linked to the illegality of their more common predecessors.

The use and misuse of illicit drugs has grown, and the use of more harmful drugs and riskier methods of use has firmly spread over the past several decades of international cooperation to end the illicit drug trade. This trade, estimated to be valued at $400 billion in 2005 (Roberts and Chen 2013: 107), was estimated to be worth $426 to $652 billion in 2017, one-third of all estimated transnational crime (Global Financial Integrity 2017). Global cocaine production increased 25% in 2017, mainly driven by Colombia despite a peace deal now in place with the FARC (UNODC 2019: 7). In 2018, the third largest amount of opium was produced since UNODC began monitoring production in 1990, and would have been higher had there not been a drought in Afghanistan, which produced 82% of the world's opium supply (UNODC World Drug Report 2019: 13).

Efforts to limit the market and supply have clearly failed but it is also important to note the greater impacts that have accompanied supply-side efforts as compared to providing treatment or supports for people who use drugs. The criminalization of drug use results in drug users engaging in riskier use, pursuing more dangerous activities to pay for illegal and expensive drugs, discourages them from seeking access to treatment and exposes them to violence and infectious disease (Degenhardt 2012: 65). As prohibitionist policies often adopt a one-size-fits-all approach, the results are similar despite differing cultural and social contexts, hurting vulnerable minorities the most.

A BETTER WAY: HARM REDUCTION

While injection drug use did not spread to most sub-Saharan African countries until the 1990s and 2000s, in Western countries, with longer histories of injection heroin use, harm reduction emerged earlier. As the AIDS crisis unfolded in the 1980s, the rates of infection among PWID rose sharply due to needle sharing. In response to government inaction, a grassroots movement to support the health and well-being of people who use drugs spread.

Harm reduction, inspired by both concern for public health and the scientific evidence that sharing needles dramatically increases the transmission of infectious diseases, was controversial when it emerged in the 1980s. Countries in Europe, however, experimented and successfully implemented some harm reduction programs that were proven to reduce transmission of HIV/AIDS and other diseases such as hepatitis C. Harm reduction practices such as needle exchanges and education within a public-health framework slowly became "institutionalized across much of northern Europe, Canada and Australia" (Gowan et al. 2012: 1252).

Although harm reduction can take on different meanings, the initial goal among harm reduction activists was simply the need to save lives regardless of drug use or misuse. Harm reduction can be complex with competing definitions. For the purpose of this study, the common definition here gives an idea of the general concept: harm reduction is a set of "policies, strategies and services which aim to assist people who use legal and illegal psychoactive drugs to live safer and healthier lives. Reduction of use is a personal choice, and can be supported, but is not expected or required" (Canadian Drug Policy Coalition 2016). This definition, however, is sometimes disputed, mainly the idea that individuals do not need to cease their drug use. As Gowan notes, "current wisdom on harm reduction with injection drug users may be moving towards abstinence as a desired endpoint" (Gowan et al. 2012: 1253). This focus on abstinence, while not an undesirable goal in itself, cannot be understood in the absence of a number of social constructs around what abstinence means and how this can be achieved.

Relapse and continued use after treatment or during opioid replacement therapy can be common. However, the belief in a final cure to this disease, and its eradication through abstinence, remains the dominant perspective in formulating drug policies. The use of the harm reduction concept, aimed at supporting the human rights of drug users, is in this way made to be simply another mode of quickly getting people off of drugs and eradicating drug use. Harm reduction can be tied to a prohibitionist approach, in which an end to drug misuse is necessary, as "the notion of a self-managing drug user inherently problematizes the epistemological basis of the drug war" (Gowan 2012: 1257). In other words, even progressive approaches to treating drug use are often practiced within a larger framework promoting abstinence and prohibition, despite this not being the end goal of activists and people who use drugs. The epistemic belief in ending drug use is so strong that it has made it difficult for harm reduction to be considered in the absence of the eventual end of addiction and drug use altogether.

Within harm reduction, there can also be tension between more fulsome and radical approaches, such as the decriminalization of illicit drugs, and more realistic approaches in a prohibitionist context which focus only on the health of people who use drugs. This tension is a result of harm reduction being opposed to common societal assumptions constructed around the use of certain drugs that are lasting and difficult to reverse. Harm reduction also goes against decades of wisdom that see drug use as a crime and source of ills. Harm reduction advocates do not focus on ending and eliminating drug use and do not pursue abstinence or view drugs as a social evil. In this way, harm reduction can be considered as possibly encouraging drug use or approving of it, a contrast to the moral judgment and stigma of criminalization and abstinence-based approaches.

Due to these challenges, the harm reduction activism of drug users, which was often explicitly antiestablishment and political, did not receive official recognition from governments early on. While the literature reflects the aspirations of a more radical approach to deconstructing drug use, early harm reduction efforts were largely volunteer-based and only received state support begrudgingly. In Canada, harm reduction programs existed for decades before the government officially endorsed even basic harm reduction measures. The Canadian policy model, while more inclusive of harm reduction approaches now, still resembles what Philippe Bourgois describes as "on the one hand neo-liberal repression, and on the other hand bio-medicalized, patronizing welfare services" (Bourgois 2003: 35). It is important to see this model as largely representative of the contradictory state of the war on drugs I describe in this book—harm reduction services offered within a realm of largely carceral and biomedical approaches.

Even as harm reduction is shown to be effective in reducing mortality, overdoses and preventable disease, promoting it remains difficult today. In order to overcome conservative concerns, harm reduction advocates often have to settle on the less controversial aspects of this approach. For example, harm reduction is often promoted as a purely public-health intervention, keeping people who use drugs alive and ensuring risks to the general public are reduced. This perspective highlights the cost efficiency of preventing HIV as compared to treating it. Despite the well-established evidence supporting these facts, which are not necessarily controversial—after all it is a proven way to save public money and provide health care to citizens—governments have often continued to oppose even these basic harm reduction measures. This lack of acceptance reveals the deep attachment to prohibition, abstinence, and individualism inherent in the war-on-drugs approach and in the making of drug policy.

Simplifying drug use and harm reduction to a medical model allows governments with little interest in the human rights of people who use drugs a way in which they can show support for drug users while not addressing any of the underlying issues. In this model which describes Tanzania well, "poor and working class drug users are treated elsewhere as zombies only curable through forced treatment" (Gowan 2012: 1258). The motive is not to improve their health and well-being, based on their own agency, but to get them off drugs as quickly as possible so they do not impact the larger society.

Despite the uphill battle, grassroots activism has achieved several victories and is the major reason for the presence of harm reduction in policy debates today. Unfortunately, these minor advances in supporting people who use drugs must exist within the larger paradigm of prohibition. The major assumptions of the war on drugs persist, emphasizing individual power to get clean through the 12-step program or through sticking to treatment. These programs may work for some people, but the underlying assumption of individual responsibility belies the "political economic and cultural forces, rather than pharmacology" that shape drug epidemics (Bourgois 2003: 31). Considering the larger contexts surrounding heroin use does not dismiss the addictive nature of psychoactive substances, but rather acknowledges what the war on drugs has erased, its socioeconomic and cultural context.

Harm reduction is favored by anthropologists but has carried less weight in advancing a progressive drug policy. As pointed out in *Drugs in Africa,* while scientific approaches have "had the desirable effect of undermining deeply held and remarkably resistant racial arguments regarding the appeal and effects of drugs, it has unfortunately also marginalized understandings of the importance of context—social, historical, cultural, economic—in shaping the patterns of drug use and abuse" (Ambler et al. 2014: 5). The science behind psychoactive substances has advanced knowledge of addiction greatly.

However, the findings can easily be co-opted and subordinated to support the ineffective policies of the past. Furthermore, scientific interventions, while evidence-based, are still subject to political and social realities that are often messier and more challenging to address.

Harm reduction is not necessarily meant to solve all of the issues associated with illicit drug use. The need for reform, however, recognizes the different contexts in which people use drugs. Expressing harm reduction as a medical treatment and curative for heroin addiction results in a one-size-fits-all approach and distorts what harm reduction is. In Tanzania, this means methadone treatment is the only choice for heroin users, despite different patterns of use, different backgrounds and different reactions to treatment. It is a victory to provide at least this level of service to people with drug-use issues. However, in the longer term, understanding the human rights and contexts of use could help support interventions beyond methadone treatment that support meaningful and better lives. Instead of working toward this expanded view, most countries prefer to simplify or keep harm reduction limited, clinging to the notion of ending addiction and drug use as the only way forward and continuing to practice the ineffective and inhumane policies that surround their limited harm reduction interventions.

LASTING NARRATIVES OF DRUG USE AND CONTROL

As is clear throughout this chapter, working to reverse the global drug war has proven difficult, despite the evidence of its failures being well known. Drug use is inextricably linked to ideologies and beliefs which create an epistemology of addiction, crisis, and control. At its most basic level, decades of working to eliminate drug use has constructed the addict as at fault for policy failures. The war on drugs paints addicts "as an isolated agent who perversely acts against his own self-interest" and removes the social context, placing drug users firmly in the neoliberal order where personal responsibility is paramount (Acker 2010: 72).

This personal weakness supports the case for criminalizing drug addiction, but also underlies scientific models which consider addiction a disease impacting specific individuals who are different from "normal" people. As Acker argues, the advancement of research in neuroscience and the reward centers of the brain to advance the disease model of addiction has furthered understanding of drug dependency, but is still linked to prohibitionist stances, promoting a model that does not answer questions of social context and systemic inequalities (Acker 2010). New forms of understanding addiction have supported progress toward more humane treatment, but have not meaningfully challenged the constructed notion of addiction which is inherently othering.

Over the past century, many concerned members of society have genuinely seen drug use as a source of social ills (Paoli et al. 2012). Given the correlation of drug misuse and mental illness, poverty and social alienation, drugs serve as an easy target on which to lay blame for the complex systemic and social inequities underlying addiction (Roberts and Chen 2013). Despite the awareness of the harms and social disintegration caused not by drugs but by discriminatory drug policy, war-on-drugs rhetoric has proven politically useful to some populist leaders. In its strong messaging and large educational component, it has created societal support for continuation of these policies—only now that overdose deaths related to opioids have reached epidemic levels has the larger public become more concerned.

The tension between the realities of drug use and addiction, which have become even more present in the West with the influx of powerful synthetic opioids, and the political usefulness of narratives associated with drug control result in a diverse range of outcomes internationally and domestically. A recent example can be illustrated in Canada, where Stephen Harper's Conservative government strongly opposed harm reduction and evidence-based policy for almost a decade, even as potent opioids and addiction rose among marginalized and middle-class citizens alike. In 2014–2015, as the leading opposition party advocated legalization of marijuana, Harper injected over $7 million into an anti-marijuana advertising campaign which, while consistent with his ideology, could also be seen as a tactic to appeal to his demographic base (Cheadlc 2015). Harper's campaign served immediate political interests, but also rehashed unscientific and dubious fears that marijuana is a highly addictive substance and legalization would endanger children (Macqueen 2015). Eventually, Canada and several other states legalized marijuana but the lasting effects of ideological framing has done little to significantly change attitudes toward drug use.

Some conservative politicians in the West have now grudgingly accepted that more support for treatment is necessary, particularly as synthetic opioids and painkillers impact society at all levels. Increased public pressure to address the crisis may have seemed a perfect moment to implement comprehensive harm reduction measures. Populists wishing to utilize the war on drugs face the challenge of maintaining the image of a tough drug warrior while also responding to real concerns over rising opioid poisoning deaths. The solution has often been maintaining legal restrictions while supporting treatment options that are focused on curing the addict and getting people permanently off of drugs.

At the center of all of this policy are the drug users themselves. The construction of the "addict" in war-on-drugs ideology remains a powerful image of deviance, potential violence, and irredeemable moral failure. Such a construction makes it easy to forget that drug users are being denied basic human rights because of something they consume themselves, a remarkable fact only due to constant social conditioning that obscures what the war on drugs is really about. The construction of the addict in this way allows redemption narratives to take hold through quasi-religious recovery narratives and, for those who cannot or refuse to stop using, the constructed idea of the addict allows the state to focus immense and violent power on those who would dare to corrupt otherwise stable societies. The process of othering and demonization through the social ideology around drug use is "forged through the intersection of media messages and images, official announcements, and community discursive activities, demonized understandings of drug users emerge that serve as a rationale not only for state punishment but for segregation, discrimination and ethnic inequality as well" (Mosher and Atkins 2007 as quoted in Singer and Page 2014: 19).

Several scholars are working to challenge this ideological construct. Bruce Alexander for example, used rats to illustrate the greater social and emotional aspects of drug dependency. His experiments, which would be famously dubbed "rat park," showed that rats increased their opioid usage in isolation and, when surrounded by plentiful food, companionship and better conditions, ceased using opioids. Alexander has long tried to illustrate that addiction is not an individual problem but is social, "a way that large numbers of people adapt to the breakdown of psychologically sustaining culture under the global influence of free-market society" (Alexander 2012: 1475). Addiction narratives are rooted in discourse on drug use yet there is little attention given to the broader causes of drug use being embedded in deeper social and economic issues. As Singer and Page note, "so compelling for them [suburban-dwelling Americans] is this constructed image [the addict], despite being loaded with inaccuracies as revealed by social scientific research, that it has helped drive continued media accounts, the enactment of drug-related laws and policies, the incarceration of massive numbers of individuals, the withdrawal of the social safety net for the poor, and the disruption of minority communities" (Singer and Page 2014: 52). While referring to the United States mainly, this quote reveals the major stakes of drug policy which has made otherwise compassionate citizens okay with the state using immense resources to target people who use drugs and deny their basic humanity. The fears around drug use are so pervasive that drug war policies, that would otherwise be horrifying, often find support among families whose own friends, neighbors, siblings, parents, and children are the target. Unfortunately, the image of the addict or the individual who dies in the drug war is thus seen as a sad, agentless victim of addiction, rather than a complex human being targeted by their own government.

CONCLUSION

The war on drugs persists as a discursive ideological framework—producing, perpetuating, and reproducing false narratives. In describing the origins of the international framework of drug control, I showed the constructed and lasting narratives that shape drug policy still. The epistemic underpinnings of the war on drugs are similar to capitalism—an alternative is so unthinkable that only minor allowances can be made to give people who use drugs the same treatment as anyone else. Just as the philanthropy of billionaires obfuscates the true inequality of modern capitalist accumulation, so does the implementation of limited harm reduction supports obfuscate the myriad of systemic attacks on people who use drugs.

In criminalizing the drug supply, governments position people who use drugs outside of mainstream society while removing the supports needed to ensure their survival and provide the basic human right to health and well-being. The creation of the addict as a criminal, a weak or a diseased individual, discards their rights and humanity and strips away the structural, systemic, and socioeconomic realities of drug use.

This chapter depicts the ideological tenets of the war on drugs while also describing the basic and obvious need for harm reduction services or rather, services that actually meet the needs of people who use drugs. In the next chapter I will show how these ideological constructs are wedded to an international system of drug control which, when combined, create a regime very difficult to overcome. This context also sets the stage for how the war on drugs unfolded in Tanzania over the past few years, why an anti-human-rights approach found purchase in the country and how a global system conspires to deny drug users rights despite their continued tireless activism.

NOTE

1. The Vienna consensus refers to the headquarters of the UNODC in Vienna, Austria, where these meetings and conferences supporting a war on drugs have been held (Boister 2016).

Chapter 2

The International War on Drugs

Regimes of Control and Mechanisms of Enforcement

The war on drugs, in addition to the strong epistemic assumptions outlined in the previous chapter, is also enshrined in real policies and institutions at the international level. Large-scale, international consensus on policy issues consists of an assemblage of actors, from the United Nations to the Drug Control and Enforcement Agency, which has branches across the globe, to the states and NGOs that participate at global policy forums on drug use and have varying levels of access and power to influence policy. Out of this large array of actors with differing and sometimes complementary motives, it can be difficult to see a coherent consensus emerge. What is clear, and what I show in this chapter, is the difference in power between those advocating for the status quo and those advocating for reform.

Despite anti-war on drugs advocates becoming more vocal in challenging the war on drugs in recent years, the consensus at the international level remains settled on the prohibitive control of drugs. States with war on drugs agendas are active, while states with real interest in harm reduction are opting out or, in some cases, simply being apathetic and allowing the war on drugs to continue. The UN is a site upon which states and civil society actors converge to contest and support war on drugs policy. While contestation exists, the global consensus forged at the UN still largely reflects the failed policies of the past.

Building on the previous chapter, I argue that the war on drugs is rooted in both ideological and material power, with greater resources and efforts aimed at continuing it rather than turning toward an alternative set of policies. The weight of supply-side efforts, as compared to the support for harm reduction, actively contributes to the epistemic belief that drugs need to be fought in the failed policies of the past. This chapter shows how the combined structural and ideological drug war overshadows the needs and perspectives of people who use drugs themselves.

I close this chapter by considering the role of African States in the global war on drugs, and how drug war narratives and ideologies are foisted upon, and discursively shaped, by Countries with seemingly little power and agency. While not often considered a part of this global war, I look at how Tanzania is situated within the broader structures and ideology of the war on drugs and begin to explore the agency of Tanzania within the war on drugs. I describe how policy in the country is influenced by international actors and how, despite the strong donor and international presence in serving drug users, the government of Tanzania pursued an archaic and dangerous drug war.

THE UNITED NATIONS OFFICE ON DRUGS AND CRIME (UNODC)

The mission of the UNODC is apparent in the epistemic linkage the name suggests, to "contribute to the achievement of security and justice for all by making the world safer from drugs, crime and terrorism" (UN Budget 2018/19). Formed in 1997, the UNODC was another iteration of global drug control, continuing the work outlined in the UN conventions and the INCB. Over the past several decades, these institutions have maintained relative policy coherence with most countries adhering to prohibitionist policies, often referred to as the Vienna consensus (Boister 2016). As late as 1998 the slogan for the UNODC remained "a drug free world: we can do it!" (Wodak 2014: 191). The year 2008 was set as the date when this goal would be realized (Jelsma 2003). Harm reduction is a difficult shift for the global body and, despite increased recognition of treatment and healthcare for people who use drugs, reducing supply and prohibition remain the main goals of the agency.

In recent years, however, authors have noted that the Vienna consensus may finally be breaking (Collins 2017; Jelsma 2016). In the 2019 World Drug Report, the executive director of the UNODC notes, "Successes identified amid the many, formidable problems that countries continue to face in grappling with drug supply and demand highlight that international cooperation works" (UNODC 2019: 2). The increased evidence of the failure of decades of cooperation seems impossible to ignore as several states are grappling with increased levels of opioid poisoning deaths.

Many countries continue to ignore this evidence, however, and reaching global consensus in tackling drug use has resulted in the production of approaches that appease more conservative countries. The power imbalance that ensures the continuation of the war on drugs does not necessarily reveal the greater influence of countries such as Russia and China in advancing repressive policies, but rather the apathy of states invested in harm reduction willing to meaningfully back this approach. Furthermore, many of the countries supposedly favoring a less repressive approach still see the value in war on drugs style policies, failing to recognize the contradiction between these policies and their half-hearted implementation of harm reduction. Countries such as Canada now support harm reduction at the federal level, yet, remain silent on repressive policies in other countries and are committed to keeping drugs and drug users illegal.

The result of disagreements at both ends of the spectrum is a growing lack of interest in working collectively. As many conservative actors remain in positions of power, there is a less concerted effort to overhaul a system and rather a number of countries opting to work within a failed system while pursuing their own agendas. As Boister (2016) argues, the current drug control system is more open to flexibility for limited change within the existing consensus rather than meaningful reform. This consensus, however, favors the status quo, as it is easier and requires less effort to overturn than a commitment to reform the system. In this context, harm reduction measures are introduced domestically in spite of the UNODC and INCB, not because of their active support (Paoli et al. 2013: 933). Only after decades of advocacy and rising overdoses due to more potent drugs did some Western countries realize the importance and effectiveness of harm reduction interventions such as supervised consumption sites.

Ultimately, the fractured consensus means there is no concerted international effort to move forward with harm reduction, and there is no country acting as a champion outside of their domestic sphere. In countries around the world, prohibition remains the epistemic assumption of policy with advocates of a different approach carving out a small niche at the bottom that does not overturn this policy framework, but rather fights to fit within it. At the same time, despite this fracturing and the increased distance between hard-line approaches and the movement to save lives through harm reduction, the need for global cooperation is still seen as important in reaching the unreasonable goal of global drug prohibition. As Barrett writes, "Advocating for a move towards policy based on the aims of the UN naively presumes genuine government support for those aims, when in fact other political agendas are more likely the drivers of current drug control efforts" (Barrett 2010: 143). As the idea of a drug-free world has persisted for decades, the current drug-control regime serves the purposes of those resistant to meaningful reform.

This overall consensus has not meant there has not been any progress toward more humane policies. For example, acceding to pressure to respond to the health and well-being of drug users, the budget of the UNODC for 2018/2019 reflected an increase of 140.5% for a balanced approach to drug use, $265 million to support the health of this population through prevention, treatment and HIV/AIDS prevention (UNODC 2019). However, in the same year, the UNODC provided $210.9 million for countering transnational organized crime through training and support of anti-trafficking activities, $45 million to counter corruption, $69.1 million to strengthen justice an legislation governing drug trafficking, $28.8 million for terrorism prevention, and $672.4 million for alternative livelihoods programs in six drug-producing nations (UNODC 2019). Taken together, these funds are four times the amount of funding put toward treatment and prevention. Furthermore, of the treatment and prevention funding, harm reduction is an even smaller portion.

From 2010 to 2018, 31% of the UNODC budget went toward countering illicit drug trafficking and transnational organized crime, 6% went toward terrorism prevention, and 8% went toward countering corrupting (UNODC 2020). 26% went toward "prevention, treatment and reintegration and alternative development" and no percentage was allocated for harm reduction (UNODC 2020). The UNODC, epistemically linked to a number of areas from corruption to terrorism and organized crime, has competing priorities which do not fit well with a harm reduction focus.

For African states, this is even more challenging as the focus of the UNODC lends itself to the greater challenges of violent conflict, corruption, and protection of resources from illicit trafficking (UNODC Strategic Vision for Africa 2030). As such, the strategic vision for Africa only devotes a small section to the health and well-being of people who use drugs which is more concerned with continuing failed efforts to limit drug supply on the continent. UNODC involvement in sub-Saharan Africa is focused on the threat of drugs to stability in the region, and to development. A 2016 UNODC report admits that "the links between insecurity and the drug trade in Africa remain largely unknown" and "the extent of drug related corruption within government structures in Africa is difficult to assess" (UNODC 2016: 9). These admissions reflect the lack of evidence to support the overwhelming focus of the UNODC on targeting corruption and insecurity as the largest threats to African states.

While increases in treatment and prevention funding are positive, it is confusing how the strengthening of criminal justice, punitive measures, and anti-trafficking efforts are not considered directly opposed to supporting drug users. These measures criminalize drug use, result in increased police harassment and limit drug supplies, increasing the likelihood of riskier use and overdose and limiting access to services. The epistemic linkage to prohibition-style approaches is so strong that legal discrimination is not seen as antithetical to providing treatment and harm reduction services, but rather a complement to a full suite of policies for drug users.

A progressive approach among politicians across the globe appears to be acknowledging drug users' humanity while maintaining their commitment to policies that rob this population of their basic human rights. What is certain when it comes to drug policy, is the lack of engagement with people who use drugs themselves in shaping the top-down measures that impact their lives.

Contradictory policy-making is magnified in the case of Tanzania where the strengthening of strong criminal justice interventions, the regulation of drugs and the harsh penalties for users seriously limit the potential positive impacts of any treatment programs.

The UNODC is stuck in an old paradigm, counter to the health and protection of vulnerable populations. While it may appear that the old war on drugs is no longer relevant, the continuation of policies associated with it provides a context and framework that can be easily utilized and revitalized in domestic contexts. The war on drugs is being revisited and seeing support from populist authoritarian leaders around the globe, who see a benefit in continuing this war for their own purposes. The way the international paradigm of drug control unfolds in the domestic environment of Tanzania mirrors this broken consensus. The government is able to pursue harsh and punitive policies against vulnerable populations while touting limited methadone and anti-HIV programs that exist in a very restricted space. Again, there is no evidence that the disproportionate amount of funding going toward counter-terrorism, anti-trafficking, and justice globally have had significant effects in either limiting drug supply or countering poor governance. As I show below in examining the 2016 meeting between UN member states to discuss drug control, these policies are not likely to change anytime soon.

THE UNITED NATIONS GENERAL ASSEMBLY SPECIAL SESSION ON DRUGS (UNGASS)

In 2016, the UNGASS took place, with high hopes that this international gathering would be an opportunity for large-scale reform of a broken system. Ultimately, the outcome document of the 2016 UNGASS was a disappointment for many hoping for more substantial change. The document illustrates the grand undertaking of changing a very long held set of international norms. As noted by a participant in the proceedings, the outcome document "reaffirms the unrealistic goal of a society free of drug abuse" and "does not explicitly mention harm reduction despite this being agreed UN General Assembly language" (IDPC 2016: 3). Indeed, the outcome document only reaffirms past resolutions, reiterating all of the misguided policies they proposed, highlighting the individual nature of drug misuse, raising concerns over criminal and "safety problems" that arise from drug use and doubling down on the determination to "eliminate the world drug problem" (UN Res S-30/1:2016).

The global make-up of the UNGASS conference showed divisions, with countries such as Norway voicing more progressive ideas and other countries remaining staunchly set in some extremely conservative perspectives. One example of the divide between conservative and progressive approaches was the push for evidence-based harm reduction by New Zealand while "Indonesia called the death penalty an 'important component' of the country's drug control policy" (IDPC 2016: 5). Russia lobbied to have harm reduction left out of the outcome document completely, and insisted on the "inclusion of language that deferred to national legislation—a carveout that appears 18 times in the document—effectively giving member states the room to ignore what the document actually suggests" (Oakford 2016).

The outcome document reasserted the need for "increased international cooperation [which] demands an integrated, multidisciplinary, mutually reinforcing, balanced, scientific evidence-based and comprehensive approach" (UN Res S-30/1 2016:2/21). The document then underscores previous conventions and leaves out harm reduction, the leading science-based approach (Oakford 2016). As a compromise among states, the opposition to harm reduction and reassertion of a prohibitionist approach led by countries such as Russia and China ensures old assumptions of drug misuse are kept alive even as some states attempt to pull back from these harsh approaches.

Collins argues that it was in fact the NGOs and civil society reformers who sabotaged meaningful reform in the process due to their "highly myopic view of political reality, an absence of understanding of what 'reform' actually meant and the active sustenance of a selective group-think" (Collins 2016: 89). Collins' view does not reflect the implementation of harm reduction over the past several decades. In the past, it has always been civil society, pushing for radical and more extreme measures to address the health and human rights of people who use drugs who have advanced dialogue, even though it often means settling for less aggressive reforms. As I discussed in the previous chapter, with a lack of political will and genuine interest from more powerful actors, these organizations must dilute their political aims and achieve change slowly and partially, resulting in the piecemeal advancements we have seen in the past decades. Collins blaming harm reduction advocates is disappointing when compared to the slowness of governmental actors to implement their suggestions. The real issue is the lack of recognition of the needs and human rights of people who use drugs worldwide, and the lack of commitment of countries to make the health and safety of this population a priority.

The continued epistemic dismissal of people who use drugs as deserving of rights and services underlies this situation. The frustration with the UNGASS outcome document was not the fault of high expectations among reformers but rather the re-emergence of hard liners and the lack of commitment among more sympathetic governments to get fully behind harm reduction. The most progressive members of the meeting were frustrated and, rather than continue fighting for a difficult consensus, simply stated their desire to pursue their own position. This was summed up by the prime minister of New Zealand, Jacinda Arden: "We have a number of challenges that are quite specific to New Zealand and particular drugs that are present, but also on taking a health approach. We want to do what works and so we're using a strong evidence base to do that" (Nichols and Mason 2018). This statement, while understandable, does not bode well for consensus on a more progressive approach forming. Perhaps, as suggested by David Bewley-Taylor (2018: 1227) in regard to the legalization of marijuana, states must begin to practice "respectful non-compliance" as a way to challenge the international drug control regime. In any case, the slow moves toward dismantling international drug control do not signify a major change any time soon.

UNGASS AND AFRICA: FURTHER CHALLENGING CONSENSUS

While the African Union (AU) does not actively align with the strongly prohibitionist approaches of some countries, the role of Africa in shaping these documents is itself riven with disagreement among member states. The African Group contribution to the UNGASS outcome document reflected a compromise between more hard-line countries such as Egypt and countries more open to harm reduction such as Kenya and South Africa. The contribution of the AU is important to highlight as, while "the global hierarchies of political and economic power that were established under imperialism and colonialism, and in which Africa was subordinated, did not cease with political independence," the AU is increasingly using its role to "exert influence" and "using common negotiating positions, in order to produce negotiation outcomes that benefit weak African countries" (Zondi 2013: 19–20). The AU documents being developed prior to UNGASS mentioned harm reduction, stating the effective approach to drug policy combines "supply reduction, demand reduction, harm reduction and international cooperation" (African Union Common African Position 2016: 4). The outcome document focused instead on hopes for a drug free world (IDPC 2016: 5).

Rogers Siyanga, head of the Drug Control and Enforcement Authority of Tanzania made remarks highlighting Tanzania's focus on harm reduction (Siyanga 2016). His comments center around health, "Tanzania's harm reduction strategy aims in reducing social and health risks associated with drug use through a set of interventions such as needle and syringe exchange,

HIV counseling and testing, anti-retroviral therapy, opioid substitution therapy, prevention and treatment of sexually transmitted infections, condom programmes, vaccination against viral hepatitis and treatment of tuberculosis" (Siyanga 2016). While promising, Siyanga's statement highlights simply the extension of regular health supports to people who use drugs, not necessarily showing any legal, social, or further interventions that would support people who use drugs. As I show in following chapters, the statement also presents gaps between international rhetoric, domestic policies, and the realities on the ground.

Ultimately, the Africa Group outcome document to UNGASS erased all references to harm reduction, reasserting the three previous UN international drug conventions and re-stating previous AU positions. The document further states "governments are encouraged to enhance close collaboration between their law enforcement authorities and their national HIV/AIDS authorities so as to ensure that the challenge of HIV/AIDS among injecting people who use drugs us properly addressed in accordance with national law" (African Union Common African Position 2016: 4). As with Russia, the importance of national law is emphasized, allowing countries to voice their commitment to combatting HIV/AIDS, while maintaining regressive laws that seriously impact populations most at risk, such as PWID. As a final contribution, the document notes that "misguided policies such as the legalization and decriminalization of certain drugs will hinder the ongoing efforts to combat the illicit production, trafficking and abuse of drugs and also the balanced approach which Member States have committed to in the global fight against the world drug problem" (African Union Common African Position 2016: 4). This reworking of a more progressive approach, directly opposed to even moderately progressive policy, was the input of several African countries to UNGASS 2016.

The UNGASS outcome document, due to the interventions of hard-liners such as Russia and contributions such as the African Union document outlined above, does not mention harm reduction and remains focused on treatment only as a means to end the threat of drugs. The document highlights a continued fracturing in the global consensus on the approach to drug use. As was evident at UNGASS, the UNODC continues to portray drugs as a criminal threat, conflating the harms caused by drugs with drugs themselves rather than the policies governing their use and trade.

At another gathering of the UN general assembly, in follow-up to UNGASS 2016, former US President Donald Trump again asserted the threat of drugs to development and stability, with no mention of development, only treatment in order to support recovery (Global Call to Action on Drug Control 2018). Trump, through a mixture of coercion and persuasion, attained 130 signatories on a document affirming the failed approaches of the war on drugs

(Nichols and Mason 2018). This strange intervention is generally reflective of Trump's scattered drug policy, but also a performance, recalling the more active days of US hegemony in the global drug war. While the United States continues to uphold fears of the drug threat, the inflammatory language of the war on drugs has become increasingly critiqued, especially in the midst of the opioid crisis and other failures their policies have wrought. Drug warriors now, with the exception of some loud populists, seem to prefer to prosecute their drug wars quietly.

Member states during UNGASS and in subsequent meetings have continued to show a lack of meaningful support for reform. Civil society actors and harm reduction organizations, sometimes made up of people who use drugs themselves remain a strong voice pushing the debate forward. Hard-line leaders and governments have been able to continue to uphold prohibition even as their countries face higher and higher levels of drug-related harms.

SETTING THE STAGE FOR DRUG USE IN TANZANIA

The inclusion of Tanzania in a global order of states participating in the war on drugs, which countries continue to support both materially and ideologically, allows for an examination of African agency in a new context. The structure outlined above, in addition to the epistemic basis of the war on drugs, is present in Tanzania and in African states which, while not often considered part of global policy formation, are constituent parts of the international system.

Before turning toward a more in-depth discussion on the Tanzanian war on drugs in the next section of this book, it is important to link the structures and ideologies presented above to Tanzania, and to African states more generally. To link Tanzania to the war on drugs is important, as the international is present in Tanzania and vice versa. This is also a novel way to explore both African agency and the global drug war. Despite the large amount of literature on both of these topics, the idea of African agency has not been applied to the war on drugs, and the global war on drugs has not been considered in analysis of the war on drugs in Tanzania.

In applying this theory to the war on drugs, the dichotomy between a policy framework foisted upon Tanzania, or a repressive agenda authored solely by John Magufuli, is replaced by a complex arena in which actors work to influence drug policy. The example of the Tanzanian war on drugs is a novel example of how the Tanzanian state, through its practices and its framing of drug use in the country, is able to participate in "processes of interaction [that] produce and reproduce social structures" and "shape actors' identities and interests" (Wendt 2000: 81). My objective in using Tanzania as a case study is to "assess the causal relationship between practice and interaction . . . the relationship between what actors do and what they are" (Wendt 1992: 424).

While I return to this idea in part III, a goal of this book is to mix the international and the domestic, exploring the interaction between international actors, local activists, political leaders and people who use drugs themselves. In Tanzania, this discursive approach involved understanding the outcomes on the ground and how policy discourses and practice constitute the identity and reality of Tanzania as a moral, strict, developmental state in which drug use is nonexistent. Deconstructing common narratives reveals that drug policies are the actual causes of corruption and criminality.

The application of African states within a global system was most popularly theorized by Bayart (2000) whose idea of extraversion focused African actors, often seen as dependent on the West or a global system, within this system, influencing and undertaking modes of action that served their own interests. While Bayart utilized this concept to discuss African politics, extraversion is also a useful way to understand how the war on drugs in African countries is applied and to how drug policy is developed. Extraversion considers African societies over the longue durée and, as I mentioned earlier, when applied to drug use, takes into consideration the economic, social, and cultural contexts in which drugs exist along with the insertion of African states into a global drug economy.

A perspective inclusive of a larger historical and socioeconomic scope avoids a war-on-drugs, one-size-fits-all discourse in which drugs proliferate in a void where generic policies, often originating in Western countries, are implemented. When countries replicate, utilize and reproduce a dominant discourse, this strategy can be considered not as a reflexive obeisance to greater powers, but a viable strategy in itself. The theory of extraversion allows for a more integrated analysis of the war on drugs in which African countries are not passive receptors of a discourse but active interpreters and promoters.

When considering the structures outlined in this chapter, extraversion situates Tanzania within a global order of states—working among a number of actors to influence policy outcomes and to be free to pursue its own domestic goals. The domestic space of African countries is subject to competing discourses in a unique way as it is inclusive of numerous actors, international and domestic, within one geographic space, collapsing distances between a simple line of external versus domestic political influence. The presence of numerous international actors within the domestic space, however, does not necessarily reduce the ability of African political elites to exert power. As Pommerolle notes, the "monopoly of international relationships enjoyed by ruling powers' was compromised, with new actors and agents, not subverting extraversion but rather making dependency and this relationship more complex" (Pommerolle 2010: 267).

Contrary to the idea that policies are foisted upon African states by pushy donors, Anderson and Fisher argue that "securitization is not something that the west has done to Africa, but rather a set of policy imperatives that some African governments have actively pursued" (Anderson and Fisher 2015: 132). Using the idea of the "donor support rationale" structure, Fisher argues,

> both donors themselves and African governments, along with other actors, interact with it [the donor support rationale]—and can therefore influence the focus and the nature of it. The securing of agency by these governments in this process might consequently be demonstrated by their successful focusing and refocusing of this rationale around donor support "narratives" more favourable to continued direct assistance. (Fisher 2013: 538)

Likewise, in Tanzania, Magufuli's illiberal project demonstrated an ability to pursue his own agenda within frameworks and narratives seemingly produced and prioritized by the West. Drugs as a development threat, a health crisis, or a source of corruption are all narratives that the Tanzanian government can actively produce and use as ways to shape foreign understandings of drug use in Tanzania and support Magufuli's desire to reduce services for people who use drugs. Jonathan Fisher argues in the case of Uganda, that the failure of donors to shape policies and Museveni's ability to pursue his own agendas despite the asymmetry of power is under-theorized in regard to other policy areas (Fisher 2015). There are linkages, and often blurred lines, between what appear to be sovereign policies—in both African and Western countries—and the discursive formation of policies between these governments. If African agency is considered in terms of the confluence of structure and agency, the war on drugs is an example where an African state, through its use of limited agency, frames drug use and justifies policies to produce structures that uphold the war on drugs.

In other words, the presence of international actors in areas such as the war on drugs, may complicate the relation of African governments to the international, but it does not always reduce the influence of African powers to steer their own course in creating and enforcing policies. For instance, the policies enacted by the Magufuli government, while still maintaining an authority and connection to the international sphere, exist among competing actors with interests both aligned and opposed to this policy framework. As I show in later chapters, drug policy in Tanzania is not only subject to a number of actors and narratives, but, is also an area where the government still exerts control, demonstrating a more complex example of dependency and extraversion in policy creation.

CONCLUSION

This chapter helps to illuminate not only the epistemic force behind the war on drugs, but also the international structures that persist in upholding this failed war. The UN system, while slowly realizing the greater need for treatment and harm reduction, is ill-suited to pivot toward a more humane policy framework. The UNODC must maintain a focus on criminality, with drug use as a global issue remaining either a criminal problem to be solved through interdiction efforts, or a medical crisis to be left to agencies such as UNAIDS. Drug use, harm reduction and greater services for people who use drugs, however, is a human-rights issue. The recognition of this again is a challenging proposition among member states that consider drug use to be a crime, a moral failure, a threat to development, and a cause of corruption.

It is also important to include African state actors within this policy framework. Both as separate entities and collectively, African states contribute to international discussions on drug policy. To date, these interventions have tended to be conservative; however, there is also rhetoric that boasts of health interventions from states such as Tanzania that contribute to these debates. In analyzing rhetoric at the international level, the confluence of international and domestic policy formation can begin to be seen. In the following section, I turn to Tanzania as a case study both in how drug policy gets translated from the international to the domestic, but also as a case of African agency, with an African state pushing an agenda within this global system. I dive deep into the domestic context before returning, in the final section, to the international to show the complex and deep ways in which international and domestic policy frameworks interact.

Part II

THE WAR ON DRUGS IN TANZANIA

Chapter 3

Maisha ya Bongo

Aid, Development, and Corruption in Modern Tanzania

In Tanzania, we had our problems, but at least we knew where we were going.

—Individual interview 14,
October 2018, Mikocheni

Since independence, Tanzania has often been dependent on foreign aid and, throughout global political trends including Cold War diplomacy, free-market liberalism and aid tied to human rights, the Tanzanian state has had a remarkable ability to manage relationships with donors, despite corruption and mismanagement. The ruling party, Chama Cha Mapinduzi (CCM), has remained in power since independence, utilizing donor supports as a source of legitimacy and control.

The rise of John Magufuli altered this path, with his more overt style of populist politics exposing the authoritarian nature of the CCM. However, this was also not necessarily a major departure from the long-standing themes of post-independence Tanzanian politics. The late John Magufuli represents continuity with the past, as he leaves a legacy of trying to erode democracy and centralize power around himself and his party. When I arrived for fieldwork, Magufuli's government was in the process of returning a party that had never fully committed to democratization to full authoritarianism, making it clear that the CCM was truly unwilling to reduce its grip on power.

My intent in this chapter is not to offer a full and comprehensive history of Tanzania since independence, which would be a book in itself. This chapter instead illustrates some of the key trends that informed Magufuli's rise to power and the government's campaign against drug users. The aid dependence of the Tanzanian ruling party and the ability of the elites to manipulate donors and pursue an agenda focused on the centralization of power is part of the reason the government has been able to crack down on drug users with little opposition.

These centralizing and authoritarian tendencies have been present throughout Tanzanian politics since independence, setting the stage for Magufuli's populist authoritarian policies and his ability to increase his control of the Tanzanian state. This authoritarianism was based on exclusion, misogyny, and the targeting of marginalized groups such as people who use drugs. This chapter establishes the main themes—aid dependence, centralized power, manipulation of donor funds and exclusionary nationalism—that have shaped the Tanzanian government's approach to people who use drugs and the broader political context of the Magufuli era, during which the war on drugs took shape.

INDEPENDENCE AND THE PARTY OF THE REVOLUTION

Mainland Tanzania gained independence in 1961 as Tanganyika, a former colony of Germany, before being incorporated into the British Empire following World War I. In 1964, Tanganyika merged with Zanzibar to become Tanzania. The country emerged out of colonialism under the leadership of Julius Nyerere and his party, the Tanganyikan African National Union (TANU). Nyerere was educated in Fabian socialist ideals at the University of Edinburgh and, after independence, he began to enact his vision of African socialism through a number of policies, most well-known perhaps is Ujamaa, meaning familyhood.

Following the Arusha Declaration in 1967, Ujamaa became official policy and Tanzanians were forcibly resettled in villages throughout the country. This process accelerated in the 1970s and, by 1976, 95% of Tanzanians lived in Ujamaa villages (Jennings 2002: 511). Ujamaa is often credited with improving basic social programs and instilling a nationalist unity that has kept Tanzania relatively stable compared to its neighbors. The forced nature of the program of Ujamaa, however, was also repressive and authoritarian. As Leander Schneider writes, Ujamaa combined "Nyerere's and other politicians' paternalistic view of the peasantry and their belief that they knew best; a framing of postcolonial politics as an ongoing struggle against neo-colonial enemies" (Schneider 2014: 319). Economically, it was inefficient and left the country in an economic crisis that was so severe in the 1980s, Nyerere chose to step down and make space for the country to turn toward market liberalization (Kelsall 2002: 56). Despite Nyerere retiring, Ujamaa left an imprint on Tanzanian politics and, as Dan Paget (2020) suggests, the unfinished nature of Nyerere's post-colonial project of liberation was taken up by Magufuli to justify his own state-led, top-down authoritarian project.

The CCM (Chama cha Mapinduzi or the Party of the Revolution), has ruled over Tanzania since independence. The party officially emerged in 1977 when the two dominant parties in Tanzania, the Afro-Shirazi Party (ASP) in Zanzibar and TANU joined to form a single party. The CCM, with its ties to Nyerere and memories of the national unity he represented, has been in power ever since, with Nyerere himself closely tied to the party until his death in 1999. Nyerere's successor, Ali Hassan Mwinyi (1985–1995), courted foreign direct investment (FDI) and opened the formerly socialist country to structural adjustment programs aimed at saving the economy through rapid privatization. While economic growth did slowly improve, the privatization of government-owned industries fostered growing economic gaps in the country and erased some of the benefits of a socialist economy such as improved education and better healthcare. The transition to a free-market economy coincided with an opening of the political system as well. In 1991, Nyerere encouraged Tanzania to allow opposition parties to participate and engage in the first multiparty elections in 1995.

This opening up did not necessarily improve the lives of Tanzanians. Under Mwinyi, business contracts were awarded in less than transparent circumstances and the rapid transition from a socialist economy to a more liberal one was more beneficial to CCM elites than Tanzanian citizens. As Sheryl McCurdy and Pamela Kaduri have pointed out, this period marked the beginning of the involvement of Tanzanian elites and organized crime in the trafficking of drugs such as heroin (McCurdy and Kaduri 2016: 313). The transition period over the 1990s set the stage for the corruption and economic mismanagement that has plagued Tanzania since.

The election of Benjamin Mkapa (1995–2005) accelerated this trajectory as he aggressively pursued foreign investment and economic liberalization. Again, this period was characterized by widespread corruption as elites benefited from the new economic environment (Warioba Report 1996). By the time Jakaya Kikwete (2005–2015) was elected, Tanzania was marred by corruption scandals and remained highly aid dependent. During Kikwete's rule, the country's Human Development Index (HDI) increased slowly, but the country is still low on the scale and is one of the poorest countries in the world. Furthermore, corruption continued to be a defining characteristic of CCM rule, implicating high-level officials and politicians in the party on numerous occasions. Elections are held every five years, and are considered by most international observers to be free and fair. However, the CCM remains dominant and has comfortably won every election despites its failures to bring development to the country and end corruption.

AID DEPENDENCE, CORRUPTION, AND DOMINANCE

The CCM won the first multiparty elections in 1995 and, though many Tanzanians maintain a deep loyalty to the party, its victories depend on patronage and intimidation. In a country that has had only one party in power since independence, the reach of the CCM into all aspects of Tanzanian life and the resource inequality between opposition parties and the ruling party, ensure its continued dominance. Authoritarian tendencies have been a part of Tanzanian politics even under the benevolent rule of Nyerere. Most CCM politicians and leaders, however, have been content to allow opposition parties to operate relatively freely. Allowing opposition is perhaps easier as these parties have never been particularly threatening. In the 2005 elections, President Jakaya Kikwete won 80.3% of the vote and the CCM took 264 of 307 seats in the national assembly (Kelsall 2007). In 2010 these numbers were reduced, with Kikwete receiving only 63% of the vote. However, no effective opposition challenge materialized (O'Gorman 2012: 318). By 2015, an opposition coalition formed and managed to garner a greater share of the vote, but the CCM still won by a comfortable margin, with 58% of the vote (Paget 2017: 153).

The CCM is deeply embedded in Tanzanian society, particularly in rural areas. Its popularity at the rural level can be summed up by a survey of farmers whose main reasons for CCM support were: "they performed well during one-party rule, they are the only strong party, they have maintained peace, they identify with farmers and they brought us independence" (O'Gorman 2012: 320). The CCM integrated itself early on into these modes through Ujamaa and one-party rule and remains strongly linked to many levels of Tanzanian society. As Tim Kelsall notes, "The sheer size of the party, its penetration of society, the administration, and the economy, means that the CCM exerts a massive gravitational pull on the political system, drawing in Tanzanians of all races, religions, regions, ethnicities and classes" (Kelsall 2007: 529). As observers of Tanzanian politics have noted, it can be difficult to find where the Tanzanian state begins and the CCM ends.

One benefit attributed to one-party rule is that, compared to its East African neighbors, Tanzania has experienced little in the way of ethnic or religious conflict and has avoided large-scale electoral violence and divisionism. Despite the peaceful decades following independence, structural adjustment and the transition to multiparty democracy in the 1990s, Tanzania has not seen the scale of development that could be expected in a country rich in natural resources. GDP increased following structural adjustment, and has continued to rise yearly over the past decade. However, development for many has continued to arrive slowly for Tanzania's over 60 million people, the majority of whom live in poverty.

The government's inability to leverage stability and access to resources for development has not been due to a lack of donor interest or support either. Tanzania has long been considered a donor darling and was often seen as a source of optimism among the donor community throughout its history (Tripp 2012; Jennings 2002). Early on, even in the midst of Cold War politics, the authenticity of Nyerere's mission was attractive to Western liberals. Ujamaa as a policy, despite its clear ideological bent and questionable economic benefit, attracted Western support, as "NGOs and activist groups, intellectuals, academics, development workers and members of the British public, all came to regard Tanzania as the great hope for the developing world" (Jennings 2002: 529). What was remarkable about this support, as Michael Jennings argues, is that, in supporting Ujamaa, a top-down, government-initiated process, groups like Oxfam "became part of a process that withdrew power and representation from the grassroots" (Jennings 2002: 530).

As I discuss below, the roots of Tanzania's close relationship with development partners is based on the CCM's powerful ability to assuage donor concerns over a lack of development, while determining donor priorities and involvement in the country. Despite decades of failed development, Tim Kelsall, writing in 2010, notes that this positivity remains and "there is considerable optimism about the country's prospects" (Kelsall 2010: 56).

According to OECD data, Tanzania has been a major aid recipient since independence, in 2016 fourth among sub-Saharan African countries. From 1990 to 2010, it was one of the largest recipients of multilateral and bilateral aid in Africa, second only to Ethiopia (Tripp 2012: 1). The relative neutrality of the country and lack of conflict have drawn donors including the Nordic countries, Canada, and the United States. Following democratization, the stability of the country and its willingness to take on structural adjustment policies ensured its continued status as an attractive aid recipient (Tripp 2012). As shown in figure 3.1, the government has increasingly prioritized independence, reducing its overall aid budget and increasing aid toward projects rather than as part of central government general budget support (GBS). However, this has not necessarily meant the government is not still highly reliant on aid through project funding and in the health sector which, as shown below, has fluctuated but remained. Furthermore, it does not mean that donor dollars previously provided, particularly in the health sector, are being replaced with this reduction.

Foreign aid is particularly important to the health sector and plays a key role in Tanzania's efforts to combat HIV/AIDS. NGOs operating in the health sector make up a large part of Tanzania's health system generally. As Michael Jennings notes, "In many African countries, the state (colonial and post-colonial) could only expand its services across large parts of their country through co-opting voluntary services, making them, in effect, a

Financial Year	Foreign Aid (USD 2015 billions)	% of central government expense	Foreign Aid as % of Health Budget
2009	3.008	70.05	unavailable
2010	2.844	70.09	37
2011	2.233	49.01	32
2012	2.629	50.78	28
2013	2.188	50.68	38
2014	2.444	32.99	26
2015	2.600	36.69	26
2016	2.349	34.83	18
2017	2.585	30.84	26

Figure 3.1 Foreign Aid to Tanzania as a Percentage of General and Health Budgets. *Source*: Author created with data from World Bank Data: Aid to Tanzania, Economic and Social Research Foundation. (2016). Percentage of Health Budget in Health Policy Plus Policy Brief. (2019).

part of the national system" (Jennings 2015: 2). Despite stating its desire at various points to develop a national health system, Tanzania is subject to the "colonization by private, albeit not-for-profit, actors across swathes of the public service sector, including and perhaps especially health. Schools, clinics, hospitals etc. have been pushed into the hand of NGOs, the state increasingly bypassed in both its funding and regulatory role" (Jennings 2015: 5). In Tanzania the colonization of the public health sector is evident, although this has not meant the government is unable to influence the sector to some extent.

In the health sector in Tanzania a major focus of donors, particularly the United States, is on HIV/AIDS prevention and treatment, reflecting the stubbornly high rates of HIV, estimated at 1.6 million in 2019 (AVERT 2019). The relationship with donors in this sector is indicative of the issue Jennings raises, as in Tanzania "the vast majority of spending on HIV and AIDS is financed by development partners—over 98 percent between 2011/12 and 2013/14" (Wuyts et al. 2017: 26). A more recent report estimated this number at 90% (Global HIV Prevention Coalition 2018: 8). While the high dependence on foreign funds for HIV response is considered a risk, especially for a government which espouses compassion for people living with the virus, the government does not seem to share this priority. Health funding in the budget decreased in 2018/19 by 8%, from 10% of the total budget to 8.9% (Sikkika 2019).

Health funding went down from 11.3% of the budget in 2015/16, and was 2,222 billion TSh, significantly underfunding the sector and not reflecting population growth and increased need (Sikkika 2019). The result is per capita funding of 37,951 ($16 US) per person in Tanzania, a huge gap in funding that continues to go unaddressed (Sikkika 2019). These figures show a government keen to allow donors to prop up the health sector, especially HIV/AIDS response. Rather than following through on calls for donor independence, in these areas, the government is not preparing to fund the sector at all. Yet, as I explore below, the policies significantly impacting vulnerable populations are being shaped by the Tanzanian government, despite its donor dependence.

Donors have largely led the drive to tackle HIV/AIDS and significant investments have helped to lower infection rates from 12% to 5% over the past two decades (Sieff 2016). The President's Emergency Plan for AIDS Relief (PEPFAR), the Global Fund, the Gates Foundation, and UNAIDS are all significant contributors to reducing HIV/AIDS transmission and providing treatment in Tanzania. The Global Fund has invested $1.9 billion in Tanzania between 2002 and 2018, and Tanzania makes up 6% of the total 2017–2019 Global Fund allocation (Global Fund Audit Tanzania 2018: 9). Tanzania's foreign aid, has addressed some of the issues challenging Tanzanian development, notably reducing HIV/AIDS prevalence. The country, however, remains low on the HDI, 154 out of 189 countries, with 68.3% of the population living in poverty (HDI Report 2018).

LACK OF DEVELOPMENT, CORRUPTION, AND THE INFLUENCE OF THE DONORS

The CCM has weathered several major scandals which, despite their prominence, did not impact electoral results. In 1996, Joseph Warioba issued an infamous report that linked corruption to almost all sectors of governance and showed that the introduction of free-market principles to the economy in the 1980s caused a rise in corrupt practices (Warioba 1997). In another study focused on local government associations, the author concluded that corruption impacted "every aspect/sector of the social fabric" (Ngware 2005: 9). In 2008, an internal audit revealed 60 million pounds in improper payments from the Central Bank to local companies (Commonwealth Secretariat 2010: 19). One high-profile CCM politician brought down in these scandals, Attorney General Andrew Chenge, resigned after taking a $1 million bribe from BAE, a British aerospace company (Norad Report 2011: 13).

Given the high number of corruption scandals, the implication of many politicians and the unlikelihood of prosecution, corruption has not been effectively addressed. Warioba's report named 70 people involved in grand-scale corruption during Benjamin Mkapa's rule and not one was ever convicted

(Kelsall 2010: 70). Later scandals were even larger and implicated several high-level officials, including former Prime Minister Edward Lowassa. Lowassa chose an unknown energy company, Richmond, to provide power in Tanzania. The government spent over $100,000 USD per day despite the company failing to deliver any services (Norad Report 2011: 13). While Lowassa stepped down as prime minister in 2008, he later ran for leadership of the CCM, lost, and then joined the opposition in the 2015 election. The CCM won this election and Lowassa has since rejoined the party, showing how accusations and proof of corruption do not result in disgrace but are simply a stage in many successful CCM careers.

Prior to the 2015 elections, the Escrow scandal implicated a number of cabinet ministers, the attorney general, and the president (Tanzania Governance Review 2014). The opposition discovered that CCM officials were siphoning off massive amounts of public funding for personal use. The scandal showed the ability of CCM politicians to act with impunity. Attorney General Andrew Chenge was not prosecuted following his misdeeds in 2008, and was able to regain a position with the CCM after stepping down. In the Escrow scandal, Chenge, along with Minister Anna Tibaijuka, improperly attained $1 million each (Tanzania Governance Review 2014: 11).

These highly publicized incidents are widely known among citizens, who are politically engaged and discuss the scandals. For many Tanzanians, however, while these scandals are larger in scale, corruption is simply a part of daily life. "Kitu Kidogo" or "a little something" is still joked about often, and citizens expect to pay small bribes to police or other public officials. As I discuss in the next chapter, many groups of drug users mentioned paying off police when caught or said that they are sometimes held by police until their family or friends can pay a bribe. It is also important to remember this context when considering the blame for corruption being placed at the feet of drug users during the 2016/17 crackdowns.

Tim Kelsall effectively sums up the situation, which has changed little since 2010: "People struggle for access to corruptly acquired resources; other people struggle to put information about these struggles into the public domain with a view to righting wrongs; and, finally, politicians, some of whom are corrupt themselves, struggle to use the discourse of corruption as a stick with which to beat their equally corrupt opponents" (Kelsall 2010: 71).

All of this "fisadi," or corruption/graft, has had a major impact on development. While illicit drugs are often targeted as inimical to development, this focus sees drugs as the causal variable. Corruption however, with or without an illicit drug market, persists in Tanzanian society regardless of the inputs. The current Tanzanian government has conflated much criminal activity, such as poaching and drug trafficking, as causes of corruption rather than the ability of CCM officials to avoid any actual consequences to their actions.

Furthermore, international influence has had minimal impact in improving governance. As Aili Mari Tripp found in her study on the impacts of aid in Tanzania, "Donors have implicitly supported a system that seeks executive expansion (albeit not as extensive as some other countries), centralized government control with the decentralization of resources that would give localities real power, and corruption taken to extreme levels" (Tripp 2012: 22).

I have described these examples of corruption and aid dependence in order to show that, even with a power imbalance in the donor-recipient relationship, Tanzania has been able to control priorities in largely donor-funded sectors, a telling example of extraversion. While Tanzania appears to be an amenable aid recipient, with goals aligned to those of their many donors, foreign aid has contributed to a system in which multiple agendas are pursued while the CCM uses and controls aid as it sees fit. As Furukawa argues, "Tanzania is a country with significant ability to manage aid and the receipt of development aid resources, despite being considered a passive donor-driven recipient" (Furukawa 2016: 282). This system "allows it to be more proactive in obtaining resources, while pursuing the development it desires" (Furukawa 2016: 282).

The results of this system, as I show below, has troubling implications for sectors that are almost entirely donor driven. For example, injection drug users, and people who use drugs more generally, largely only have access to a small portion of foreign HIV/AIDS funding, most of which, is still aimed at supporting the general population. No other large-scale government funding, or programming specifically to address addictions is available. Furthermore, the government sets priorities in which key vulnerable populations are not important and organizes funding accordingly. As I discuss in the next section, President John Magufuli, with his strong desire to end aid dependence and his advancement of Tanzanian nationalism, worked to further distance himself from donors' goals while maintaining their actual support and pursuing his agenda.

MORALITY, AUTHORITARIANISM, AND CONTROL: ENTER PRESIDENT JOHN MAGUFULI

John Magufuli, the former minister of infrastructure under President Kikwete, was a relatively unexpected candidate for the leadership of the CCM. Prior to the 2015 election campaign, he rose to prominence in the CCM leadership contest. His main adversary, former PM Lowassa, a long-time CCM member with popular support, had since returned to the party and was expected to win the CCM leadership. Magufuli, however, was a contrast to Lowassa, with a clean record and upstanding reputation. He surprised the country by being selected to lead the CCM and, despite opposition gains, won the general elections of 2015, preserving CCM dominance. (Paget 2017)

John Magufuli, unlike other CCM members, emerged as a champion of ending the culture of corruption in Tanzania, a welcome change following the Escrow scandal and the failures of Jakaya Kikwete to reign in abuses of power. Foreign and domestic observers alike applauded Magufuli's initial focus on cleaning up the bureaucracy, combatting corruption and improving the lives of Tanzanians. Magufuli followed through on this promise, immediately cracking down on high levels of corruption in the public service, visiting bureaucrats unannounced, and sacking several high ranking public officials. This turn in a country long mired by corruption earned Magufuli the hashtag #whatwouldmagufulido and some observers drew favorable comparisons between him and Julius Nyerere (Mkony 2016). The disruptive change was taken seriously by many, as one interviewee noted, "There was a sense of fear, nobody is sure of anyone anymore. This was a time when you know Magufulication is happening, he is firing everyone, nobody is sure and they [government employees] were scared" (Interview 14, October 2018, Mikocheni).

The initial excitement over Magufuli's activism and war on corruption quickly began to sour however. According to Dan Paget, "Since early 2016, it has become apparent that Magufuli is not just waging war on corruption—he is also declaring war on democracy" (Paget 2017: 2). While his policies initially seemed to be positive ways to deal with endemic problems in the Tanzanian political system, Magufuli's approach began to look familiar to previous CCM leaders. As Tripp (2012) noted, the centralizing tendencies of the CCM have been a long-standing theme in Tanzanian politics, preventing the growth of a strong opposition and healthier democracy.

The shock of John Magufuli's death during his second term, announced in March 2021, has left many scholars and political observers grappling with the authoritarian legacy of Magufuli and what this will mean to the CCM. Magufuli's policies not only reinforced centralized control of the state by the CCM but also his own executive power. He worked to ensure the CCM had increased oversight over several key sectors, and over ministries and departments. In controlling ministers, and his willingness to silence critics, Magufuli was the most active president in pursuing centralization since Nyerere. The mystery surrounding his actual death, where and when it occurred, amplify the risk to this party with an absent strongman. The CCM elites benefited from Magufuli's populist belligerence, and quietly won huge majorities in elections and in Parliament with Magufuli as the public face of the continued failures of the CCM in alleviating poverty and responding to major health crises, such as COVID-19.

Magufuli's approach drew both admiration and derision, with liberal publications such as *The Economist* (2018) heralding his anti-liberal and anti-foreign investment policies as profoundly dangerous. In March 2018, it noted that "Mr. Magufuli is fast transforming Tanzania from a flawed democracy into one of Africa's more brutal dictatorships" (*The Economist* 2018). Other scholars such as Goran Hyden have compared this approach to Ethiopia and Rwanda, countries pursuing a developmental state model focused on development rather than democracy (Hyden 2017). As Michaela Collord points out, Magufuli stepped into a false dichotomy of state versus market, heavily favoring the state and intervening in a number of aspects of the economy (Collord 2019).

Unfortunately, the developmental state model includes a reduction in press and democratic freedoms. The loss of some rights of expression in this model are a trade-off, worthwhile in the short term as long as economic development increases. Whereas Rwanda received donor aid and invested in lucrative industries such as information technology and tourism, Magufuli's erratic policies have had mixed results.[1] For example, Magufuli charged Barrick Gold subsidiary Acacia Mining plc. with a $190 billion tax bill, which eventually resulted in a payout of $300 million (*Financial Post* 2017). While this was a success in advancing Magufuli's goal of increased state presence in the economy and improved economic outcomes, his pledges to end tax evasion and corruption to increase investor confidence are not leading to similar success (Norbrook 2019).

Ending corruption, and enforcing taxes and regulations in an informal sector that has functioned without much interference for decades, presented a major challenge. The imposition of regulations can have the effect of shuttering businesses unable to function in a formal setting, or causing businesses to struggle with taxes that are suddenly imposed and enforced with regularity. Furthermore, with the loss of numerous public-sector jobs, and the money spent by these employees in the informal sector, circulation of currency slowed. Tackling corruption will be a long process and, in the interim, poor and vulnerable members of this informal economy are still subject to police and authorities that continue to exercise power unfairly. Once optimistic investors have been scared away by new regulations and FDI has fallen 18% since 2014 (*Washington Post* 2018). In pursuing these policies, Magufuli created a narrative that presents Tanzania as the victim of greedy multinationals, which is certainly true to an extent, but obfuscates how his own party has benefited at the expense of the rural poor since liberalizing the economy in the 1980s.

In alignment with the blame he assigns to foreign interests, Magufuli also worked toward ending aid dependence. His statements on ending foreign support are more connected to his desire to pursue his own agenda, however. For example, Magufuli called for an end to aid dependence immediately following donor condemnation the unfair elections in Zanzibar in 2015. Again, when donors disapproved of his attacks on gay men in 2018, Magufuli called for an end to foreign influence in Tanzania. Cloaked in old pan-Africanist rhetoric, the calls for aid dependence were strongest when Magufuli wanted to abuse human rights or centralize his own power. In 2016, he called for Tanzanians to "work hard and end the country's dependence on donor money as a United States government agency confirmed its cancellation of a $472 million aid package due to Zanzibar's disputed election" (Shekighenda 2016). While the motive is self-interest, it does recall the spirit of the Arusha Declaration of 1967 in which Nyerere called for African socialism independent of Western interference. This call for independence is in interesting contrast to the historical, and continued, aid dependence of the country (Anyimadu 2016: 5). Issa Shivji remarks that this is likely because Magufuli's end goals were different, "although he rhetorically used the term uberu (imperialism), it is doubtful he ever understood it as a system. He hardly ever talked about ubepari (capitalism) or for that matter ujamaa (socialism)" (Shivji 2021).

Magufuli initially gained support from Tanzanians in his calls to end aid dependence and in his desire to pursue a more state-led approach. *The Economist* and organizations such as the International Monetary Fund (IMF) reacted predictably, lamenting the turn away from market-based principles implemented after Nyerere. As Collord states (2019), these arguments seem to paint a picture in which market or statist economies can only exist independently, rather than as a mixed strategy. In Tanzania, neither a purely state-led approach or a strong market-based approach has worked, yet Magufuli staked himself as a Nyerere like leader who will return power to the state or, more accurately, to the CCM. It is impossible to judge his popularity by electoral returns, including Magufuli's re-election in 2020 as this election was not free or fair. The election was a profound reminder of the one-party nature of Tanzania and how the once optimistic commitment to multipartyism is very much a distant memory.

In projecting the image of an independent, strong state, Magufuli drew parallels as a successor to Julius Nyerere. Many Tanzanians still revere Nyerere as the father of the Nation and he casts a long shadow on politics. Furthermore, Nyerere's calls for familyhood and kujitegemea (self-reliance) also continue to be an important theme in Tanzanian politics (Hunter 2008), which Magufuli was intent to uphold. Disputes over who "owns" Nyerere's legacy have persisted since his death in 1999, with both opposition parties trying to show how the CCM is no longer Nyerere's party, and the CCM working to maintain their link to him as their founder (Becker 2013; Fouere 2014). The CCM has often won this battle, giving it an important advantage in rural politics where nostalgia for socialist rule and the incorruptible Nyerere remain strong (O'Gorman 2012).

Magufuli explicitly patterned himself on the Father of the Nation, more so than past leaders, drawing a straight line to a past that conveniently ignores the hardships it wrought. Dan Paget (2020) describes this comparison as "restorationist developmental nationalism," a post-colonial project started by Nyerere which has yet to be completed and which, just as it did under Nyerere himself, justifies top-down state control and authoritarianism. In emphasizing and repeating discourses utilized during one party rule, the CCM under Magufuli "embraced the claim that the nation has strayed from its developmental trajectory and promised to restore it" (Paget 2020: 1251). With his absence, it is unclear how the CCM will maintain the populism embodied in Magufuli. What is clear is that the CCM continues to have no intent to loosen its grip on power and Magufuli was not a single actor in enforcing the authoritarianism and control of the CCM. As is often said of American President Donald Trump, Magufuli was not a cause of authoritarianism and moral nationalism, but a symptom of post-colonial Tanzanian politics which, though cloaked in the benevolence of Nyerere's socialist mission, is actually based in repression and authoritarianism.

Interviewees regularly remarked on how calls for accountability have increased, with more reporting requirements in line with top-down mechanisms of policy control. As Anyimadu notes, "The selection of more permanent secretaries [in Cabinet] than in previous governments suggests a desire to hold direct authority over the technocratic aspects of policy implementation" (Anyimadu 2016: 8). Magufuli tried to sell his interference in this sector as a way to reduce corruption. Ultimately, while remembered as a staunch anti-corruption advocate, his targets were wider ranging and increased obstacles for NGOs which already faced greater oversight and were forced to align with top-down goals set by the CCM.

QUESTIONABLE TACTICS AND INCREASING CONTROL

Magufuli's focus on economic nationalism, discipline, and state-led economic growth during his first term were accompanied with the same authoritarian tendencies that characterize other so-called developmental states. Magufuli publicly cracked down on members of his own party, the opposition, and even popular public personalities such as the pop singer Diamond Platnumz (*The Standard* 2017). Members of the opposition have been harassed, arrested under questionable charges, or simply restricted in movement. Zitto Kabwe, a member of the opposition in Parliament, was imprisoned multiple times and banned from traveling outside of the country (Wako 2019). Wealthy members of Tanzanian society were targeted with charges of drug trafficking or improper conduct (Sixpence 2017), or have mysteriously disappeared. During my fieldwork in 2018, Mohammed Dewji, one of Tanzania's richest men was abducted for 10 days and then returned. There was no investigation or arrest of any responsible party.

In a telling example of the move toward state control, Magufuli outlawed any statistics not published or vetted by the government, making the government the sole source of statistics in the country. When the government reported positive GDP figures, they were questioned by Zitto Kabwe who was promptly detained by police (Sandefur 2018). Twaweza, a nonprofit organization that conducted polling studies, published a report in 2018 showing a major downturn in the approval ratings of the president, from 80% to 41%. The government revoked the organization's research permit and accused it of not having appropriate clearance from COSTECH. The head of the organization had his passport revoked pending investigation (Elias 2018).

Magufuli worked to become the sole power and arbitrator of knowledge in the country through the production of his own truths and the repression of other opinions. Such was his success in achieving this goal that, when he took ill in February 2021, his whereabouts and condition were a complete mystery. The lack of information is a clear result of the tactics he undertook while alive. In March 2019, Magufuli banned *The Citizen* for one week for violation of "an obscure regulation regarding reporting on the Central Bank" (Chambers 2019). This paper is the leading English language news source in the country, serving as my main source in many cases given the lack of other independent English publications. It is certainly not known for controversy. In 2019, Amnesty International and other observers of press freedoms in Tanzania such as Journalists Without Borders raised concerns over the imprisonment of journalist Erick Kabendera, who is also having his citizenship investigated (Maclean 2019).

Magufuli was clear on his belief in traditional values and conservatism, as evidenced by many questionable public comments including statements criticizing young women who are pregnant, supporting legislation banning them from schools, noting they may encourage other young girls to engage in premarital sex (Githaiga 2017). Magufuli also stated that "outsiders who promote birth control are giving bad advice, and that people who use contraceptives are lazy" (*The Guardian* 2018). He then banned family-planning advertisements, announcing "women should stop using contraceptives because Tanzania needed more people" (*BBC News* 2018). In 2019, Magufuli urged women to "set their ovaries free," a bizarre idea to boost the economy through increasing the population, many of whom remain poor and unemployed (Ng'wanakilala 2019).

Magufuli also maintained an extremely conservative stance toward gay men since gaining power. I discuss crackdowns specific to gay men with

HIV/AIDS below. However, his willingness to attack homosexuals so publicly is unprecedented. As several NGOs noted, gay civil society leaders have either fled or stopped advocacy activities (Individual interviews 4, 6, 10 and 11, August–September 2018). In November 2018, Magufuli's close political ally, Paul Makonda, declared that homosexuals needed to be rooted out of Tanzanian society and encouraged the sharing of information on individuals engaged in these activities (Kirby 2018). While this declaration was only an escalation of Magufuli's preoccupation with gay men as many advocates had left the country already, it is a definite intensification in a country known for a more peaceful and tolerant approach. Previously, while gay men were certainly not accepted in society at large, they were not actively hunted. Ironically, despite Magufuli's invocation of African values, many of these laws originated during the colonial era and are simply being brought back to prominence by Magufuli for his own purposes, recalling the invention of tradition (Akumu 2018).

As mentioned above, Magufuli was willing to take on foreign donors in his calls to end aid. Following the Escrow scandal, donors initially halted aid, holding back $558 million in general budget assistance though not for long (Makoye 2014). The World Bank withheld $300 million over concerns with Magufuli's policy toward women and girls (*CNN* 2018). In both cases however, through negotiation the government was able to reach an agreement for the aid without reversing its position. These are just two examples that illustrate the limitations of donors seriously challenging Magufuli's course, as cutting aid impacts the poorest and most vulnerable (*The Daily Nation* 2018).

While all of the actions above show a government committed to restricting political, civic and moral space, the actual ability of the Tanzanian state to express its will across society remains in question. From my own fieldwork, Magufuli's ability to dictate policy and the ability of the Tanzanian government to make policy a reality on the ground was surprising. In my previous experience, Tanzania was a state with weak power at the ground level yet, the statements of the CCM leadership translated into vulnerable groups being increasingly targeted and facing increased repression. Furthermore, the words of other members of the CCM, including Paul Makonda, Health Minister Ummy Mwalimu and Prime Minister Kassim Majaliwa, all reflected the harsh tone of John Magufuli, revealing a surprising level of cooperation among CCM elites. This cooperation is even more notable given the reversal in tone in the statements of Minister Mwalimu, who previously did not attack harm reduction.

The supposed inability of the Tanzanian state to pursue a top-down agenda may help explain why the current government is so focused on vulnerable populations. To date, the government's targeting of vulnerable individuals is enabled by their presence in Dar es Salaam, where the coercive power of the state is strongest and by the relative lack of support and regard for groups such as drug users, who have been constructed as morally deserving of harsh treatment.

Furthermore, as this chapter illustrates, the project of the Magufuli regime represented continuities with Tanzanian politics but also evidence of a new and concerted push toward authoritarianism. The Tanzanian government used a mix of discourse, policy change, and performance to bolster its authority. While the Tanzanian state is far from a fully realized authoritarian government, the tactics of sporadic enforcement, fear-based rhetoric, and performative crackdowns have real impacts on the ground. In pursuing authoritarianism as the CCM does, "People are degraded not because of the content of the norms [produced by authoritarianism] but because, although no one believes in them, everyone enforces them…ideology is insidious because it allows people to hide their reasons for obedience from themselves" (Wedeen 1998: 513). As I show in later chapters, the mutually constitutive power of rhetoric and policy change together create an environment of repression.

The CCM has always been able to exercise a high degree of flexibility while maintaining huge levels of foreign support as is evidenced by its ability to control elections and commit human-rights abuses. As I discuss in depth later, Tanzania receives significant funding in the health sector and this has had a major impact in reversing preventable disease and HIV/AIDS prevalence. However, the government maintains relationships with donors while continuing to impose major restrictions by groups in great need of assistance, such as key vulnerable populations. As long as aid can be subordinated to the goals of the ruling party to maintain power and absolute control over the direction of the country, the CCM will continue to pursue an authoritarian agenda while not prioritizing those in society who need the most help.

These developments represent a troubling move toward authoritarian consolidation with popular appeals to morality and individual responsibility. The death of Magufuli will not change the CCM's relentless drive to hold onto power. As I expand upon in this section, the rhetoric of the government had two immediate impacts: ensuring those working with vulnerable groups are aligned to the central government, not their clients (not to improve effectiveness of programming but rather to ensure these groups do not encourage homosexuality or contravene any laws); and, making the lives and situation of vulnerable people in poverty including PWID, gay men and women and girls, much worse.

CONCLUSION

The CCM is ingrained in the Tanzanian state and many of the legacies of the one-party era remain. In this chapter, I outlined this background and these themes to show the context in which the government of Tanzania has pursued policies addressing illicit drug trafficking and use. The aid dependence of the Tanzanian state, particularly in the health sector and in HIV/AIDS response, has left this sector vulnerable and exposed to changes in funding and priorities. Furthermore, the current authoritarian government is able to pursue its own priorities in regards to illicit drugs while foreign funding supports the majority of programming available to drug users, making the sector vulnerable to policy change.

While fondly remembered, Julius Nyerere presided over a one-party state with centralized control. After stepping down, despite moving toward multi-party politics, the CCM maintained a firm grip on political power in Tanzania. Magufuli did not reinvent Tanzanian politics but rather returned the CCM toward absolute one-party control, utilizing the existing political and legislative power established by his predecessors to implement authoritarian policies. In 2015, Magufuli presided over the slimmest victory in the CCM's history, which still was a sizeable win. In November 2019, however, the CCM gained 99% of the vote in local elections and, in 2020, the CCM won re-election with 84% of the vote. Tanzania is not witnessing the establishment of a one-party state, but is rather seeing the realization of a trend in Tanzanian politics that had seemed to be losing salience in a time of increased openness, tolerance and development.

While Tanzanian politics is complex, the lasting impacts of Magufuli's tenure represent some of the underlying elements of Tanzanian politics that have hobbled the state since independence: authoritarianism, aid dependence, and discriminatory nationalism. In this context, Magufuli was not an aberration even though his moral politics were more extreme than previous leaders. Drug users, gay men, girls and women and other groups deemed immoral are trapped in an authoritarian project deeply rooted in the history of the Tanzanian state, where they are excluded.

NOTE

1. See Golooba-Mutebi and Kelsall (2012).

Chapter 4

Maskini, Maskani na Matatizo (Poverty, Hot Spots and Problems)

Using Drugs in Dar es Salaam

> *Many people using drugs in Tanzania, their families are very poor and the stigma for the people that are using drugs is very high because they don't know anything about addiction. They think that life, you choose it. The people in the government don't know anything about addiction. We are going everywhere but they don't know how to help. This program, and the people that help me, [are the] addicts. We stop using and start to help [one] another. There is no professor here, only addicts.*
>
> —Individual interview 17, October 2018, Kigamboni

In the past three decades, the quantity of heroin being trafficked through East Africa has steadily increased as it is transported to major markets in Europe and North America. In Tanzania, the beginning of a larger-scale heroin trade began in the mid-1980s, coinciding with the disruption to social and economic life brought by the transition to a multiparty democracy and the liberalization of the economy. The increase in heroin availability during this time led to local use around trafficking routes, mainly in coastal towns along the Swahili coast including Dar es Salaam. Heroin use continued to rise in the later 1990s and, by the 2000s, injection drug use was prevalent and spreading in Dar es Salaam and Zanzibar. As drug use increased, so too did methadone programs and harm reduction services, mainly aimed at preventing HIV/AIDS transmission. These ground-breaking programs in East Africa have been widely studied, but not from the lens of the larger social, political, and economic context which is all the more important given the tenuous support for harm reduction in Tanzania.

In this chapter, I explore the programs made available to people who use drugs in Tanzania over the past decade. Building on the context established in the last chapter, I look at how progressive programming was established with the support of international organizations and through local activism. Despite the very positive step in establishing methadone programming, I also look at the gaps in Tanzanian drug policy and programs from the perspectives of those who work within these systems.

My focus below is to show the challenges this population faces and how a lack of political will to provide adequate supports resulted in increased vulnerabilities. I examine these vulnerabilities and the experiences of people who use drugs to illustrate the setting in which John Magufuli's crackdown and policy revisions took place. In Tanzania, heroin use occurs within the context of high levels of poverty and low employment, meaning it is often risky and can have major adverse impacts for those who get into patterns of misuse. As I illustrate below, heroin use in Tanzania can cause a number of challenges for people who use the drug, with most of the adverse effects caused not by the drug itself, but by poor policies and a lack of support. With this context, the full negative impacts of what appear to be minor policy changes and a temporary crackdown, can be seen as highly impactful on a population already facing many obstacles.

BACKGROUND

The heroin being trafficked through Tanzania is mainly destined for European countries and the United States, drawing the focus of these powers and the UNODC on improving anti-trafficking measures in the region. However, despite the increased efforts at reducing this supply, heroin continues to be readily available in Tanzania and is relatively cheap, especially compared to prices in Western countries. Furthermore, efforts to control opium production in Afghanistan, the main source for global opium production, have had the opposite effect of reducing supply. Alternative crop incentives and military intervention only resulted in more opium from Afghanistan being produced than ever before.

With a large supply to export, the Indian Ocean route continues to be utilized by drug traffickers, bringing large amounts of heroin to Tanzanian shores (see figure 4.1). Increased enforcement has only led to temporary disruptions in trafficking or to the creation of new routes, including one now in place through Pakistan and Iran to the Indian Ocean (Rweyemamu 2018). The heroin trade shows no signs of slowing. The UNODC reported that opium production in Afghanistan reached 10,500 tonnes in 2017, the highest amount recorded since 2000 (*The Economist* 2018). The UNODC measure of drug seizures reported in Tanzania was 14 kg in 2004, the highest seizure of heroin between 1990 and 2005 (UNODC 2018). In 2010 the seizure of heroin was 190 kg and in 2014, total seizures reached 400 kg (UNODC 2018).

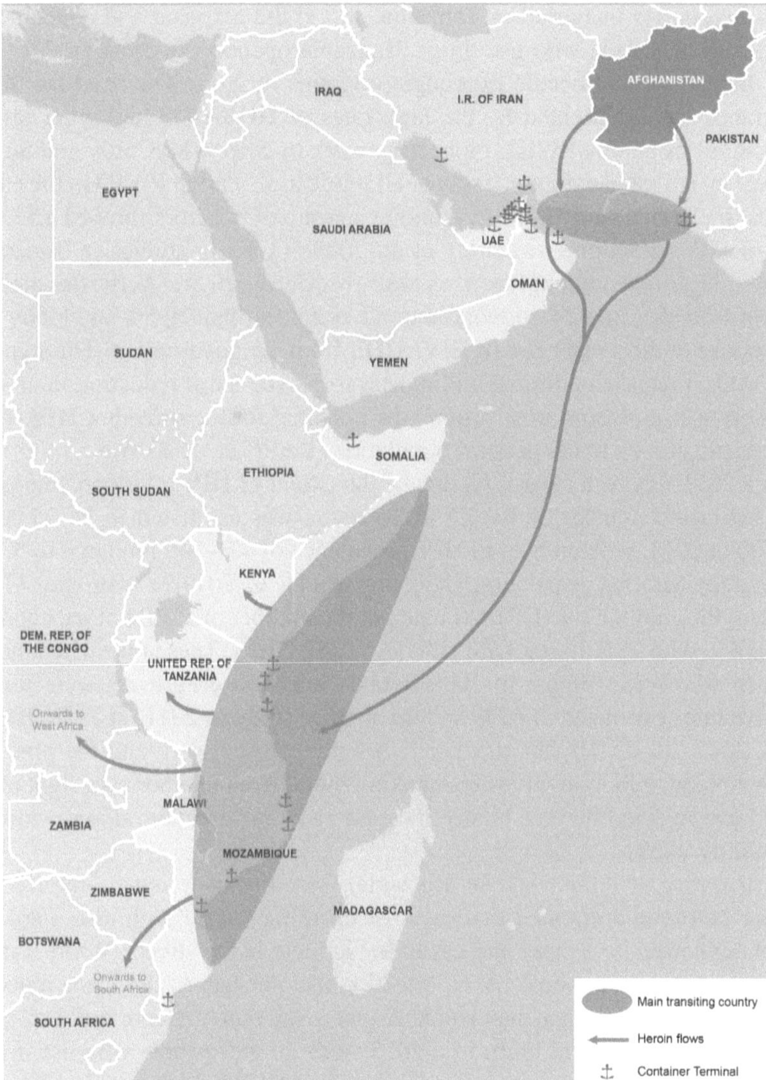

Note: The boundaries and names shown and the designations used on this map do not imply official endorsement or acceptance by the United Nations. The final boundary between the Republic of Sudan and the Republic of South Sudan has not yet been determined.

Figure 4.1 Indicative Afghan Heroin Trafficking Routes by Maritime Means to Eastern Africa. *Source*: United Nations Office on Drugs and Crime. (2016). *The Afghan Opiate Trade and Africa—A Baseline Assessment 2016.* Vienna: United Nations Office on Drugs and Crime.

As heroin use increased in Tanzania, so too did activism and concern for the health of people who use drugs. Tanzania opened sub-Saharan Africa's first methadone and needle exchange programs in 2011. The need for these programs was highlighted by the high rates of HIV/AIDS and other infectious diseases among PWID. Pioneering work by Sheryl McCurdy and Susan Beckerleg revealed extreme levels of HIV infection among PWID in the early 2000s. In 2005, a study in Kenya among a group of injectors showed a 52.5% rate of HIV infection (Beckerleg et al. 2005: 1). Early studies in Tanzania showed high rates among users as well (McCurdy 2006). Activists, mainly people who use drugs, also worked to advocate for their rights and lobby for a response to the steady rise in HIV/AIDS from the government. Throughout the 2000s, increased political willingness to pursue harm reduction interventions grew as concerns arose around the potential for the spread of HIV from vulnerable groups to the general population (Ratliff et al. 2016).

In a 2011 report, a clearer picture of the extent of HIV infection emerged. The estimated number of PWID in Tanzania was estimated to be 25,000–50,000 in 2011, with an overall HIV prevalence of 42% as compared to 5.1% among the general population (Nieburg 2011). In 2014, a National AIDS Control Programme (NACP) estimate put the number of PWID in the country at 30,000, with 35% living with HIV (AVERT 2016). These rates rise among women who inject drugs. In 2009, female injection drug users were found to have rates estimated at 62% and, in another study in 2011, at 71% (Balaji et al. 2017: 2094). Higher risk behaviors such as sex work and the practice of flashblood, which involves re-injecting blood from another user right after they have injected heroin, highly increase risks of infection among women (McCurdy 2009).

A majority of individuals in Tanzania, from my interviews, preferred to smoke heroin and claimed that most of those they used with also smoked. Smoking heroin is cheaper and easier to facilitate in the streets. While it may appear dangerous to some users, injection use persists as the same amount of heroin injected, rather than smoked, enters the blood stream quicker, providing a more powerful high. In a 2015 study of 480 people who use drugs in Mwanza, 13.5% of respondents injected (AVERT 2018). A 2018 study showed that, in 436 interviews, "most primary key informants reported smoking 'cocktail' described as a combination of ground-up cannabis, tobacco and heroin" (Tiberio et al. 2018: 23). However, PWID, as the most at risk population, attracted far more attention at first from international donors and NGOs concerned with high rates of HIV/AIDS. The first methadone clinic in Tanzania at Muhimbili National Hospital was open to injection heroin users only (Saleem et al. 2015: 60).

Foreign donors such as PEPFAR almost entirely fund the methadone program (Ng'wanakilala 2013: 89). The clinic was the result of years of growing concerns and local advocacy. The Tanzanian Network for People Who Use Drugs (TANPUD) was an early instance of a network of users hoping to spread education and understanding (Jensen 2016). In discussions with one of the original members they described how, given the difficulties faced by people who use drugs in everyday life, organizing was a challenge at first (Individual interview 4, August 2018, Mikocheni). Syringes were (and remain) illegal, drug use was criminalized and life for many people who use drugs was a constant series of obstacles and problems (Individual interview 4, August 2018, Mikocheni). This member told me about the difficulties of forming an organization among people who use drugs without external support, and noted that the group was not a popular choice for funding. Other organizations that were bigger, but did not have as comprehensive an understanding of harm reduction, were better able to organize themselves to access foreign funding (Individual interview 4, August 2018, Mikocheni). Fledgling activist organizations have remained an important part of advocacy and have even been invited to consult with the government. The election of Magufuli, however, had a severe impact on the advocacy work of these groups.

Other organizations formed and became more active in 2011 to support outreach and safer drug use. Some organizations, such as Methadone Families Advocating Against Drug Use (MEFADA) formed with direct connections to the methadone program, working to connect people who use drugs to the program. The French NGO Médecins du Monde (MDM) began a needle exchange program in Temeke district (McCurdy and Kaduri 2016: 315). These interventions, the result of advocacy and education, slowly gained the support of the government. The results of these interventions also proved effective in reaching some people who use drugs and connecting them to needed supports. As these supports grew, however, it also became clear that much more support was needed. Between 2011 and 2016, an estimated 1000 clients were enrolled in the methadone program (Saleem et al. 2016: 60). New methadone clinics in Mwananyamala and Temeke neighborhood have helped increase access and the expansion beyond syringe users has increased enrolment in the program. While the methadone program grew, accompanying wrap-around supports and outreach worked with limited funds to keep up.

A major focus of methadone treatment is to ensure that PWID can access anti-retroviral therapy (ART) should they be HIV positive while ending risky drug use practices. Given the high rates of HIV among this population, the implementation of these services was of major importance even if it did not address the root causes of addiction. When the program began, the aim was not only getting individuals on treatment but also simply testing individuals to get a better understanding of the scale of the problem. The rate of HIV diagnosis, with those diagnosed aware of their status, is lower in Tanzania compared to its neighbors, at 78% (AVERT 2019). Of this 78% that have received their diagnosis, around 92% are receiving treatment. The rate of treatment for KVP, however, is not known (AVERT 2019). These challenges underline the importance of testing, informing patients, and supporting their access to treatment. The improved numbers in Tanzania also reflect the overwhelming focus on achieving the 90-90-90 target, which focuses on ensuring 90% of people know their status, are receiving treatment and are viral suppressed by 2020. While this focus is important, it is not always suited toward the inclusion of KVP.

In terms of reducing HIV/AIDS prevalence and facilitating access to treatment for PWID, the methadone program was a major step toward enhanced health services for people who use drugs. Many proponents of the program, however, including local NGOs and academics, anticipated that the program would develop and grow beyond a simple medical intervention. As noted by Ratliff et al.,

> In Tanzania, methadone is a substance designed only to reduce HIV transmission: it is one component of this harm reduction strategy along with comprehensive health services, individual and family counseling and occupational training. It is not intended to treat addiction and foster recovery as in other settings or systems. (Ratliff et al. 2016: 12)

This position reveals the limitations and issues that have persisted with the provision of methadone in Tanzania.

During fieldwork in 2018, methadone was provided with little support beyond the daily dosage. Individuals enrolled in the program are required "to commit to a treatment plan, which includes abstinence from alcohol and illicit drug use" (Ng'wanakilala 2013: 90). While this rule is to be expected, in the everyday context of Tanzanian life, and in the absence of social and economic supports, sticking to this program can be challenging. Methadone patients are required to present themselves respectably when they appear for their dose every day, regardless of their circumstances.

Pointing out the limitations of the methadone program is not a critique of the program itself, but rather a critique of the practice of implementing one aspect of a more comprehensive and needed health and human-rights intervention. The medicalization of addiction through the provision of one program in the absence of other supports has major impacts on people who use drugs. Most importantly, people who use drugs have little option in accessing other services such as mental health supports, outreach, counseling and supportive treatment centers, all of which cannot be funded with the limited dollars present in the sector.

The focus on methadone allows donors to maintain their goal of reducing HIV transmission, even as people who use drugs require more comprehensive supports and better options. The continuation of the program also can be trumpeted by the government as promotion of its "harm reduction" approach, which apparently consists of providing methadone to "solve" the problem of addiction. The concern that "isolated epidemics never remain concentrated among drug users" but reach the general population (Bruce et al. 2014: 24), drives this intervention, not the human rights and right to health of PWID. In other words, "dispensing methadone is acceptable harm reduction activity because it also corresponds to the values of prohibitionists in reducing the demand for heroin" (Ratliff et al. 2016: 13).

Framing harm reduction as a strictly medical practice contributes to altering its meaning, and making its implementation a seemingly straightforward medical intervention. Recommendations in 2016 for improving methadone treatment were only focused on HIV prevention and highlights "the importance of higher doses of methadone to maximize HIV treatment benefits for PWID" (Lambdin et al. 2016: 47). Calls for greater supports often have not gone beyond a focus on how to get individuals in the program and retain them, rather than considering other important needs that address the everyday realities of people who use drugs. Comprehensive harm reduction involves basic healthcare, outreach, mental health and social supports and, most importantly, should be based on the principle of meeting the needs of drug users and not promoting abstinence.

The danger of this single-minded focus, as pointed out by Caroline Acker in regard to syringe exchange, is that interventions are "stripped of the symbolic charge surrounding illicit drug use, syringe exchange is simply good, old-fashioned infectious disease control: a pathogen has been identified; its life cycle has been studied, and how it is transmitted from one body to another understood; and syringe exchange interrupts that transmission by providing drug users with sterile injecting equipment" (Acker as quoted in Gowan et al. 2012: 1252–1253). Similarly, with methadone, a population of individuals with various challenges, histories and experiences are considered a vector for disease control, without any meaningful interventions aimed at increasing chances for recovery and improved health outcomes. As noted by McCurdy, "socioeconomic and educational investment are the key to responding to the triple threat of the crack, heroin and HIV/AIDS epidemics. In other words, to effectively respond to this epidemic we must address its socioeconomic determinants" (McCurdy and Kaduri 2016: 317). During my time in Tanzania, this sentiment was echoed by every drug user and activist I talked to, many of whom are accessing methadone despite poverty, lack of opportunity, and stigma.

Despite the focus on reducing HIV/AIDS, even in reaching this goal several barriers persist, including lack of support at point of contact, limited social supports, and stigmatization (Saleem et al. 2016: 63). The stigmatization and barriers are particularly prevalent among women who use drugs who are estimated to make up 33% of PWID but only make up 8% of methadone clients (Balaji et al. 2017: 2094). Women face a huge number of obstacles in accessing services, often facing intimate partner violence, sex work, stigma, and having no or little income (Balaji et al. 2017). The difficulty of addressing drug use through methadone at public health institutions, with less focus on individual patterns of use, is evidenced by those who choose not to attend, who continue to use while attending treatment or who end up going to sober houses where they can receive more social and mental health supports. The drive, for example, of the Global Fund to enroll 400,000 people in ART (Waititu 2018) is important but changes little for the most vulnerable who face stigma, obstacles to treatment, low prospects of employment and lead very difficult lives. The result, as shown in a more recent estimate, is that only an estimated one in five injection heroin users are accessing treatment and methadone (AVERT 2019).

In 2015, the methadone program needed expansion and support, but found in Magufuli a very reticent sponsor. The continued support for people who use drugs seemed possible, even though this idea appeared to be more of an afterthought in the largely clinical literature focused on reducing HIV transmission among injection drug users. Furthermore, the MDM needle exchange program was set to expand through Dar es Salaam from its base in Temeke district. Outside harm reduction organizations such as Mainline looked into operations in Dar es Salaam and even undertook preliminary studies on establishing harm reduction supports in the country. Service providers and scholars saw that methadone was not a holistic solution but part of a greater human-rights based approach toward drug use. Prior to Magufuli, advocacy in this direction was well underway, and the government was listening.

PATTERNS OF USE AND THE EXPERIENCE OF PEOPLE WHO USE DRUGS

While it was not my intent to describe the personal stories of people who use drugs in Tanzania, many of the people I interviewed discussed their histories with me. I use these histories to illuminate how experiences are discursively shaped in the context of wider policies and social environments. I also use these interviews to provide a brief glimpse of some of the realities of drug use I would not have been otherwise able to discover, such as the cost of drugs and the ideas and beliefs of those who use them. During my interviews, I asked questions that related everyday experiences to the larger political context and interactions with the government. In most cases, government policies were inadequate or directly opposed to improving the lives of people who use drugs. I found this to be the case with existing programs available and in terms of the stigma, police harassment and the large gap in health services available to people who use drugs.

In several interviews, people noted that the first drug they used was bangi (cannabis), which is cheap and widely available in Tanzania. One man at a sober house began using drugs by dealing heroin across the Indian Ocean to Kenya and Comoros from Zanzibar and Dar es Salaam (Individual interview 39, October 2018, Kigamboni). Since he transported drugs by swallowing them, he would sniff heroin to reduce the possibility of a bowel movement, and eventually began sniffing regularly regardless of his trafficking duties. Soon he became what he described as a mteja (client or junkie) and his employer lost trust in his ability to continue his work (Individual interview 39, October 2018, Kigamboni). In another case, a woman had dropped out of school and was using bangi for some years before trying heroin, as she believed it was just a different kind of cannabis (Individual interview 28, October 2018, Kigamboni). Another former drug user at the sober house also started with cannabis before feeling the need for something stronger. Since the people she spent time with had access to heroin, social connections increased this desire for something stronger, "There was peer pressure and people would use heroin around so I started using it too, I was 15 years old" (Individual interview 26, October 2018, Kigamboni).

Some interviewees noted that they were around other people who use drugs and transitioned over several years to higher doses of heroin. While this may sound like a confirmation of the "gateway drug" idea that marijuana leads to heavier drug use, this is not the case. I only talked to those who became heroin dependent, not the huge majority of others who tried and abstained from marijuana or heroin, nor those who continued to only use marijuana, a very common drug in Tanzania. Poverty, lack of opportunity, and boredom impacted people's decisions to use, while other factors were the same as anywhere, curiosity, trauma, peer pressure, or a desire to have fun. From my limited experiences in Tanzania, the higher levels of poverty and unemployment did not seem to have the impacts predicted in some sensationalist literature, where people with limited hope of a better future resort to heavy drug use. Drug use was just as common as any other country, albeit in a different context.

The smoking of a cocktail, which as mentioned is a mix of cannabis, heroin and tobacco, appeared to be the most common form of use among interviewees and in hot spots as it is cheaper and easier to do in a vulnerable setting, often among homeless individuals. Injection use was avoided by some because of the known risk and the ability to continue to have needs met by smoking. In discussing the transition from smoking heroin to injecting in Kenya, Dimova et al. note how "agency is produced and enacted within these structural pressures through the creation of a logic of economic constraint that shapes how transitions are understood and managed" (Dimova et al. 2015: 7). This statement points to multiple levels of reasoning, from social networks to economic constraint that shape transitions from cannabis to heroin, and from smoking heroin to injecting heroin.

In interviews with both outreach workers and former users themselves, the most common reason for the transition to injection use I found was based on economic calculation. The economic choice behind the switch points to the influence of a structural component over behavioral. However, agency is present in the need to increase use as tolerance rises. Dimova et al. (2015) rightly point to the multilayered reasons for a transition, but economic pressure and rising prices can motivate a switch. As one interviewee noted, they could hustle all day and get enough to smoke a few times. However, rising dependence and higher costs mean that you could also just inject providing a more direct high (to the bloodstream) for less money (Individual interview 26, October 2018, Kigamboni). Inland, where costs are higher, a hit of heroin could be from 5,000 to 7,000 Tsh (US$ 2–3). A person with high tolerance could smoke easily 30,000 Tsh worth in a day ($12) but if they are injecting they can have a more powerful effect for the same cost (Individual interview 5, October 2018, Kigamboni).

The income and poverty levels in Tanzania put the costs of drug use in sharp relief. In 2015, the World Bank estimated the number of Tanzanians below the poverty line to be at 28.2% using a figure of 36,482 Tsh ($15.84) per adult per month (World Bank Poverty Assessment 2015). This poverty line is now at 26.4% according to state-sanctioned statistics (Masare 2019). In contrast, the cost of drugs and the average use for many heroin users easily outstrips average incomes. One man at a sober house noted that for one day he could spend 50,000 Tsh ($22), "Because I am using crack cocaine which is 5,000 Tsh ($2.20) for one hit, heroin is 2,000 or 3,000 Tsh ($0.85 or $1.30) so if I want to get high I need to have 10,000 Tsh ($4.40) in the morning. I need this to avoid withdrawal, and if I don't have it I have to maybe beg the pushers" (Individual interview 5, October 2018, Kigamboni). Another former injection heroin user who now worked in outreach told me he often stole as he was spending upward of 40,000 Tsh/day ($17), and some days could even spend 100,000 Tsh ($43) (Individual interview 44, October 2018, Kinondoni).

These sums are extremely high in Tanzania and many individuals resort to differing means to support this. At one hot spot I saw men disassembling electronics to extract any valuable parts, likely for a small return (Mwenge Hotspot participant observation, October 2018). In others, men prepared to begin a day of hustling in Tanzania's informal economy, and spend the day doing small odd jobs to avoid withdrawal. Several interviewees told me that when they were using, thoughts of treatment or getting clean were far from their mind as the need to avoid withdrawal and get money to survive the day was paramount. A main goal for people who use heroin is to avoid withdrawal, or dopesickness (rusto), which means ensuring adequate supply in the morning to stave off sickness and then hustling to make money for the next hit.

In general the costs of heroin in Dar es Salaam were reported as around 2,000–3,000 Tsh ($0.85 – $1.30) per dose which, depending on tolerance could mean spending well over what most Tanzanians make in a month in one day. These costs are just for the heroin and do not include other basic needs meaning a major objective for people who use drugs is simply scraping enough together for the day and repeating the cycle the next day. Many people at hot spots have to weigh the options of getting enough money together to stave off withdrawal against the burden of attending some treatment. In cases of medical need, filariasis,[1] malaria, and other easily treatable diseases are common, but medical services also cost money in Tanzania.

For women, getting money for drugs can often lead to prostitution. Almost every former female heroin user I talked to discussed informal sex work as a means to make money. In focusing on abstinence and not reaching people who use drugs in ways that combat stigma and are more accepting, this challenge will remain. The stigma and challenges facing women reflect the realities of how drug use impacts populations differently, and how interventions cannot be a homogenized service for everyone that does not recognize this fact. Foreign donors may prioritize women and girls in other sectors, but not women who use drugs. As a former heroin user told me,

> You are going to do outreach you see women without money, many are prostitutes with STIs. I was a sex worker when I used drugs, I needed the money. That is normal for the addict. The money can go, but me I do it. It is dangerous. We have a house for women I stay with them there, we have many we take them in the past we had a house women only. And then some women come here. (Individual interview 17, October 2018, Kigamboni)

The overlap between women who use heroin and female sex workers is not known, but the much higher rates of HIV among women who use drugs illustrates the greater risk factors they undertake to pursue the habit. While male injection drug users have an estimated HIV prevalence of 28%, females have an estimated rate of 62% (Tan et al. 2015: 2). As one interviewee noted, it is "very hard here to get drugs, very expensive. You have to go sell yourself. Sometimes you use a condom, sometimes it is very risky you know. [It is] very risky to get HIV. Some men offer you a lot of money to not use a condom" (Individual interview 46, October 2018, Mwananyamala). Women who use drugs in Tanzania and sex workers are highly stigmatized and have lower rates of participation in all programs.

USING IN HOT SPOTS ("MASKANI")

In Dar es Salaam, "maskani" or hot spots emerged as sites where people who use heroin spend their time, using together, supporting each other, hustling and buying drugs. While not all people who use drugs spend time in these places, maskani are areas where drugs can be purchased and are sometimes used, creating makeshift communities in poorer neighborhoods. I visited six hot spots in Kigamboni, Mwenge, Mwananyamala (outside the methadone clinic), Temeke, Kinondoni, and Manyanya. These sites ranged from highly social areas with dozens of people, to small groups using together in various spots around the neighborhood. I visited some areas more than once, and accompanied outreach workers from methadone support organizations, sober houses, and with one international NGO.

The first hot spot I visited was in Kigamboni, an area in Dar es Salaam reachable by ferry or across the new Nyerere toll bridge. Kigamboni is a poor area known for higher levels of drug use. The hot spot was among boat builders and repairers, with some individuals using and others who had just smoked or injected nodding off. There were over 100 people in the spot, beginning their day and, for some, staving off dopesickness with their first hit. Notably, this was one spot where I noticed a man dealing, with a large wad of money. In conversation with the outreach worker I was with afterward, the dealer is apparently able to pay off police if needed (Kigamboni ferry hotspot observation, October 2018).

Visitors to offer support were uncommon. The outreach worker I was with discussed the lack of supports available in the spot, a sentiment shared among those living and spending time in Kigamboni. The outreach worker pointed out several individuals who required medical attention for infections and parasites. The focus on HIV is important, however, there are a number of other less serious illnesses that are very common in Tanzania, from malaria to water-borne pathogens. The maskani showed both the complexity of supporting a highly vulnerable population and the impacts of changes in policy which can reduce outreach or raise the cost of drugs, upsetting the tenuous daily balance many of these individuals face.

I went to these hot spots as a participant observer both with workers from sober houses and with organizations meant to support a transition to methadone treatment. I also went on one outreach trip with the needle exchange program in Temeke, which was more harm reduction focused and included cleaning up needles at hot spot locations. Many outreach workers were former users themselves and had different experiences, as the methadone outreach teams had all used methadone to get clean and were hopeful about supporting others through this process. The sober house outreach workers were less keen on methadone, as it did not work for them, but did not focus on abstinence either in their outreach. The goal of the methadone outreach teams was to encourage people to start treatment. The outreach worker used experience, rhetoric, and a mixture of cajoling and enthusiasm to encourage individuals there to come with him and get clean (Mwenge Hot Spot observation II, October 2018). At one hot spot, the small group of men we visited all said they would like to quit drugs but the prospect of interrupting their ability to find money and the fear of withdrawal was difficult to get past.

One local NGO director told me, "Everyone wants to quit of course, my experience is that 90% of people I talk to want to quit" (Individual interview 24, November 2018, Temeke). Similarly, while many interviewees who continued to use in hot spots told me or outreach workers they aspired to quit and wanted to be in sober houses, they obviously did not have the means to do so. As I outlined above, the prospects of going through the processes required to begin methadone treatment would be difficult for most. The aspiration of quitting versus the realities of doing so, are an issue for people who use drugs in general, not just in Tanzania. However, the supports in Tanzania are far from adequate even though a more effective model of harm reduction and outreach could have been better developed by now.

THE METHADONE PROGRAM IN TANZANIA AND HARM REDUCTION

Since its inception in 2011, the methadone program has grown to support several thousand clients, with outreach organizations also supporting people who use drugs to access services. MEFADA, one of the main organizations doing outreach work, has reportedly supported 1,154 clients since opening in 2014 (Individual interview 2, October 2018, Kindondoni). Outreach work involves getting beneficiaries connected to supports and easing their access to methadone treatment.[2] Ensuring beneficiaries are successful in graduating from the initial outreach sessions and remain committed to getting their methadone treatment daily, can involve a lot of work. Once the week of preparation is complete, further supports are not as available as when beneficiaries begin the program. There are many more clients than can be adequately served by outreach organizations which have to continue finding people to get them on treatment and then doing follow-up work should they relapse.

The process of doing outreach to encourage people who use drugs to attend treatment makes sense on paper as a harm reduction intervention. Beneficiaries are supposed to enter counseling to prepare for methadone, reducing their likelihood of quitting the program and receiving education to help them on their journey. The reality of this process can be messy and challenging. During my first outreach trip with the methadone support outreach organization, I watched as the outreach worker I was with spent over an hour discussing the benefits of methadone treatment with a group of young men using heroin. Encouraging these men to interrupt their day and begin treatment did not appear very convincing (Mwenge Hot Spot observation, October 2018).

The outreach worker ultimately convinced three beneficiaries to return to the NGO office with us to begin the process of starting treatment. This process begins with counseling and registration. When we caught up with this group the following week, they were back where we found them in the hot spot. They related how, since it had been too late to get to the methadone clinic on the day they received counseling, they had to return the following day and were then forced to wait several hours. This process was not easy and took time away from their limited window to make money and avoid withdrawal (Mwenge Hot Spot observation, October 2018). To be clear, getting off drugs and on methadone is a desirable goal, but it was unclear what the people receiving services wanted, how they wanted to be served, and if this process was meeting their needs. In other, similar outreach trips of varying success, the need for a spectrum of services was clear.

The methadone program receives the majority of harm reduction funding, reducing funding available for other supports. The organization I accompanied to do outreach received its funding from the Global Fund. The organization had a humble office building and outreach workers were volunteers. The importance of this work, including counseling and education essential to supporting beneficiaries through the methadone process, was not reflected in their funding. I was surprised to see how hard it could be to get people to access treatment. Deciding to start treatment is already difficult enough without the considerable obstacles people who use drugs face in Tanzania. In Temeke, I found the needle exchange program to be less focused on getting people to methadone, and more on establishing connections and practicing harm reduction. However, the more expansive services offered were due to the fact that this organization had different, more substantial funding and was able to offer other services at its office, such as a drop-in, basic medical services and some counseling. While this program also supports people in accessing methadone, it is not necessarily the goal.

In other areas, methadone can be difficult to maintain. One man at the sober house noted that, "When you use heroin you can feel it, you can't feel the methadone so at the same time I was using cocaine because you can feel the high. So most of us who are taking methadone, we are also taking cocaine. One day I skipped (methadone dose) so I was banned for one week and I found myself using again" (Individual interview 5, October 2018, Kigamboni). This statement does not mean methadone does not eventually work or that all people who enter methadone continue using other drugs. As an individual on methadone for two years told me, "At the beginning I was using methadone and drugs, then later I realized this was not good so I stopped drugs and use only methadone. The methadone is helping me" (Individual interview 45, October 2018, Mwananyamala). Two people I talked to had been on methadone for over four years, and one of these women stopped and has been on methadone again for eight months (Participant observation and interviews 45–49, October 2018, Mwananyamala).

One man at a hot spot in Kinondoni told an outreach worker he was on methadone but had continued with other drugs. He had developed a dependency to methadone but also complained that going every day cost him money and time he could not afford (Participant observation, October 2018, Mwenge). Several people I encountered at hot spots told outreach workers they had tried methadone and it had not worked. Methadone of course works for some, however, the question of whether it "works" or not is misleading. Methadone can provide long-lasting and sustainable substitution for drug use, or it can do so for a time and be returned to after a relapse. The linear mentality of a biomedical cure obscures the often complicated path to sobriety. The lack of support for greater harm reduction intervention reveals an evolution toward one method of treatment, with the intention of stopping and eradicating drug use which, for many, may not be possible.

A major area where I discussed methadone and use was outside of the Mwananyamala hospital, one of the sites in Dar es Salaam, along with Muhimbili and Temeke, where methadone is offered. The neighborhood is known for being poor and outreach is regularly undertaken as the area just outside the clinic is where people gather after having taken their methadone dose. In the morning the area was busy, with at least 100 people gathered, talking and visiting. Several people I talked to discussed how, as methadone is their daily routine, they spend time here after taking their dose in this place, with their friends.

The community aspect of hot spots is a feature I have not seen considered in the literature, or more generally in works on homelessness, vulnerability, and drug use. In the absence of meaningful counseling, psychological or social supports from the methadone clinic, former drug users in the program gather to support each other. As a key factor in both gaining and maintaining sobriety, social support is a remarkably under-theorized aspect of recovery. Most of the literature on methadone in Tanzania does not mention it at all. As I discuss later, drop-in centers closed by Magufuli's government were one area where both former and current drug users could gather to support each other. With the closure of these centers, the area outside Mwananyamala is a site that emerged in their place.

When I asked one woman who had taken her methadone dose a couple of hours before why she was still spending time outside Mwananyamala hospital, she said "Where can we go? When we are finished drinking methadone we come here, we talk to each other . . . when we go home, what are we supposed to do at home? You sit with your friends, you talk, change your minds, give a little bit of advice. Some people are still using, some people they don't use" (Individual interview 46, October 2018, Mwananyamala). The need for social support and lack of meaningful work mean people prefer to stay, even if they are around drug use. The alternative of being at home, facing the challenges of being bored and not being able to go to work are potentially worse risk factors for relapse. As another woman at this spot told me, "When I'm home I'm bored, the whole time I'm at home I have nothing to do and then I started to use. I still come here, I stay for a while and then I go to my house . . . these people they're my friends, they are friendlier. That's why we are here" (Individual interview 47, October 2018, Mwananyamala).

With the lack of employment, every interviewee that day noted their preference to stay at the clinic and visit. The burden of attending every day showed a real commitment among some interviewees wanting to get clean. While return bus fare is only 1,500 Tsh ($0.65), for individuals without real employment (like many other Tanzanians most work in the informal sector), this is a cost that adds up. The cost of transport is exacerbated for women who have children to care for. Traveling by dala dala, as the buses in Dar es Salaam are called, often involves waiting for the bus to fill before departure. There are no strict schedules and dala dalas are not always quick which takes up time during the day—and for methadone users this is every day—that could be spent working. However, everyone still wants employment and some are able to fit methadone treatment into their schedule before work. In interviewing people who use drugs themselves, everyone requested better services, financial support, and work. The main issue confronting people who use drugs in Dar es Salaam, whether they have completed time at a sober house or are in methadone programs for years is social and economic support.

It is difficult to criticize the methadone clinics, as they do important work and methadone can be a path to sobriety or a healthier life for some people who use drugs. I showed the difficulties of using methadone as a single intervention for people who use drugs not to dismiss opioid agonist therapy as a crucial intervention, but rather to point out that it cannot be the only intervention. The issue is not the clinics themselves, nor the service providers who work in them, but rather the lack of harm reduction supports around these clinics and a lack of work to address the economic and social barriers to access. These barriers could be addressed in part by scaling up the needle exchange programs, providing more counseling and undertaking small interventions such as the provision of basic medical services. In Temeke, the goal of the outreach organization is to provide options, as methadone is not for everyone (Individual interview 18, November 2018, Temeke). Unfortunately, the government has chosen a one-size-fits-all approach which exists with little support beyond foreign donors.

SOBER HOUSES, 12 STEPS AND APPROACHES TO HELP PEOPLE WHO USE DRUGS

Through connections built with local NGOs, I heard about a former heroin user who spearheaded the sober house movement in Dar es Salaam. Learning about the movement was unexpected as there have been no academic studies that I was able to find on sober houses other than a planned future study from Volda University. Sober houses started in Zanzibar and are a mix of 12-step approaches borrowed from the United States, harm reduction and a grassroots effort to provide some supports for people with drug use issues. They have become more common in recent years, led largely by former heroin users or others with substance misuse issues. I met with some of the sober house volunteers and staff and was able to observe their program. This program, while abstinence based included outreach that sounded like harm reduction, with the recognition that most people were unable to attend a sober house and in the interim require understanding and help. Many of these houses have formed networks that are mutually supportive and are founded in the hope of reaching people who use drugs, helping them better understand their addiction and make improvements in their lives.

The first sober houses in Tanzania opened in 2009, founded by a man named Suleiman Mauly, with supporters from the United States (Warner and Boswell 2015). The first sober house in Zanzibar was called Detroit Sober house, owing to its roots in American 12-step programs. One man I talked to currently at a sober house, started his recovery there in 2009 as "detroit sober house, that was the first place of the sober houses" (Individual interview 39, October 2018, Kigamboni). Since this time, the model spread into Dar es Salaam and some other towns in Tanzania. A proposed project from Volda University numbered sober houses at seven in Zanzibar and three in Dar es Salaam (Volda University 2019). During my time I visited three houses in Kigamboni, a lower-income area of Dar known for drug use, but also heard of another site south of Dar and one that had opened in Dodoma. There seemed to be a growing movement as the supports are in high demand and exist in the absence of any other social supports or meaningful approaches that address addiction beyond a medical model. Sober houses offer people who use drugs some tools to understand drug addiction.

The development of sober houses is a novel process in Tanzania, where heroin users are more often treated as criminals or medical clients. As I noted previously, mental health supports are weak and are far from enough to support people who use drugs that require these interventions (Individual interview 12, October 2018, Muhimbili University). The lack of training within mental health education also presents a major obstacle. In fact, the woman I talked to who organized the sober houses in Dar had done so because of her experience with mental health:

> A long time, I used for 12 years and before the 12 steps I was in mental hospital. In 2003 I was in mental hospital, that time there is no sober house, no other treatment here. I go to mental hospital, they treat me like I am mentally ill. They tell me I have substance abuse and then next time bipolar or mania. In 2006 I went there three times. They treated me with mental illness but I'm not. They don't talk with us or treat drug use. (Individual interview 17, October 2018, Kigamboni)

While this experience may be unusual, it depicts the lack of understanding in medical training at that time of substance misuse. No other interviewees received any mental health interventions. At the methadone clinic, I talked with a social worker at Temeke, one of three who sees between 15–25 clients per day (Individual interviews 21,22, October 2018, Temeke). This number is out of close to 1,000 beneficiaries enrolled there. In our discussion, the social worker outlined how they support planning treatment, connecting with family to discuss the needs of the client and intervening in the case of relapse (Individual interviews 21,22, October 2018, Temeke). The health-centered approach for injection drug use and drug dependency more generally does not receive much attention in official health policy, despite the growing methadone program. While mental health care is often an important component of treatment for drug use, mental health services in Tanzania are inadequate, with over 80% of mental health work being done by traditional and faith healers (Tanzania National Health Policy 2017: 9).

In this context, where drug use is not discussed, these houses offer a spot away from use with a community of people who have shared experiences. Many interviewees noted their desire to attend a program at these houses where there is an understanding of their experience. 12-step programs are based on abstinence and a higher power, but they also offer peer support, something that is lacking in Dar es Salaam. As with the supportive communities of former users around methadone clinics, sober houses are a reaction to a lack of other social supports available.

I found that sober houses really are the only other option available in Tanzania for people who use drugs, or for any people with substance misuse issues. I also found the community that had developed in these houses to be an important network in continuing involvement and encouraging mutually supportive relationships, as sober house volunteers often follow up with beneficiaries even though many return to drug use. Sober houses have people who found sobriety and swear by the process as the only way to move forward. There are also high rates of relapse as is the case with many drug addiction programs. The 12-step program, though abstinence based shares a unique perspective with harm reduction, in recognizing the challenge of overcoming addiction and expecting and forgiving relapse, which is a part of the recovery process. In the context of the limited options available for people who use drugs, at sober houses there is at least an attempt understand addiction itself, forgive and break down the stigma around drug use. In the absence of government supports, sober house volunteers play multiple roles role including outreach, support, and advocacy.

All of these roles and work are done without any government support or any foreign or donor funding. In discussion with one sober house director, he described how random sources of funding sometimes became available when private individuals took interest and offered short-term funding for periods of three to six months (Individual interview 19, October 2018, Kigamboni). With no sustainable sources of funding, attendees at the clinics are required to pay for their stay, depending on the sober house this can range from Tsh 300,000/month to Tsh 500,000/month ($130–$220 per month). These costs are extremely high for the average Tanzanian, let alone vulnerable people who use drugs. There are few ways to pay these costs for the majority of people who use drugs, unless they are able to rely on family or friends to pay their way. Many interviewees lacked these connections. The staff at sober houses try to support as many people as possible even when they cannot pay. In one sober house with room for 10 clients, only two were paying the full costs, six were paying half, and two were not paying at all (Individual interview 19, October 2018, Kigamboni).

The efforts of sober houses to include individuals who cannot pay, and likely could not repay their stay after attaining sobriety, is due to the high demand and an understanding that most people truly cannot afford to stay at a sober house. Many people want to attend but can only do so through sponsorship by friends or family. The model is similar to the United States, where treatment is offered through numerous private clinics, often based on intensive counseling, trauma-based care, and a 12-step program to abstinence. This, now multibillion dollar industry in the United States, has been a cornerstone of drug treatment for decades in the West, despite the mixed evidence on their effectiveness. Treatment and sobriety are difficult, and require continued support. In one sober house, rates of relapse were estimated at 30–40%, which is quite low. However, this number is based on relapsing and leaving during treatment, not on experiences afterward where clients can face even greater challenges.

Interestingly, the overlap between harm reduction, abstinence, and methadone in sober houses appears to be based less on hard ideological lines and more on the need to simply do something. The motives guiding activists, in contrast to the Tanzanian government, are not based on ideology and more on lived experience. As with grassroots organizations across Dar es Salaam, the need to get involved and work toward some level of supports is a genuine desire among former drug users who recall the difficulties drug users face. I found sober house staff also undertook outreach that was not focused on preaching abstinence but rather seeing what individual needs are, visiting and sometimes providing a little support. The outreach I witnessed was not highly organized but very appreciated in the hot spots, even in the absence of material support. There is less pressure and more openness, and the shared understanding, based on the volunteers' own experiences, that sometimes understanding and hope is all they can offer. The flexibility required in working with a variety of individuals, with unique histories is reflected in this outreach, rather than the one-size-fits-all, top-down approaches favored by war on drugs ideologues who tend to view this population as homogenous.

CONCLUSION

Over the past three decades, heroin use has increased in Tanzania and efforts to slow the traffic or influx of drugs into the country continue to fail. The literature on heroin use in Tanzania has tended to focus on HIV/AIDS. However, the greater context in which use takes place can help guide interventions and better meet the needs of people who use drugs. In this chapter, I showed some of the complexities surrounding drug use in Tanzania and describe some individual experiences that could guide the implementation of better services for people who use drugs. In outlining the experiences above, my goal was to show the unique trajectories and lives of people accessing services, which better illustrates the efficacy and weaknesses of existing programs in place in the unique context of Tanzania.

I found some common threads throughout these stories, as the combination of poverty, lack of opportunity, and the expense of drug use produce vulnerabilities that are not being addressed by current programming. People who use drugs are at increased risk of contracting HIV/AIDS, a number of preventable and treatable diseases, face random police harassment and are criminalized, which I describe more in the next chapter. All interviewees needed much greater support, whether it is accessing and maintaining methadone or getting some basic, inexpensive medical treatments. From the perspective of people who use drugs, the common refrain was a desire for greater opportunity. This is not a shocking finding, yet people who use drugs are so often denied agency that it is important to highlight.

I also note that existing services, including methadone and sober houses, are not enough to support people who use drugs to build my argument in this book that harm reduction is being simplified and imposed upon people who use drugs. Existing supports are underfunded or not funded at all, resulting in people who use drugs organizing ad hoc communities of support that require much greater support. The experiences of drug users should be the basis of interventions which are purposely excluded by the government of Tanzania. The voices and concerns of drug users are not included in shaping the policies that affect them, a fact that is common in many countries despite the strong, evidence-based voices of activists with lived experience.

The lack of opportunity, economic development, and widespread corruption in the country place people defined as criminal by the state in precarious positions. Despite the lack of government support, people who use drugs have organized themselves and are continually advocating for greater support, even in the face of an increasingly repressive government. Methadone treatment, sober houses, informal and formal networks are only in place due to the activism of people who use drugs themselves. However, the government takes credit for available supports, while not addressing the underlying concerns and much greater needs among this population. The election of John Magufuli in 2015 should be understood with this context in mind. The services available for people who use drugs prior to him were far from perfect. However, the Tanzanian government since 2016 has only introduced fear, along with unhelpful policies, that are not improving life for people who use drugs. In the next chapter, I explore how this happened.

NOTES

1. Lymphatic filiarias "is a parasitic disease caused by microscopic, thread-like worms. The adult worms only live in the human lymph system. The lymph system maintains the body's fluid balance and fights infections. Lymphatic filariasis is spread from person to person by mosquitoes. People with the disease can suffer from lymphedema and elephantiasis and in men, swelling of the scrotum, called hydrocele. Lymphatic filariasis is a leading cause of permanent disability worldwide. Communities frequently shun and reject women and men disfigured by the disease. Affected people frequently are unable to work because of their disability, and this harms their families and their communities" (Centers for Disease Control and Prevention 2020).

2. In Tanzania, individuals accessing supports from NGOs are referred to in English as "beneficiaries."

Chapter 5

Performance and Reality

The War on Drugs in Tanzania

> *Because this guy knows how to perform, he makes people to have this fear, he does this purposely to make people afraid of doing anything so he can do what he wants to do.*
>
> —Individual interview 39, October 2018, Kigamboni

Early in his tenure as president, while still enjoying a reputation for being tough on corruption and "cleaning up" Tanzania, John Magufuli began cracking down on vulnerable populations. In 2016, the Tanzanian government targeted female sex workers and gay men. At the same time, the government initiated a review of policies toward these populations and their access to life-saving anti-retroviral treatment (ART) and harm reduction supports. In 2016 and 2017, Magufuli then very publicly declared a war on drugs and drug use in the country. Within months, following the arrest of many low-level drug users and accusations against several higher-profile targets, including members of opposition political parties, the government announced its success in tackling the issue of drug use in Tanzania (Kamagi 2018).

The official stories told by the government and the impacts of this crackdown on the ground, however, were quite different. While pursuing a war on drugs was clearly performative and fit well with Magufuli's greater drive to "clean-up" Tanzania, the crackdown was not successful in eliminating drug use and made life for people who use drugs worse. Despite the lack of success in fully eliminating drugs, the high level of cooperation between the Ministry of Health, the Drug Control and Enforcement Agency, District Commissioner Paul Makonda, and the police resulted in drug users being targeted on multiple levels, legally, socially, and in accessing health services.

Referring to the Kenyan government's pursuit of its own war on drugs, Margarita Dimova argues that "Kenyan political leaders perform the war on drugs in order to shore up their image . . . a locally led war on drugs thus offers a whole new set of smokescreens and discursive planes through which to manipulate public perceptions and to bolster donors' confidence" (Dimova 2016: 238). Dimova's argument about the performative aspects of the war on drugs and its use as a way to shape perception is important. However, from my fieldwork, I found Magufuli's performance not only created a sense of fear and anxiety but that this strong rhetoric was mirrored in government policy, with high-level ministers aligning with his vision and many levels of government working together to enact new, harsher policies that broke with previous ones.

In this chapter I show that, while a war on drugs aligned with Magufuli's particular brand of moral populism, the government of Tanzania also implemented policy changes targeting people who use drugs. The CCM has a long history of aid dependency, leaving responsibility for the delivery of services to vulnerable Tanzanians almost exclusively in the hands of foreign donors. The KVP population relies on foreign funding for the limited services they receive which leaves a precarious sector exposed to risks should there be any changes to funding levels. In spite of the difficult situation fostered by the Tanzanian government, local NGOs have worked hard to advocate for better services. However, these local NGOs have also faced new challenges, as the Tanzanian government avoided real consultation and paid little attention to the grassroots work being done to address the gaps in service caused by decades of aid dependency and government inattention. The crackdown on drug use is a visible manifestation of the war on drugs; however, the government also targeted people who use drugs by dismantling progressive health policy and harm reduction supports, effectively reducing access to services and weakening the already limited services available.

THE CRACKDOWN: MAGUFULI'S WAR ON DRUGS

In February 2017, President John Magufuli undertook a number of policies to enact a war on drugs, enlisting the Dar es Salaam Regional Commissioner, Paul Makonda, along with the armed forces to root out the "social cancer" of drug use (*Famagusta Gazette* 2017). Magufuli made clear that "no one is too prominent to be arrested even if they are politicians, security officers, cabinet ministers or the child of a prominent person . . . even if my wife, Janeth, is involved she should be arrested" (Shaban 2017). Magufuli also launched crackdowns on sex workers and gay men which continued periodically during his tenure.

The appearance of control, while also causing chaos and confusion among targets of a crackdown, is a useful tool in asserting and establishing a position of power. Dimova (2016) similarly explores how crisis narratives around drug use in Kenya were utilized by the government during elections to create a similar effect. Magufuli engineered "a crisis," as drug use and gay men were present previously, using powerful rhetoric to raise these issues to prominence and give them the appearance of major social problems. In doing so, Magufuli began the work of shaping narratives around drug use in the country, echoing war-on-drugs ideology.

The Government of Tanzania, at the same time, took action to change policy that, in many ways, reflected Magufuli's harsh rhetoric. Policy change included the implementation of the Drug Control and Enforcement Act in 2015, replacing the Drugs and Prevention of Illicit Traffic in Drugs Act and empowering an agency, the Drug Control and Enforcement Agency (DCEA), to prosecute and enforce it (*Xinhua News* 2017). The DCEA order includes provisions allowing for harsher penalties for people in possession of drugs or involved in drug trafficking. The punishment for anyone caught trafficking or producing drugs can be life imprisonment, and anyone caught with drugs may face a sentence of up to five years or be fined 500,000 to 1 million Tanzanian shillings ($217–$435), depending on the type of drug (DCEA 2017). Furthermore, the onus is put on any individual caught with small quantities of drugs to prove they are not for sale or distribution (DCEA 2017) which can be a difficult task that is subject to interpretation by law enforcement. Syringes and other drug paraphernalia are illegal, as is the act of using drugs itself.

One aspect of the Act that appears to support people who use drugs is a new provision that allows users to avoid up to three years in jail or a fine by going to government recognized treatment. The realities of enforcing the Act are already unrealistic, as police do not have the time or capacity to arrest every single drug user. Seen from the perspective of people who use drugs, however, being forced to attend treatment can be equally unrealistic. As one director of a harm reduction organization told me when asked if this provision was a positive, "No, because methadone is not for everyone. Now police have to enforce more. It doesn't work anyway because even if they are caught and have to go on methadone, we have to prepare them and we try to give them options" (Individual interview 24, October 2018, Temeke).

Treatment is of course better than imprisonment, but the focus remains not on the individual and their needs, but on enforcing a single option for people who use drugs, which is required rather than chosen. Furthermore, treatment still ignores the myriad of challenges faced by drug users and it is unclear to what extent the police have really followed through in supporting treatment. Most people I interviewed or people who use drugs at hot spots were not given the option of treatment but rather, as always, were simply harassed or temporarily detained.

The creation of the DCEA and the government's stated commitment to ending drug use for the betterment of Tanzanians helped foster the appearance of an activist leader and citizens were called upon to come together and contribute to support the war on drugs. A *Tanzania Daily News* editorial reported in September 2018 "We should join forces in the anti-drug war" (*Tanzanian Daily News* 2018). In Mwanza, northern Tanzania, Prime Minister Kassim Majaliwa warned that 10,000 people needed rehabilitation and requested "Tanzanians to work closely with the Drug Control and Enforcement Authority (DCEA) to thwart the network of narcotic trade" (*Xinhua News* 2018). The *Tanzania Daily News*, a paper often supportive of government initiatives, pitched this battle in epic terms: "Perpetrators of the illicit drug trade are virtually human satans. For their machinations are hugely costly to the human race, through wrecking the health of may {*sic*} potentially resourceful individuals who would otherwise contribute immensely to the social welfare enhancement and economic development of particular countries" (*Tanzanian Daily News* 2018).

The calls for Tanzanian citizens to support a national drug war is simply a way of framing drugs and the people that use them as a social problem to be removed. Despite a largely pro-government media, many activists and NGO workers challenged the narrative of the drug war. In some interviews, I was told that Magufuli's crackdown was a cynical attempt to increase his own control over NGO work. Some individuals even noted that the war on drugs may be a way for the corrupt Tanzanian government to gain greater control over the drug trade itself. Dimova found a similar discourse in Kenya, as people view the government as "both complicit in transnational crime and the most effective antidote to it" (Dimova 2016: 232). While Magufuli appeared genuine in his desire to end drug use, the idea of the government itself trying to displace major drug dealers and earn money from the illicit drug trade is plausible. Such a theory is impossible to confirm, but few, if any members of the CCM were implicated in the war on drugs, despite their longtime hold on power.

The Tanzanian government instead targeted high-profile individuals with less obvious links to international drug trafficking. In 2017, the government accused the main opposition leader of CHADEMA, Freeman Mbowe, of involvement in a drug trafficking ring (Musiyo 2017). The charges were dropped but Mbowe has faced numerous charges since then, including prison time for illegal protesting, part of the CCM's focus on eliminating political opposition. The government never produced any evidence of his involvement in drug trafficking. The CCM also accused Yusuf Manji, CEO of Quality Group Limited and Chairman of YANGA FC, of heroin use among other charges (Sixpence 2017). These are just a few of 65 high-profile individuals, including celebrities and a pastor, that the government accused of involvement in drug trafficking or possession, none of whom were subsequently found guilty (Musiyo 2017).

While high-profile accusations made the news, a major push to nab low-level drug traffickers and drug users was also underway. Prime Minister Majaliwa claimed 11,303 suspects were arrested between July 2016 and January 2017, with 9,174 suspects found guilty and 238 found not guilty (*The Citizen* 2017). By the time of my fieldwork, the prime minister declared the war on drugs a triumph, estimating a 90% success rate, a strange statement possibly referring to drug supply (Kamagi 2018). The *Tanzanian Daily News,* without any supporting evidence, repeated these claims as facts, "It [the government] has scored high marks in the anti-drug war. This is borne out emphatically by the 90 percent reduction rate of illicit drugs trade in the market and illicit trafficking" (*Tanzanian Daily News* 2018). Apparently, Tanzania had done what other countries with greater resources and capacity could not and successfully ended the war on drugs.

While there was some evidence during my fieldwork 2018 of disruption to the drug supply, the trade and use of heroin appeared to be largely back in place. The crackdown in 2016–2017 impacted drug supply, causing large-scale traffickers to adapt by lying low or temporarily continuing operations remotely from another region or country. Lower-level dealers faced increased scrutiny and potential arrest if caught. Ultimately, however, the supply limitations did little other than force people who use drugs into more difficult circumstances. From interviews undertaken with people involved in working with drug users or who were themselves using at the time, it seemed more likely that long-term impacts on drug supply would be minimal, while the short-term impacts on marginalized people who use drugs were much greater. NGOs noticed some clients resorting to use of other drugs, going further to find drugs and participating in riskier behaviors such as needle-sharing, flash-blood or using other, more dangerous, substances. When the trade did return to pre-crackdown levels prices remained slightly higher and the disruption left lasting fears of arrest and discrimination.

A 2018 report described the political economy of the drug trade in Tanzania as "a disrupted criminal market" due to the impact of reforms undertaken by President Magufuli (Haysom et al. 2018: 3). This report highlighted how Magufuli did not end the illicit drug flow but rather transformed it (Haysom et al. 2018), a reality borne out by my fieldwork. At MEFADA, an organization supporting drug users' access to methadone treatment, one employee noted an increase in users seeking treatment as drugs became more difficult to access due to fears of being caught using or selling drugs. As mentioned, the DCEA contains a provision for the "identification, treatment, education, after care, rehabilitation and social integration of drug addicts" (DCEA 2017). While this appears to be a humane policy, there is little effort put toward rehabilitation, education, after-care, or social integration.

Forcing people into treatment is antithetical to a harm reduction approach. Furthermore, forcing treatment as the alternative is not a meaningful reform as, out of fear and the need to continue using, many individuals opt to avoid treatment through bribes, continue using while on methadone or commit to treatment and return to use. One thing is certain, Magufuli's interventions in the drug war "created a feeling of huge insecurity for anyone who has been involved, or could be accused of being involved in the drug trade or corruption" (Haysom et al. 2018: 6).

The ability to pursue a war on drugs requires the cooperation and support of a number of levels of government, none of which opposed the repressive drive of John Magufuli to attack vulnerable people. The war on drugs, as a project of the Tanzanian state, reveals the overall efforts made by Magufuli during his tenure to bring various sectors of the Tanzanian government under his control. Now that he has passed away, many scholars reflecting on his legacy agree that the Magufuli era turned the CCM back toward its authoritarian roots. In the war on drugs, while Magufuli was far from able to exert authoritarian control completely, the cooperation of the government with a directive from him to target vulnerable populations was a major factor in disrupting the lives of already vulnerable drug users.

The level to which the Tanzanian government has successfully been able to set priorities for people who use drugs can be seen in both levels of access to harm reduction services and the experiences of people who use drugs. While Magufuli's drug war entailed a highly rhetorical performance, the war on drugs sets impossible goals and the Tanzanian state is in reality limited in its capacity to truly eliminate drug use. In 2020, the UNODC commended Tanzania for its ability "to control and monitor its borders in collaboration with international security agencies by conducting special operations that have hugely helped to control the illicit trade" (*Xinhua News* 2020). Similar statements were made during my fieldwork, yet there is no evidence at all behind the idea that control of drugs has been effective and drug use continues.

People who use drugs represent an easy population to target, especially when stigmatized as part of the endemic corruption that has saddled Tanzania over the past decades. The manufactured linkage of drug use and corruption provides the government a useful tool to depict a war on drugs as a measure necessary in taking down the "big fish," the corrupt drug trafficking elites perceived to be involved in the drug trade and the corruption that is supposedly slowing Tanzanian development. Due to this idea of tackling high-level corruption, I found in interviews that some NGOs initially welcomed the crackdown on drug use and even some individuals using drugs at the time saw the crackdown as a positive step in addressing the corruption in the country (Individual interview 19, October 2018, Kigamboni). Some interviewees saw the government as actively involved in the drug trade and supported Magufuli's pledge to take down corrupt elites. The strength of the linkage between corruption and drug use can almost automatically justify any means to end the trade, while conveniently letting the CCM off the hook.

Ultimately, the actions described above show how the war on drugs became a site for a demonstration and performance of the president's power in tackling a seemingly ever-present social issue. While this performative aspect is important, the policy changes undertaken made the war on drugs a reality for people who use drugs, empowering the DCEA to actually implement the harsh directives of the president and reveal that the Tanzanian war on drugs is not just performative.

BEHIND THE CRACKDOWN: SHIFTING POLICY AND MARGINALIZATION

A key focus for foreign donors aiming to prevent and treat HIV/AIDS in Tanzania is reaching Key and Vulnerable Populations (KVP). It is through the funding provided by these donors that much of the harm reduction available in the country, including methadone treatment, is possible. Prior to the election of Magufuli, the sector was relatively free to determine the supports needed to reach and provides services to KVP, including harm reduction services such as needle exchange and provision of lubricants. Magufuli's war on drugs involved a re-evaluation of available harm reduction supports and a review of the delivery of programs to KVP in the country.

In 2016, Magufuli's government was also disrupting the aid sector, putting program delivery on hold as the new government worked to adjust laws governing KVP and HIV/AIDS transmission. While incarceration, lower supply of drugs and police harassment can be temporary, changes to aid and support for KVP have longer lasting impacts. During a period of almost six months in 2016, several NGOs, both local and international, described being unable to meaningfully engage with KVP and offer services during the review period, and many are still dealing with the impacts of the Tanzanian government turning its back on harm reduction.

The review of supports to KVP was one of the first major actions by the Tanzanian government and it was immediately apparent that this review was not intended to bolster harm reduction services. The result of the review was a disappointment for more harm reduction oriented groups focused on KVP, but it did seem to be an improvement for HIV/AIDS interventions more generally. The government loosened previously restrictive policies supporting HIV/AIDS interventions, allowing the work of major NGOs such as JHPIEGO and ICAP to reach more people and provide better treatment. Major concerns impacting all Tanzanians, such as the fact that many Tanzanians with HIV/AIDS do not know their status, drove the government to increase flexibility and capacity in testing.

However, the review also included some notable reverses toward services available for KVP. While funding for HIV/AIDS is limited, the expansion of testing and treatment for all Tanzanians did not need to include any cuts for KVP. Funding was not the issue, as the review was clearly ideologically driven. Health Minister Ummy Mwalimu, describing the findings of the review, found that "despite the good intention of the Government and its HIV and AIDS partners to start provision of HIV and AIDS services at community level . . . some implementing partners were promoting homosexuality, contrary to the laws of the land" and reports had "provided detailed evidence of existence of homosexuality promotional activities" (United Republic of Tanzania 2017).

The findings of the review came after the government's active involvement in intimidating homosexuals and threatening organizations that worked with them in 2016. Some local NGOs reported being subject to raids if they did not get rid of lubricants (Individual interview 24, November 2018, Temeke). The other KVP populations did not fare much better. PWID, already facing increased harassment and intimidation due to Magufuli's drug war, now saw their options for treatment and support narrowed. The government shuttered harm reduction centers, where drug abuse was supposedly rampant, and a fear of reprisals led PWID with HIV or other infectious diseases to not seek treatment. The government did allow the Médecins du Monde (MDM) needle exchange to continue. However, they also restricted its expansion to other areas of Dar es Salaam. During outreach in 2018, MDM was still unable to provide needed and effective services beyond Temeke and limited its outreach services to other hot spots. NGOs had to adapt to these laws, submit reports and not act contrary to the penal code. Minister Mwalimu's statement also directed health-care providers to provide service free of discrimination. It is unclear, however, how unbiased service can be achieved given the discriminatory stance of the government.

The revision of KVP policy reduced evidence-based practice and went against advice given to the government by local advocates to reduce HIV/AIDS among KVP. Many grassroots activists and service providers advocated for evidence-based interventions, such as "promoting and providing condoms for MSM and FSW [Female Sex Workers], promoting the use of water-based lubricants for MSM, screening and treating STIs, harm reduction techniques for IDUs (e.g., needle syringe exchange programs), and HIV counseling, testing, and early treatment initiation" (Mpondo et al. 2017: 4). The need for these services is evidenced by the fact that, while HIV/AIDS rates went from 5.1% in 2011 to 4.6% in 2018, rates among KVP remain stubbornly high as these populations are subjected to politically motivated policy directives that severely hinder their access to healthcare. The government has ignored the recommendations above and has instead focused on a limited and partial approach.

The tension between supporting KVP from a healthcare lens, while also making their existence illegal, illustrates the state of harm reduction in the country and is an issue facing many states across the globe. With PWID, the need for interventions is clear. However, the possession of any quantity of drugs or any drug use equipment is illegal, raising major questions as to how services can effectively be delivered to these people who are in constant violation of the law. While the government presented the KVP revision process as inclusive consultation in order to improve harm reduction services, the perspective of those involved in this process told a different story.

A VIEW OF THE PROCESS FROM THE GROUND

Among many service providers, there were hopes that Magufuli's tough approach would clean up a number of sectors, tighten up the practices of local and international NGOs, and ensure funding reached the areas it needed to. Corruption was considered an issue impacting all sectors, including local NGOs. Improved oversight, better tracking of outcomes and a realignment of available funding toward efficient and high-performing NGOs indeed could have been a step forward in improving services to KVP.

Magufuli's initial statements and involvement in the sector reflected a move toward these improvements. As one local NGO found, once Magufuli was in power, bureaucrats were on notice, and were worried about keeping their jobs. The random spot checks made by Magufuli in certain departments made civil servants nervous and therefore responsive. As a director at one NGO I visited noted, "There was a time when Magufuli is firing everyone, nobody is sure. During this time we were conducting a survey and we had the best cooperation [with the government] because they were scared" (Individual interview 14, October 2018, Mikocheni). In this case, a process that previously may have been delayed became easier to undertake. This example, however, was one among many other instances where I heard of government obfuscation and confusion as an unruly bureaucracy, long used to getting its own way, was reformed to follow a number of new processes, or at least appear to be following Magufuli's dictates.

Increasing oversight in the NGO sector may not be a bad thing; however, under Magufuli, it was motivated less by concern for a well-functioning NGO sector and more by a need for control. A legal and human-rights focused NGO described how previous relationships with top-level bureaucrats, who had worked in these sectors for years and were often experts, were disrupted as Magufuli removed longtime bureaucrats with experience and appointed unknown candidates with questionable expertise (Individual interview 14, October 2018, Mikocheni). The removal of experienced civil servants helps to explain the change in direction from support by those who understood the issues, to a political project enacted by government allies.

The crackdown and the KVP revision process outweighed any of the potential benefits from a temporarily more responsive bureaucracy. A major problem was fear, in both the public service and among politicians, of engaging in issues that are not priorities for the current government or on sensitive topics such as methadone. One foreign harm reduction organization, hoping to begin operating in Tanzania, found it difficult to connect with anyone interested in supporting their entry into the country to provide needed services. This organization found initial support from the Health Ministry, but this support dissipated during the KVP revision process (Individual interview 1, September 2018, Conducted remotely). When I talked to the director of this organization, she noted how the government seemed disorganized, and believed that the lack of engagement seemed to be less a tactic of disengagement, but rather an uncertainty and sensitivity as to what the government could support. The difficulty in operating in Tanzania during this time was echoed by other NGOs already working in the country, unsure about what guidelines would emerge, how new policies would impact them, and whether they would be able to continue their work.

While some NGOs were asked to participate in the KVP revision process, the development of the new policy guidelines was ultimately a top-down process. In several interviews, participants in the process told me that the discussions were a one-sided exercise in dictating terms rather than engaging in meaningful consultation. The head of a local drug users support organization noted that the process was very much driven by a focus on HIV/AIDS treatment only, not broader services. Local NGOs, willing to focus only on HIV/AIDS prevention and treatment were eligible for more funding, while the government considered those organizations in favor of greater harm reduction efforts outside of the focus of the KVP revisions (Individual interview 4, September 2018, Mikocheni). The head of a sober house network who was also involved in the process emphatically told me:

> I was part of this process, we talk so many times, even now we talk, but we just see them [government officials] and they don't know anything, they don't know

> what we do. I worked with the government on guidelines about the MSM [men who have sex with men] and other KVP but after this government comes, and the election of this president, they say they don't want to give them support. I am the addict, others were there, and there were a lot of discussions the government was trying not to accept. But we try our best, that's why these [guidelines] are not strong, but if you are not there, there are more problems. (Individual interview 17, October 2018, Kigamboni)

The revision of guidelines impacted local organizations greatly, as many are small with little or no funding. For larger NGOs with greater ability to access funding from partners such as the Global Fund, concerns over working with MSM required a need to choose language carefully. The director of one NGO noted that there is less flexibility than under former President Kikwete, and HIV/AIDS is a more useful narrative to access funding, from both donors and the government (Individual interview 10, August 2018, Mikocheni). Harm reduction is a goal for agencies such as the Global Fund but, in this case, framing work as medical and HIV/AIDS focused was a result of intimidation by the Tanzanian government, not the desire of these agencies.

Some organizations accepted this new reality, indeed there was no other choice, as the government dismissed the rights-based approach being advocated by grassroots organizations in favor of focusing only on HIV interventions. This restriction of services coincided with the active harassment and arrests of people who use drugs. A human-rights based approach was not possible and, despite some advocacy, it was clear that the government would only allow for methadone treatment to continue (Individual interview 2, October 2018, Kinondoni). The work of outreach organizations supporting people who use drugs also continues. However, the focus on getting people on methadone is more pronounced, reducing the services being offered at hot spots. Even larger organizations involved, funded through PEPFAR or the CDC, had less of a say, as one CDC employee told me that it was clear some things would not continue such as giving lubricants to men who have sex with men (Individual interview 13, September 2018, Dar es Salaam city center). An epidemiologist I spoke to at Muhimbili University summed up the whole process of intervening in the provision of services to KVP frankly: "The KVP revision process was absolutely politically driven with too many discussions around behavioural issues" (Individual interview 15, October 2018, Muhimbili).

The political sensitivity around the issue of drug use, in a country like any other where many people have friends and family impacted by illicit drugs, appears manufactured. The renewal of conservative stigmas around drug use is part of a larger process pursued by the Tanzanian government to align organizations with a moralistic vision for the country. Magufuli's government refocused issues around vulnerable people such as young women, gay men and drug users, sometimes under the guise of morality and other times simply revealing his deep resentment of these groups, the most vulnerable in Tanzanian society. During my time in Tanzania, most people involved in supporting drug users, or even those who knew people who used drugs, did not seem to fully share the sensitivities and issues surrounding methadone. It appeared that any sensitivities or concerns emanated from the government, as if providing supports to drug users is taboo and needs to be shrouded in secrecy.

The reverberations of Magufuli's opinions echoed down the channels of power in his government. While some interviewees felt that politicians formerly supportive of harm reduction changed their opinions to appease Magufuli, it was unclear to what extent ministries actually opposed Magufuli's directives. For example, the minister of health's KVP guideline statement encourages the streamlining and centralizing of service provision through health centers only, and introduces stringent reporting and registration requirements for all NGOs in the sector (Tanzanian Ministry of Health Statement on KVP 2017). Furthermore, the document "urges" regional officials to "closely supervise activities undertaken by NGOs working to fight HIV and AIDS in their respective areas" so they "adhere to their geographical scope" (Tanzanian Ministry of Health Statement on KVP 2017). Finally, as illustrated above, policies and directives are in place and being followed by many levels of government. The separation between an independent civil service working to support evidence-based approaches and an ideologically driven government does not appear to be prominent.

As mentioned above, even international NGOs with greater resources experienced disruptions. In aligning with the Ministry of Health, NGOs must "ensure that they do not act contrary to the National laws, including the Penal Code" (Tanzanian Ministry of Health Statement on KVP 2017). NGOs faced a difficult situation. The politically driven process of targeting vulnerable people in Tanzania is an example of the major tensions between legal and moral strictures and the provision of harm reduction services. When practiced as a medical treatment without consideration of the larger restrictions being put in place, harm reduction cannot fully address the needs of people who use drugs. Some NGOs I talked to saw some basic harm reduction support as better than nothing, even if their work was compromised in some ways. As the director of one organization noted,

> That's why you see we have very weak KVP guidelines. At the NGO level, we fear we would be tracked down because we had supplies of lubricants. We don't have them, they are illegal now so we had to pack them. It did affect the community we served. MSM used to come, they would come to the office, the

> drop in centres. You cannot get them anymore. They are gone now you can't see them. We are living with them but you can't see them. (Individual interview 23, 24, November 2018, Temeke)

This director also discussed how the fears induced by the government led to riskier practices such as flashblood, sharing syringes and using other substances in secret. As the 2018 harm reduction report on Africa states, "In Tanzania, NSP provision remains poor and high risk behaviour such as needle sharing and the practice of flashblood have been reported, with an estimated 15.6% of people who inject drugs practicing flashblood and 14.2% sharing a needle with another at last injection" (Harm Reduction International 2018: 165).

The services available for drug users in Tanzania at the time of my fieldwork, seemed to increasingly reflect Magufuli's antipathy toward drug use and his misunderstanding of the realities of addiction, which are shared by the government generally. The personal failures represented by people who use drugs are the opposite of Magufuli's story, which emphasizes hard work and moral rectitude, dismissing the benefits or privileges he has experienced along the way. Drug use was simply not a good fit within his moral universe or his vision for Tanzania. While some interviewees remained confident that he would not disrupt the methadone program, many often admitted he was successful in limiting greater supports beyond this singular program.

Similar to authoritarian governments across the globe, blame for the rise in stigma against vulnerable populations is denied even as the leader of the country, and his ministers, regularly use stigmatizing language. There is a discursive relationship between people actively disapproving of those who use drugs, and the government producing and perpetuating this disapproval. From my fieldwork, I noted that the scourge of drug use amplified by the Tanzanian government did not seem to be filtering down to the neighborhood level, where community bonds and relationships exist. While this observation is based on limited experience, it does raise questions for future studies on how the government's war on drugs has succeeded in shaping public opinion.

In framing the issue as a moral one, Magufuli went against the previous government's approach. One interviewee related how supportive former President Jakaya Kikwete was, albeit with limited resources. This interviewee told me that Kikwete had personal experience with friends of his having problems with drug misuse and therefore understood the issue better (Individual interview 12, October 2018, Muhimbili). As mentioned previously, Kikwete originally did not understand the drug problem in the country but grew to see harm reduction as a solution. While certainly not a zealous advocate, according to the NGOs I interviewed, Kikwete listened and was open. Of course, the openness of Tanzania during Kikwete's regime was not necessarily a good thing, characterized by Issa Shivji as "one of the most laissez-faire periods in [Tanzania's] history . . . the party and the government lost any semblance of coherence . . . policymaking was erratic. Donors ruled the roost" (Shivji 2021). That said, the erratic nature of 2005–2015 allowed a niche in which progressive drug policy could take hold.

As should be clear by now, when the eyes of the state focus on drug use, the outcomes are not better. The war on drugs and the conservative narratives being used by the Tanzanian government frame drug use as a moral problem where people who use drugs are not seen as individuals with different stories and histories of drug use. Despite drug use not necessarily worsening since Kikwete, the focus of the government and by Magufuli on drug use reframes and revitalizes the issue. One individual, who had been in and out of sober houses for 10 years and on methadone, summed up his thoughts on Magufuli as, "he [Magufuli] talks a lot about drugs, but people they know, people they are still doing drugs. He hates drug addicts, drug dealers he hates them. You get caught it is 30 years but its full of drugs in Tanzania, any kind of drug" (Individual interview 39, October 2018, Kigamboni).

A good example of the Tanzanian government successfully reframing the issue as a moral one was the shuttering of harm reduction centers. I had not noticed any mention of them in the literature. However, they operated quietly and were described to me as drop in centers where KVP could go and access services, and also simply have a safe space to spend some time. The revised KVP guidelines officially closed these drop-in centers stating, "The use of drop in centres for provision of health and HIV services to KVPs will not be allowed. When necessary, outreach services through the use of service providers from nearby health facilities will be used" (Tanzanian Ministry of Health Statement on KVP 2017). Again, this centralization allows only the government to be in charge of these services and only organizations with a narrow focus on HIV prevention to be involved, hence the overwhelming focus on methadone.

I received mixed messages about these centers as official voices from larger NGOs and the government did not see their benefit, while almost every grassroots organization did. One interviewee at the CDC told me that the centers were closed because they were being abused by beneficiaries and, while admitting their closure meant these people had nowhere to go, they were being used by homosexuals to have sex and by drug users to use drugs (Individual interview 13, September 2018, Dar es Salaam City Center). Local NGOs involved in these had different opinions and spoke of their benefits as harm reduction centers:

> The drop in centres were very important for beneficiaries. They were harm reduction centres. They have information, supplies . . . no they are not using

> drugs. It's a lie. In rare cases if you don't include the beneficiaries themselves in the management of the centres, but if they are included no one is abusing the drop in. (Individual interview 24, November 2018, Kigamboni)

Even an official at the UNODC, which has a small presence in Tanzania, discussed how drop-in centers were places where people could go and feel safe and access services, but the change in political environment made them untenable (Individual interview 25, November 2018, Msasani).

The contradictory accounts were difficult to reconcile. However, it is possible that, in the absence of other safe spaces, people may have used drugs or felt comfortable enough to attend these centers while using. Not turning away people who use drugs and not requiring their abstinence to access services is common harm reduction practice. Furthermore, having safe spaces where individuals can access services regardless of their sobriety is important in overcoming stigma and being able to connect and establish relationships with individuals. Providing services only to sober people is similar to only providing poverty alleviation to those who are no longer poor. In any case, the government gave no evidence of the supposedly rampant abuse of drugs at these centers. Their closure is an example of how moral ideology can override evidence-based practices and create narratives of people who use drugs as out-of-control, moral failures undeserving of services and justify a shift toward punishment and abstinence.

The government of Tanzania clearly focused its' interventions on reducing and limiting the types of services available to people who use drugs. As I outlined in the previous chapter, services available prior to the crackdown were not comprehensive enough. The reversal of greater, more comprehensive progress while maintaining methadone has helped to obfuscate how little the government is doing to support people who use drugs. The approach of implementing a single harm reduction practice, without comprehensive supports does not effectively improve the well-being of people who use drugs. Foreign donors remain involved and, in some cases, NGOs explicitly asked me not to use their interviews for fear of being unable to continue operations in the country. While this policy process was underway, drugs continued to come into the country and people continued to use them.

CONCLUSION

As with his other crackdowns on sex workers and gay men, Magufuli did not have a state apparatus capable of effectively combatting drug use. No state is able to do this effectively. The government of Tanzania did, however, have the capacity to disrupt the lives of people who use drugs and to manipulate and control access to the sector for foreign and local NGOs. The war on drugs, conducted in a low-income country, with its own histories of drug use and its own political priorities, fails similarly to Western countries. There is a lack of consistency in how it is applied, when arrests are made, when bribes are taken and when, in essence, the rules are applied. This lack of consistency has not greatly altered drug supply or demand, but it has made people afraid and aware that they are targets.

While the minister of health and the DCEA gave voice to equitable health care and comprehensive harm reduction services, in reality these departments are involved in removing the rights to health of people who use drugs and enforcing legal restrictions. The war on drugs is a discursive space, where performance and belief meet and mutually support each other. It is in this space that the Tanzanian government worked to create narratives, which I explore more in this next chapter, that there are comprehensive supports for people who use drugs and that drugs can be eliminated through a tough approach. As I showed in this chapter, neither is the case, but the framing of drug policy along abstinence and prohibitionist lines would be useful in intimidating and appeasing foreign agencies involved in the sector.

It may be impossible to discern the reasons for why people continue the war on drugs, but it is possible to look at the real actions, rhetoric and threats they use to uphold this war which have real-world impacts and are not abstract or performative. These impacts are why continued work is needed to interrogate leaders, policy makers, and citizens on the reasons for their continued use of bad policy. The contradiction in making claims of equitable health-care provision ring hollow when considered in the context of drug policy overall. As I argue in the next chapter, international drug policy continues to disregard this context in creating drug policy, a lasting effect of the conservative war on drugs that removes socioeconomic, cultural, and historical background from policy making. As states have tried to impose their vision of a drug-free world on society, people who use drugs are further marginalized.

Chapter 6

Finding a Way to Cope

Supply, Survival, and Resilience in Dar

We were laughing you know, how come everywhere there are still drugs? So the major kingpins were caught but the drugs are still there? 90% [success in the drug war], I don't know how they base these statistics.

—Individual interview 27,
October 2018, Kigamboni

The previous chapter showed the strategies taken by the government of Tanzania to marginalize drug users and weaken their support networks. During my fieldwork, I discussed these changes with many of those targeted by these policies and actions, trying to understand often neglected perspectives. As with crackdowns anywhere, many of the outcomes are obvious and appear straightforward in official government narratives—drug users are imprisoned, drug supply is disrupted, and those who choose a better life for themselves get treatment and are redeemed. There are, however, a myriad of outcomes not included in these official narratives.

By establishing what life is like for people who use drugs in Dar, it is more possible to understand the deeper impacts the focus of the state can have on vulnerable populations. People who use heroin in Dar were not only harassed by police and incarcerated temporarily, they also saw the price of drugs rise; the scarcity of supply made their daily struggle to stave off dopesickness more difficult and previous support networks evaporated with a strict methadone treatment taking the place of peer supports.

The government ensured drug users became fully responsible for their own failures and weaknesses, despite the path to redemption being mired with major obstacles. The idea of "getting clean" is challenging enough when one has access to funding, support networks, and multiple treatment options. Heroin users in Tanzania, however, must bear the full costs of accessing treatment—from the daily transportation to the clean clothes needed to appear responsible at the clinic.

This chapter outlines the impacts of the drug war on the community of drug users and activists in Dar, and their resiliency in coping with these changes. I argue that the government of Tanzania made life worse for drug users by disrupting local and international partnerships, cracking down and stigmatizing people who use drugs. As I mentioned previously, my expectation of donor influence curtailing the excesses of the drug war and challenging policy changes was proven untrue by the situation on the ground. In this chapter, I look at the experiences of those working with people who use drugs to show the extent to which the Tanzania government achieved its goals of punishing drug users and making longer-term policy changes reducing their access to needed services.

IMPACTS OF THE CRACKDOWN

The fear of being caught during the initial crackdown was very real. As one sober house volunteer who had been using drugs at the time stated, "There was a change because the government just dealt more with people selling drugs and people bringing drugs in the country and this Regional Commissioner Makonda named all people selling drugs publicly" (Individual interview 5, October 2018, Kigamboni). One organization believed that major drug traffickers left but were just waiting to come back, and the decrease in supply was temporary but resulted in people who use drugs turning to more dangerous use, other substances or to methadone (Individual interview 1, August 2018, Mikocheni). This reduction in supply was commented on by most interviewees. Supply reduction, however, as is the case with any attempts at prohibiting substances, was temporary and partial. The increased pressure and reduction in supply drove up costs, a typical result of the war-on-drugs approach. One individual, staying at a sober house to treat his marijuana addiction, noted that the price of cannabis went up from approximately 800 to 2000 Tsh ($0.35–$0.85) for one joint (Individual interview 27, October 2018 Kigamboni). However, he always had access to drugs even when the crackdown was at its most intense.

Another individual noticed a difference, as the low-level dealer he worked for quit due to pressure and increased police presence (Individual interview 30, October 2018, Kigamboni). As this individual was using at the time, the result for him was simply more time spent searching for drugs, "We went to Kindondoni, people who were bringing the drugs found it harder. The price went up from 2,000 Tsh ($0.85) to 3,000 Tsh ($1.30) and even up to 5,000 Tsh ($2.20). But now they have come back down" (Individual interview 30,

October 2018, Kigamboni). The rise in price and the temporary reduction in supply does not signal a success in the drug war. People who use drugs are simply forced into greater hardship, needing to seek out different areas to find drugs and undertaking riskier behavior to avoid dopesickness. In the case of the individual quoted above, Kigamboni is a ferry ride and a bus ride away from Kinondoni, adding to the difficulties already faced in finding and paying for heroin.

In several interviews, people who use drugs and work in the sector were not opposed to the crackdown netting higher-level drug traffickers. These higher-level traffickers are seen as contributing to corruption in the country and profiting off of addiction. However, in Tanzania there was little evidence the crackdown netted any "big fish." One notable drug baron, nicknamed Shkuba, ran a major trafficking ring and was arrested and extradited to the United States (Kapama 2017). He was arrested in South Africa in 2014, prior to Magufuli's war. Otherwise, many interviewees commented on the lack of effectiveness of the crackdown in either eliminating drug supply or really capturing high-level traffickers. The bragging of the government, including the high levels of incarceration and their successes in stopping supply, did little to net anyone other than high-profile businessmen or members of the opposition.

The result of failing to tackle drug traffickers meant the continuation of the drug trade which, after 2016/17, had returned to previous levels. Prices remained slightly higher than before Magufuli had come to power, but whether this was due to a crackdown or simply a rise in price was unclear. When I was in Tanzania, it appeared that the old norms of drug use and trade in the hotspots had returned. When asked the reason for this return to normalcy, many interviewees saw this as a failure to meaningfully tackle the politicians and businessmen acting with impunity (Individual interview 4, August 2018, Mikocheni). The outcomes of the government of Tanzania's failed drug war are not unique, as the war on drugs has failed globally. The government, instead of taking of responsibility, however, has framed the project in a way that makes them appear successful. The successes the government highlights are not truly addressing drug use in the country but rather increasing the vulnerability of people who use drugs.

Police were also at the forefront of enforcing Magufuli's war on drugs. However, after the initial arrests and crackdowns, it appeared the old cycles of bribery, temporary detention, and the informal understandings between police and users had returned. Magufuli, in attempting to tackle corruption, did not address underlying issues such as police pay. Corruption persists and does not seem to be changing. As I observed, drug dealers were visible and not concerned with hiding their actions. As one outreach worker and former heroin user told me, "Laws should help us. I was already hurting from the drugs, so why do they [government] punish me too? Police go to maskani [hot spots] they bother them [people who use drugs] they try to get some money then they leave. They are not scared. He sells drugs, pays the police so sometimes I say that police are dealers too" (Individual interview 44, October 2018, Kinondoni). Police, as before, add an element of chaos to hot spots, appearing and retreating randomly. Given the lack of consistency, it is no surprise that interactions with police are shaped by individual police officers who may have relationships with NGOs or be more supportive of not repeatedly arresting the same people.

The experience of stigma and violence in hot spots persists. Almost everyone I talked to said the police come, "they disturb us. They catch us. They don't take us to jail but the post [a local station], they keep us sometime and then let us out" (Individual interview 47, October 2018, Mwananyamala). This common experience for low-level users is getting temporarily detained until you can pay a bribe or, if you can't, simply being detained to make a point. At a sober house, one man told me,

> When police come we all run. Anytime they catch you, you get hit. I have been caught 4 or 5 times. You stay at the police for some days and then first thing you go to sleep. Sometimes, if they catch you, maybe they might have seen evidence like the syringe, they can't hold you they can take it from you, they just keep you at the post for some time, but not to court. (Individual interview 26, October 2018, Kigamboni)

One interviewee who had worked in the methadone program offered the metaphor of low-level drug users as moto drivers or Bajaj (small, three-wheel taxis) drivers who don't get pulled over because they can't pay much (Individual interview 15, October 2018, Muhimbili). Unfortunately, by this principle, higher-level pushers are "pulled over" but can afford to pay off the police. This example reveals the complexity of the Tanzanian government presenting itself as tough on drugs, when its ability to effectively control these situations is limited. Even inconsistent police actions can have impacts on people who use drugs, however. One man had been arrested three times, the second time he had been detained for almost two weeks with no access to methadone or naloxone, undergoing an extreme withdrawal (Individual interview 30, Kigamboni, October 2018).

The word that came across most often in interviews was "-sumbua" (to disturb, annoy) or "wanatusumbua" (they disturb/annoy us). This word reflects a shared experience, as people seemed to be less worried about serious criminal repercussions and more about the disturbance that unexpected and sporadic incursions into hot spots would entail. These incursions could lead to serious withdrawal or simply interrupt time that could be spent earning money. At no point did it appear the police were working with the well-being of citizens in mind. The current government seems to be content having "performed" its crackdown, with a return to the more sporadic and occasional use of police to keep people who use drugs aware of their status as immoral and deserving of punishment.

Tanzanian police do have a reputation for rushwa [taking corruption]. For many of those I interviewed, bribery is so common that it is simply another aspect of life. Many car drivers ensure they have proper amounts of cash so if they are threatened with a ticket they can strike a deal with officers. It is the most vulnerable, however, that are more often targets of harassment and subjects of surveillance and control. As Transparency International reports, "Corruption and impunity are deemed to be pervasive in the Tanzanian police force . . . a factor contributing to high incidents of bribery among the police force is their low salaries—they are paid an average salary of less than US$40 a month. In fact, bribes in the force are so common that there are directives for tourists on how to deal with officers demanding payments" (Transparency International 2019). The lack of trust in police and institutions is a result of decades of corruption. In many interviews, there was so little faith the government could achieve its goals that other motives were given for why they would attempt a crackdown. Many interviewees even insinuated the government was in fact benefiting from the rise in drug prices.

A more plausible benefit than directly involving itself in the drug trade, was perhaps the appearance of the government being able to extend its power into all reaches of Tanzanian society. In my own experience during this trip to Tanzania, the appearance of control sometimes felt real and overwhelming when compared to my previous visits. In a country with a weak judiciary, corrupt police and a government actively targeting people who use drugs, it didn't matter that the government was not actually capable of catching all of them. It was enough that the government cared enough to ensure they were at least sporadically targeted, and more of a target than in the past. The impacts for people who use drugs were entirely negative. A former drug user who now runs a grassroots advocacy organization stated this clearly: "Many people, those most vulnerable, were scared and resorted to riskier use and sharing needles [syringes are still illegal in Tanzania], outreach became difficult and many people were being sent to prison. This impacted the small dealers and people on drugs the most, this was done to make politicians look good while many suffered" (Individual interview 2, August 2018, Mikocheni).

On the other hand, the government also worked to appear to be compassionate to people who use drugs who were accepting of treatment and could achieve redemption and reintegration into society. While boasting of prevention efforts, methadone outreach and even posing for photo ops at sober houses, the government does not fund any part of the sector. Participating enough to appear involved and engaged makes the level of support seem greater that it actually is. In reality, much greater support is needed, and government intransigence is the major obstacle to increased foreign funding and involvement. While there are issues with low funding for harm reduction and lower donor interest than in other areas, a lot more could be done and is available were the government to choose this approach and get behind it.

Harm reduction supports persisted in spite of John Magufuli not because of him, but could have expanded much further without his interventions. The framing tactics of the Tanzanian government—that it is providing comprehensive services that it is not, and that it is "cleansing" Tanzania of drug use, even as supply and police harassment remain the same—are effective tools in fooling outsiders and ensuring little media or international attention is devoted to the reality

As a result, supports in hot spots have dried up with nothing put in place to replace them. During my visit to Kigamboni ferry hot spot, a volunteer related how outreach workers used to come but have stopped in the current environment. While there was mention of services starting again, specifically under a local organization slated to spearhead needle exchange and harm reduction in the city, progress was slow and, in the meantime, nothing was available (Individual interview 32 and participant observation, October 2018, Kigamboni ferry). During this same visit the outreach worker I was with showed me an X-ray and explained how the people using in this area had pooled money to contribute to this as it cost 10,000 Tsh ($4.30) as the individual who needed it did not have enough money (Individual interview 32 and participant observation, October 2018, Kigamboni ferry). Apparently, some medical services were previously funded through outreach, or at least individuals were given some support in accessing medical services and health care.

At the Kigamboni ferry hot spot there were many health concerns that were now not being supported, such as diarrhea, malaria, and parasites. Despite the funding restraints globally in harm reduction, in contrast to the large amounts of funding being put toward perpetuating the war on drugs, a small amount of funding could go a long way in helping people who use drugs. However, people who use drugs remain a low priority, exposing the real and lasting mentality the Tanzanian government, and governments across the globe, have toward drug use.

FAILING PEOPLE WHO USE DRUGS: RHETORIC AND REALITY

While the Tanzanian government receives the majority of funding for methadone and drug treatment programs from foreign donors, control over this funding is still largely influenced by the government. As Magufuli's priority was state-led development, less funding was available for social programs and projects needed to increasingly align with the country's priorities, which were largely focused on infrastructure. Magufuli positioned himself as a state-led project leader, focusing on development at all costs, similar to the models being pursued in Ethiopia and Rwanda. State-led development projects, as modeled in these countries, do not usually focus on marginalized groups. As one sober house director told me, there are no funds because of other priorities and the DCEA is stretched too thin (Individual interview 19, October 2018, Kigamboni). The result is a haphazard network of sober houses undertaking work that is possibly beyond their scope and capabilities.

With a complete lack of supports for people who use drugs other than methadone, sober houses are combining outreach with harm reduction and mental-health interventions. One man I spoke to was found on the street with severe problems in his legs from injecting with old syringes and brought to a sober house by an outreach worker. The director of this sober house told me that their sober house, which receives no financial support from the government, paid his full medical costs, over 1,000,000 Tsh ($434) (Individual interview 17, October 2018, Kigamboni). The sober house covered all costs for the medical treatment of its beneficiaries without financial aid, whether this was 20,000 Tsh ($8.50) for malaria medication or 72,000 Tsh ($31) for antibiotics (Individual interview 17, October 2018, Kigamboni). These costs are far above what an unfunded sober house is able to pay.

Similar to physical ailments, the lack of mental health services sometimes leaves places like sober houses in charge of clientele with complex mental health issues as well. One man who had attended sober houses in Zanzibar and in Dar stated, "There is a difference between a crazy person and a drug user . . . there are some limitations to some people affected totally" (Individual interview 39, October 2018, Kigamboni). It was unclear how widespread the inclusion of severely mentally ill people in sober houses was. With a lack of understanding of the true extent in which mental health issues are prevalent among drug users, it is likely volunteers at sober houses will face challenges with certain clients. There is nowhere else for people to go.

While the lack of outreach and mental health supports made sense given the government's abstinence focus, I was surprised to see very little being done in terms of prevention. Prevention, mainly educating youth around the dangers of drug use is often a cornerstone of the war on drugs, and is complimentary to abstinence based-approaches. During the Reagan era in the United States, the "Just Say No" campaign was a major policy pillar. In Tanzania, however, the government was not even doing basic education. Several interviewees told me that children are not taught the difference between major drugs and end up using drugs that they may think are marijuana or different forms of it.

During one of my visits to a sober house in Kigamboni, the director was organizing an outreach trip to a local school near which drug use occurred. The government included prevention in its planning, which would include education on drug use to youth. The session, however, was organized through the sober house as little government programming had actually been put in place. The sober house was actively doing this work in the absence of a concerted government effort to reach out. This important work was noted by the teacher:

> It is really sad because there are a lot of people out there and we really expected the government would do more. I think we need someone who knows these things and can talk to the whole school, 500 students and 60 workers. Students were interested and it was new knowledge. I have a different perspective now. Most people see them [people who use drugs] as outcasts, I didn't know there are a lot of factors. (Individual interview 18, October 2018, Kigamboni)

The efforts to provide some preventive education are being undertaken without official support. The prohibitionist stance of the government would seemingly be in great support of prevention efforts, but no funding was available.

Ultimately, prevention is a low priority for the government, as are supports for people who use drugs and efforts to meaningfully addressing the challenges they face. Despite the lack of government involvement in supporting the sector, however, NGOs are required to align with the government's goals and report in great detail on their activities. This issue of reporting came up in several interviews, as the reporting requirements have increased to the point that it appears that the government wants greater control over all sectors in the country. As one interviewee noted, "Now we must provide, in addition to our annual report and audited financial reports, further information on where funds are coming from and the contracts we have signed. NGOs also need to explain how much their projects align to country priorities" (Individual interview 14, October 2018, Mikocheni).

Sober houses also have strict reporting requirements to the government, even though there is no financial support. In discussion at the DCEA I was told that increased control over sober houses was meant to increase accountability and support the implementation of best practice as these sites. So far this increased oversight has only increased the reporting burden on volunteers and the minimal staff at these sites, however, and the government still is not committed to any supports despite identifying the need for more training, mental health education and funding at sober houses.

METHADONE AND HARM REDUCTION: PERSISTENCE AND CHANGE

With the crackdown, the methadone program, out of political design, emerged as the dominant and often only option for people who use drugs to access treatment. The program presents a compromise, as it is a harm reduction initiative focused almost solely on healthcare rather than supporting a full suite of services. The presence of methadone and one needle exchange are reported upon in international reports such as the Harm Reduction International report card on harm reduction 2020. In such reports, Tanzania appears ahead of other African states with these, most basic supports, present. Yet, as I outlined in the past two chapters, the reality on the ground is different. The presence of these services obfuscates the real lack of support for people who use drugs. Drug replacement therapy is scientifically proven to support people who use opiates to live more productive lives and act as a measure to treat and prevent HIV. However, methadone alone is not a cure for a disease, but rather a replacement therapy meant to support people who use drugs should they choose to get clean.

I was repeatedly told in interviews that the government would not interfere in the provision of health services, including methadone. Other harm reduction supports such as needle exchange or mental health services that would increase adherence to methadone treatment are apparently not considered health services. As Tim Rhodes points out, methadone is a subject invested with "recovery potential" which is "an assemblage of relations; of connections between various social, affective and material forces which flow between, and thus make up, both the objects of methadone and recovery" (Rhodes 2018: 72). In other words, methadone cannot be separated from its practice and it is often connected to narratives of recovery.

The treatment itself, while sometimes seen as a purely medical intervention, is invested with a number of connections making it not just a simple intervention, but part of an assemblage of relations between the substance itself, the drug user and the social context in which it is offered. Methadone is a site for narratives that can both support a government, such as Tanzania, to pursue discriminatory practices against drug use while also touting itself as a champion of harm reduction. Depicting methadone as medical is itself ascribing a narrative to the treatment. In divesting methadone of its intended position within an array of resources and supports for people use drugs, the potential for the treatment doing what it is intended to do, drug replacement, is replaced by what it is not intended to do, offer a medical cure for addiction.

Among the people I talked to who were now sober, I found a full array of perspectives on, and experiences with, methadone. These perspectives and experiences were colored by my selection process but do reveal some interesting aspects of lived experience with this program. I talked to people who had been on methadone, recovered and now did outreach work to support others; some still on methadone while using drugs; others on methadone living their lives; and some at sober houses who considered methadone as another form of dependency who wanted to be completely clean. These narratives are not about the efficacy of a certain treatment, but rather show the complexity of drug use and dependency.

Recovery is possible, but the lived experiences listed above were often shared at some point by people who use drugs. The narrative of a linear path to sobriety, getting on methadone and being cured, was not an experience shared by any of the people I talked to. The reality of "getting clean" can often involve being on and off methadone and in and out of treatment numerous times. As I mentioned above, the purpose of methadone is drug replacement along with other supports that can help a drug user choose sobriety when they are ready, not as a one-time cure. The main thread underlying these experiences are the universals of job loss, alienation, impoverishment (or exacerbating existing poverty) and stigma, none of which are meant be, or are in reality, addressed by methadone.

Methadone is successful for some but even those in the program for an extended period still face challenges. One woman, on methadone for two years, described her current experience:

> No, the only support we are getting really is methadone. For other medical services, me or my baby, we have to pay. It is very hard, I don't have a job. My baby dad he helps, but he doesn't have a job. He has a small business which is not enough. We have to pay for a room every month, 30,000 Tsh ($13) every month, you pay every 6 months. My husband doesn't make enough for us to eat. Pay for a room, support baby when she is sick, you know all that. I am happy because I have beat drugs and it is good I am happy with that. (Individual interview 46, October 2018, Mwananyamala)

Methadone is not aimed to fix every aspect of a person's life and it is certainly not a way to address deep rooted socioeconomic inequality. However, the lack of supports beyond giving people a daily dose is a weakness in the program. Many interviewees had aspirations and goals in their lives which are out of reach, from starting support organizations to operating cooperatives (Individual interviews 45–49, October 2018, Mwananyamala). Even outreach workers I talked to who supported methadone saw the gaps in existing services:

> It is still easy to get drugs still. He [Magufuli] makes it up. Many can still use up until now. Many use now, he is doing nothing. There are still problems. At the

> methadone we need other services, they have problems there, other sicknesses. They use methadone but they are not busy. They have to go methadone and then they need to be busy and have jobs. Harm reduction is really centred around HIV, but drug users have bigger problems. HIV is full support, drug users are supported through HIV but drug users don't get their own program. It's not enough, we need full support. Government doesn't want this. Little NGOs like us try to raise up our voice and our government its slow. They help so little. (Individual interview 44, October 2018, Kinondoni)

The government's approach to drug use in Tanzania is not client-centered. As one outreach worker, who had quit drugs with methadone, told me, "Counselling helped me more. They [beneficiaries] can't meet their goals, but if they come here they win. They think most about finding money, not future. They drink methadone but they can't eat, they can't help themselves. If you miss the education you lose" (Individual interview 44, October 2018, Kinondoni). In focusing only on the agency of the person using drugs, the government accepts none of the blame for individuals who are not successful in the methadone program, even though they face numerous systemic obstacles to success.

The head of a larger harm reduction organization pointed out, "There are not options. It is very hard when you see beneficiaries cannot go to sober houses. They want something easy for them in daily life, methadone is free and legal. The motivation is to stop the drug use, that is the major motivation . . . we had to work on methadone sites because it wasn't well envisioned. It wasn't client centered. For example, you could be punished for being late, even being late" (Individual interview 24, November 2018, Temeke). This statement revealed some of the early challenges with methadone that the program that advocates are working to address.

At Kigamboni ferry hot spot, the outreach worker I was with discussed the challenges of supporting clients in accessing methadone. We talked to one man who described how outreach workers come and test for HIV and, once finding someone is HIV positive they are told to start methadone (Individual interview 30 and participant observation, October 2018, Kigamboni ferry). Again, this depicts getting on methadone as a simple course involving just deciding to stop using heroin and get on methadone. The reality is difficult, however, and some at the hot spot either chose not to leave or kept using methadone and then returning to the hot spot to use more heroin, a dangerous mix (Individual interview 30 and participant observation, October 2018, Kigamboni ferry). The push to support methadone, driven by the idea of abstinence and curing individuals of their addiction has realigned priorities along a war on drugs epistemology in which greater supports can encourage increased drug use.

The drop in centers, outreach, and provision of harm reduction materials in hot spots and prevention have been essentially replaced by methadone. While programs can exist concurrently, the limited resources available mean a diversion in one direction reduces the availability of resources in other areas. Outreach organizations are aware of the issues, as they are usually comprised of former drug users with a genuine desire to improve people's lives but limited in their mandate. Outreach workers have no resources and are not able to provide any services at the hot spot, driving them to encourage people in the hot spots to come with them. This approach is markedly different than the needle exchange, where basic medical services can be offered and syringes are cleaned up.

The needle exchange program in Temeke, once seen as ready to expand, may still do so in coming years. However, expansion could have occurred much sooner and saved many more lives. Furthermore, the revision of legal restrictions could also have reduced the sharing of syringes. One local advocate noted how hard this still can be, as police enlist pharmacies to keep an eye out should someone return often to purchase a syringe (which many already can't afford) (Individual interview 4, September 2018, Mikocheni). As one former injection drug user at a sober house told me, "When you are around a lot of syringe it is easy, sometimes it gets late and shops are closed so you go and try to find a syringe you used before but it is not there. Then you share. Even at the pharmacies there are difficulties" (Individual interview 26, October 2018, Kigamboni). It should be noted here that this individual had only come to the sober house due to outreach workers noticing the swelling and abscesses in his legs, caused by using old or dirty needles.

The needle exchange program offers more services than methadone, as people with minor injuries can be treated before they become serious. Methadone is part of a continuum of services, the intent of which is meant to be focused on the improved health, dignity, and well-being of people who use drugs. A needle exchange is often considered a first step in this continuum. Testing can also take place at the outreach stage and support the development of a community network. This network can improve relationships and follow-up with individuals. The relationship built between Médecins du Monde (MDM) and local partners is significant. More than this, the work helps to reduce stigma and break down barriers. As several people told outreach workers at hot spots, Temeke hospital was the most comfortable site to access methadone due to their relationship with MDM.

The provision of harm reduction has reduced the barriers in Temeke hospital, such as stigma and a lack of understanding of addiction, and facilitated positive interactions where people who use drugs feel safer and more supported regardless of their failure or success in the program. The expansion of this model to other hot spots would only increase similar outcomes in other neighborhoods. Furthermore, the needle clean-up was appreciated by residents of Temeke and also reduces risks and stigma. The holistic model of harm reduction is clearly a positive step in helping those who use drugs; however, it is contrary to the stigma and ill will Magufuli and his government cultivated. The grassroots work of harm reduction activists could achieve so much more in terms of improved health and well-being of people who use drugs, if it were to receive official support.

CONCLUSION

In examining the multiple sites in which this war on drugs is taking place, it is possible to see the impacts as part of a coherent whole. In short, Tanzania's war on drugs has meant a removal of supports from people who use drugs and further marginalization. The crackdown impacted individuals across Dar, who were forced into hiding, saw drug prices rise and struggled to find their usual supply. The war on drugs was connected to Magufuli's overall push to "clean up" Tanzanian society according to moralistic and conservative norms. This connection cemented the belief that drugs, and by extension, people who use drugs, need to be cleaned up as they are part of a corrupt and immoral Tanzania.

In this chapter I showed not only that the visible crackdown hurt people who use drugs but also the results of a one-sided, top-down policy change foisted upon the only sector through which people who use drugs receive support. The persistence of methadone clouds the reality of a single treatment provided for people who use drugs and reflects larger, global attitudes toward drug policy which—rather than focusing on real, sustainable change, is instead still compromised by old assumptions of curing drug use and removing people who use drugs from society. The minor efforts made to support people who use drugs do not meet their needs and are confusingly implemented within extremely hostile policy environments where the very existence of drug use is violently repressed. Moving toward meaningful change requires thinking beyond people who use drugs as deserving of basic HIV/AIDS treatment and actually understanding that they are people, as any other group in society deserving of an array of supports, services, and policies that are developed with their perspectives in mind.

In the past few chapters, I charted a course through Tanzanian drug policy in the recent past. A deep dive into the specifics of the Tanzanian drug war reveals continuity and change, as drugs will continue to be available, while characters like the late John Magufuli can arrive on the scene and influence drug policy in ways that have lasting impacts. In the next section, I focus on the international involvement and reaction to the war on drugs in Tanzania.

Linking together the chapters on the international war on drugs with Tanzania, I draw out similarities with and linkages with this international system and drug policy in Tanzania. While it may be easy to say that policy makers simply do not care about drug users, what I reveal is that there is still a commitment to punishing people who use drugs and that harm reduction, in its true intent, is a long way from being fully realized.

Part III

TANZANIA AND THE INTERNATIONAL WAR ON DRUGS

Chapter 7

Tanzania, the War on Drugs and International Influence

Shaping Perspectives and Policies

> *In Tanzania it is different than places like Kenya, the focus is on reducing use as well as reducing risk. We want to see behavioral change. Harm reduction will reduce use and users. There are challenges. Funding is limited, and there is no support for social, economic activities or income generation. Many return to the same conditions as before and struggle.*
>
> —Individual interview 2,
> October 2018, Kinondoni

In a globalized world, the international is domestic and, as I have shown in Tanzania, the implementation of drug policy includes numerous local and foreign actors. In the previous section, I argued that Tanzania is shaping policy toward people who use drugs and described how the government there effectively shapes the realities for people who use drugs. My findings are in contrast to assumptions that "weak state capabilities" often "contribute to an inferior position [of African governments] in the international system of states" (Andreasson 2013: 143).

This idea, which results in the "shifting dynamics of international relations" being driven by external agency (Andreasson 2013: 143) should mean that Tanzania is unable to pursue its agenda, which goes against the goals of donors to advance human rights and reduce the spread of HIV/AIDS. In this section, I expand on this idea to argue that Tanzania, rather than being influenced by international actors as a weak, aid-dependent state, pursued a war on drugs with little interference, using tactics of intimidation and appeasement to exploit a neglected policy area.

In opening up space to explore how this agency is exercised and pursued, I show how the Tanzanian government implemented policies within the space of the international consensus on drug control, where there remains flexibility to adapt this consensus to support the war on drugs. In raising how the Tanzanian government has undertaken its own war on drugs, I question the influence of external actors in the war on drugs in Africa and illustrate the agency of an African government in upholding a global policy framework. This chapter describes the practical steps taken by the government to pursue its agenda. I show how political hostility from the Tanzanian government and donors prioritizing other areas left people who use drugs without the advocacy and support needed to stop the shift from policies inclusive of harm reduction to policies focused on abstinence and punishment.

I begin with an overview of John Magufuli's fraught relationship with foreign donors. While Tanzania has long depended on foreign aid to prop up multiple sectors, Magufuli challenged donors directly and leverages aid independence as a political ideal for Tanzania to follow. The response to HIV/AIDS and support available to drug users is almost entirely funded by foreign agencies and Magufuli's threats to foreigners were experienced by these agencies as well. Below, I show how the Tanzanian government sidelined these foreign agencies through threats and harassment to silence opposition to crackdowns on drug users and policy changes reducing access to services provided to drug users by these agencies.

MAGUFULI AND INTERNATIONAL NGOS, A WARY RELATIONSHIP

In December 2019, President John Magufuli expressed his frustration with foreign agents "sabotaging" Tanzanian progress, stating "they [foreigners] use NGOs and CSOs (Civil Society Organizations) to push their agendas, pretending they are teaching us democracy and human rights while, in actual fact, they are the ones who are breaking them by creating oppressive systems . . . through their operations, they interfere with other countries' sovereignty, creating chaos" (Kimboy 2019). Foreigners were a favorite target of Magufuli's, whether it was donors interfering in his agenda or a nonprofit sector with different values. As mentioned in chapter 3, Magufuli's antagonism of donors appeared less connected to the old pan-African ideal of aid independence but rather the desire for absolute political control. By the time of his death, the CCM was again in a position of absolute dominance with the opposition in disarray, a trend his successor Samia Suluhu Hassan appears content to continue.

I found during my fieldwork that the focus on controlling priorities impacted the nonprofit sector across domestic and international lines. The "Magufulication" of civil society was marked by increased oversight over all sectors, more reporting requirements and less certainty over what was allowed. One major local NGO employee noted this change with their international partners, stating "Visas are denied, we say there is a shrinking civic space, there is a shrinking humanitarian space, even the UN, the organizations under the UN find it difficult to work" (Individual interview 14, October 2018, Mikocheni). In interviews at Muhimbili University, the lack of space directly impacted the research being done and what could be explored. As one researcher told me, the "environment is a bit difficult, there is confusion at the moment on research permits and very little funding" (Individual interview 15, October 2018, Muhimbili University). The lack of support for research created difficulties for researchers and NGOs wanting to work in areas that do not align with Tanzanian government priorities focused on state-led development projects.

One director of a harm reduction NGO based in Europe described to me the real obstacles faced in trying to begin operations in Tanzania. This organization has an explicit harm reduction focus and, during fieldwork, the need for both their advocacy work and the funding they could provide to better support the needs of people who use drugs was apparent. In order to begin work in Tanzania, this organization undertook a study and needs assessment and planned operations in the country before obstacles and issues with government arose. Instead of interest in accommodating the NGO, the difficulties of applying to work in the country multiplied. The experience of this organization, at the time I talked to them, exemplified the dashed hopes of organizations planning to build upon successes in Tanzania prior to Magufuli. Harm reduction advocates and organizations were now being met with obstacles and difficulties, if not outright refusals (Individual interview 1, September 2018, conducted remotely).

The obstacles faced by this organization were such that work planned to begin in 2016 was only getting underway in early 2020, albeit very slowly. In follow-up, I learned expansion of the Needle and Syringe programs beyond Temeke district also began in late 2019. In advancing better harm reduction services, the arrival of more funding and an active and supportive organization in Tanzania may finally advance initiatives that should have begun years ago. These delays show how the Tanzanian government was an obstacle to the progress of harm reduction, slowing down the development of the more comprehensive supports that could have been established years ago.

International organizations in the country before Magufuli also faced obstacles even though, despite interruptions due to policy reviews, they have largely been able to remain in the country. Similarly to local NGOs facing increased reporting requirements and scrutiny, international NGOs have been subject to increased control and oversight over their operations. In chapter 3, I made it clear that Tanzania's status as donor darling is not a result of its success in implementing donor goals or even its amenability to donor priorities. Despite its long-standing relationships with foreign donors and NGOs, Tanzania has largely pursued its own agenda.

A departure with Magufuli, however, is that the country was once considered flexible to certain donor-driven solutions. The sector of illicit drugs is an example of this. While sometimes drawing the interest of the state, Tanzania under Jakaya Kikwete appeared to have little interest in the sector, allowing the growth of harm reduction services funded by foreign NGOs. The connection of donors and local activists spurred a collaboration that led to the growth of harm reduction services between 2010 and 2015. This relationship is in some ways an example of positive extraversion. Local Tanzanian activists used their lesser position in a limited global harm reduction sector, to leverage support for methadone.

The election of John Magufuli interrupted this fruitful partnership. While Magufuli did not halt the continuing work of advocacy, as was clear from many of the vocal activists I talked to, the freeze on harm reduction in the country slowed the progress underway. Advocacy work persists but Magufuli created a "climate of fear" that has made this work more difficult (Jerving 2019). In 2019, Human Rights Watch released a report noting how "his government has adopted and enforced laws and practices that severely restrict activities, resulting in the arbitrary deregistering or suspension of NGOs—including on accusations of violating Tanzanian 'ethics and culture'—and the arrest and harassment of NGO workers" (Jerving 2019).

During fieldwork, I certainly noticed a chilling in this sector, especially among NGOs working with sensitive populations. As one foreign NGO employee stated, "There continues to be major gaps [in services for people who use drugs] outside of Dar es Salaam. In Tanzania, there is some support among different politicians but there is a reticence to discussing it, people are nervous about touching these issues" (Individual interview 1, September 2018, conducted remotely). In sectors where donors are providing the only services to KVP, there appears to be the observation that, were major HIV/AIDS donors to retreat from Tanzania, the government would likely not replace these services. Certainly, in the case of KVP, the Tanzanian government has made it clear they have little interest in offering any support.

The retreat of donor influence shows the impact of the Tanzanian government framing the issue in a way that limits the expansion of harm reduction in the country, an example of extraversion and also the insertion of the Tanzanian government's agenda into a global policy debate. In limiting the conversation to drugs as a threat and a medical problem, the vocal activists who call for human rights and greater socioeconomic support for drug users is silenced. Funding is also impacted, as the framing of the debate subsequently frames the priorities of donors who divert funding to reach more accessible goals, such as reducing HIV/AIDS transmission among the general population.

A UNODC representative in Tanzania blamed the lack of funding for people who use drugs squarely on the government, noting how organizations working with KVP face harassment and are in fear of greater government reprisals (Individual interview 25, November 2018, Msasani). International organizations facing complications around regulations and arbitrary restrictions have other priorities. There is a growing recognition that the Tanzanian government, if it continues its current course in targeting vulnerable people, will be a bad partner in advancing even basic outcomes such as encouraging HIV/AIDS testing among the general population.

In a sector with fewer actors and high global need for programming, the government's lack of interest and use of intimidation results in a more general lack of donor engagement, especially in working with KVP. The Tanzanian government sets the priorities and threatens harassment or arbitrary bureaucratic obstacles to silence NGOs that may challenge its agenda. As one outreach worker told me, "The problem is our government, donors are not the problem. They are ready to help. I can't help you if you don't help yourself. Our government doesn't support drug users so how will donors support you? We support but government don't want us to support. But we want it" (Individual interview 44, October 2018, Kinondoni). Several interviewees told me the same story: money provided for outreach is minimal and needed funds that local organizations had planned on using to expand supports are not available. I explore this more in the next section; however, it is important to note that while KVP have been a particular target, the larger context of international NGO involvement in Tanzania was subject to challenges as well. The result is less advocacy for improved services.

SERVING PEOPLE WHO USE DRUGS, AN INTERNATIONAL PERSPECTIVE

While the twin goals of supporting the health of people who use drugs in Tanzania while also ceasing drug supply remain the drivers of international interventions, interest in expanded needle exchange and improved harm reduction has grown since 2010. In neighboring Kenya, drug user networks expanded from 2012 onward, taking the example of Tanzania as a model and groups such as the Kenya AIDS NGO Consortium (KANCO) are continuing to expand the harm reduction supports in the country. The growth of organizations such as KANCO are to such an extent that harm reduction programming in Kenya is now more comprehensive than Tanzania. In Tanzania, foreign support continued to focus on supporting PWID with HIV/AIDS;

however, this funding was also being used flexibly to grow outreach programming with the understanding that reaching these populations is difficult and reducing stigma and easing restrictions on access to services is necessary in reaching vulnerable populations.

It is clear that the Tanzanian government-driven process resulted in changes to how services were prioritized and delivered for people who use drugs. The ability of the Tanzanian government to sideline international influence, despite being established and largely funding supports for drug users, relies both on competing funding priorities, in which drug users are not a high priority, and the control of narratives by the Tanzanian government, appeasing and intimidating foreign agencies. In more concrete terms, for these foreign agencies, the Tanzanian government's intimidation and appeasement, resulted in their inability to influence policy outcomes or curb the excesses of the crackdown. There is a continued inability to challenge the existing frameworks of drug policy in the country and services remain framed within a context of ongoing criminalization and marginalization of people who use drugs.

The scale of funding from the Global Fund outmatches many smaller organizations and, although harm reduction is not the main focus, the Global Fund is advancing harm reduction policy and does include harm reduction in its vision for comprehensive services to reduce HIV/AIDS. A challenge with major funders, as noted by some of the local NGOs I talked to, is that the government controls this funding and funnels it through the DCEA and the Ministry of Health.

Since 2015, these government branches have not been friendly to improved harm reduction supports. The opportunities for smaller, less organized groups such as the network of people who use drugs, to link directly with these foreign agencies is limited. There are only a few organizations that operate internationally in support of harm reduction, besides larger NGOs such as Harm Reduction International, which mainly operates in advocacy and research. For people who use drugs in developing countries, besides organizations such as Mainline and Médecins du Monde, there is little focused funding for harm reduction available.

In 2016, the government actively inserted itself into several areas impacting the work on international NGOs. The crackdown, while not directly aimed at foreign donors, stigmatized and targeted the populations they work with, making an already difficult population to reach even more unreachable. International NGOs could not interfere with this domestic political situation. As it became clear that this was not just a temporary crackdown, international actors were forced to wait and see what their futures in Tanzania would look like.

The Tanzanian government's decision to target KVP and people who use drugs had direct impacts on how organizations could continue outreach and support for vulnerable populations (Individual interviews 4, 6 August 2018 Mikocheni). However, a more lasting disruption which donors appeared to be unable to influence was the KVP policy overhaul. Organizations such as Jhpiego and ICAP, with major funding from PEPFAR, awaited the outcome of the revision to the guideline, unsure of the extent to which it would impact their work (Individual interviews 7,8 and 9, September 2018, Mikocheni). Jhpiego, associated with Johns Hopkins University are large contributors to work with KVP. Jhpiego, for instance, received $73 million from 2015–2020 to provide HIV tests for gay men and sex workers and was the top USAID partner in 2019 (Sieff 2016). During the crackdown, the NGO faced obstacles in reaching these groups, and was unsure of what its work would look like going forward. Jhpiego was also forced to get rid of all lubricants and submitted to government searches ensuring this was the case.

The size of this NGO and its ability to influence decisions appeared very low considering the funding envelope. The uncertainty of the period during the revisions shook donor confidence in achieving goals for HIV reduction in the country, especially among KVP. Prior to this, gay men already faced numerous obstacles in accessing testing due to stigma and fear. This policy revision further complicated how meaningful engagement and ongoing treatment with HIV positive and already vulnerable Tanzanians could be achieved. To continue operating in the county, even a well-funded organization providing highly needed services in Tanzania was required to play by the rules being set by the Magufuli government.

In interviews with ICAP, the KVP team mentioned a six-month suspension to some of their work while the government reviewed KVP guidelines (Individual interviews 7,8, September 2018, Mikocheni). During this time, while not all services were restricted, the government restricted their work with KVP. While reaching KVP is an important part of the work of ICAP, HIV/AIDS in Tanzania remains a huge issue among the general population and the focus of organizations funded through Center for Disease Control (CDC) or the Global Fund, facing the prospects of diminished funding, is the general population. The director told me that the number of people tested is low, therefore the priority is getting the entire population tested, and then getting them on treatment (Individual interview 9, September 2018, Mikocheni).

The employees I talked to at ICAP in charge of the KVP program did feel they could continue work unimpeded, but also admitted the government imposed restrictions making KVP hard to reach (Individual interviews 7,8, September 2018, Mikocheni). The understanding among several interviewees was that health funding would not be cut. However, when all other areas impacting the lives of people who use drugs are being targeted, health care is impacted as well. In the context of preventing the spread and increase of HIV/AIDS, reaching and effectively treating key populations will remain a major challenge. INGOs recognized this fact, however, they decided to focus on general population goals in the hope that KVP outreach would improve eventually. The continued inclusion of methadone program assuaged some anxieties even though the limitations of this service was also recognized. The growing difficulties over 2016/17 in getting visas, work permits and being able to work unimpeded, also led to organizations wanting to avoid antagonizing the Tanzanian government.

The focus of major organizations, where KVP are only a subsidiary part of their larger goals, can leave more sensitive subjects behind. Whatever strategy is followed, it will take some time to meaningfully address the considerable task of testing, treating, and monitoring all people with HIV in Tanzania. Harm reduction practices beyond methadone, such as distributing lubricants, syringes, expanding outreach, and advancing decriminalization are all simple and cost-effective measures to immediately prevent more cases of HIV that will need to be treated in the future. Harm reduction, inclusive of measures deemed by the Tanzanian government as immoral practices are, in fact, healthcare. Yet, this simple truth did not curb the government's highly ideological and abstinence-based policies.

The methadone program persists despite the government's attacks on drug users' human rights. Magufuli's crackdown, however, may result in the further removal of services to KVP. As I noted above, the success rates for testing and treating HIV in Tanzania do not reflect the sizeable investments, especially as compared to similar countries. No doubt the lack of success is, at least in part, due to the lack of support in reaching KVP. The combination of a new moral code, uncertainty over what kind of work can be done and the lack of political will from the Tanzanian government is challenging some agencies, with limited funding and unlimited need across the globe, to rethink their work in Tanzania.

For instance, PEPFAR has faced cuts due to Donald Trump's overall reduction of foreign aid, with a 11% cut in FY2018, 16% in FY2019, and a proposed 25% cut in 2020 (Rose and Keller 2019). As shown in the chart below this has not necessarily impacted Tanzania, which is a priority country for PEPFAR with strong bilateral ties. Figure 7.1 illustrates that funding for HIV/AIDS makes up the large proportion of United States assistance to Tanzania, largely provided through PEPFAR which is Tanzania's largest international donor and "will finance 64% of Tanzania's HIV treatment and care" (AVERT 2020). However, the request for 2020 reflects the disappointment of PEPFAR in achieving its goals in the country and is a 30% reduction over FY2018 (Rose and Keller 2019). The actions of the Magufuli government exploit an area of low priority for donors, and it is much easier to work in reaching KVP in countries more amenable to foreign agencies' priorities. The Tanzanian government is thus not only successfully reducing services in

	Global Fund ($US)	United States total funding for HIV/AIDS*	United States total funding for Health
2020	138,969,076	266,610,000	335,110,000
2019	174,280,149	464,500,000	537,000,000
2018	95,408,413	470,000,000	513,000,000
2017	241,780,731	393,580,000	496,670,000
2016	219,560,697	393,580,000	494,910,000
2015	155,422,982	372,380,000	475,220,000
2014	182,762,770	330,040,000	431,670,000
2013	231,217,111	344,300,000	440,500,000

*Total Funds represent overall funding from the United States only, including PEPFAR, Global Fund and any other sources. The totals provided for HIV/AIDS funding reflect funding almost entirely through PEPFAR which also provides funds to the Global Fund.

Figure 7.1 Global Fund and the President's Emergency Plan for AIDS Relief (PEPFAR) Yearly Funding Allotments to Tanzania ($US). *Source*: Author created with data from Global Fund data portal and US foreign assistance dashboard.

the country with little opposition, in the coming years it may eliminate the remaining services altogether.

At the beginning of 2019, Ambassador Deborah Birx, introducing the 2019 PEPFAR operational plan for Tanzania, wrote:

> Only 61% of persons living with HIV infection (PLHIV) were aware of their serostatus. This result, the lowest in Eastern Africa, is deeply disappointing in light of the cumulative $4.5 billion investment of U.S. tax dollars since 2004. It is also disappointing given that substantial increases in PEPFAR funding over the past 3 years have not yield commensurate achievement . . . It is noteworthy that the PEPFAR/Tanzania program faces unique structural impediments to its progress. Formal and informal policy developments in Tanzania undermine efforts to diagnose and treatment persons most vulnerable to HIV infection, including arrests of sexual minorities, anti-contraception messaging, and the expulsion of pregnant adolescent girls and young women from school. (United States Department of State 2019)

This statement shows how global funding levels specific to this sector already face pressures. Furthermore, the majority of this funding is already aimed at major partners such as ICAP and Jhpiego, which focus on HIV/AIDS in the general population, not KVP. Magufuli's rhetoric and policy did not eliminate aid, but impacted aid arriving for the most vulnerable who are not necessarily the top priority for major donors either. Interestingly, the statement does not include specific mention of drug users, highlighting again their lack of importance even among organizations focused on KVP.

Despite the recognition of the importance of harm reduction, INGOs are not involved in treating drug use which is outside of their mandate. At the CDC, entirely funded by PEPFAR, the lead of the Key and Vulnerable Populations program discussed how the main focus currently is peer outreach in order to undertake HIV and other communicable disease testing and then connect individuals to the methadone program (Individual interview 13, September 2018, Dar es Salaam City Center). CDC focuses on injection drug users mainly, and PEPFAR pays for the methadone program entirely. As with the approach to the general population impacted by HIV/AIDS, the focus is understanding the scope of the problem, diagnosing HIV, and driving forward the medical-based approach that has gained the support of the Tanzanian government and the police (Individual interview 13, September 2018, Dar es Salaam City Center). A medical approach to drug use sounds reasonable, however, it also does not fully consider the challenges people who use drugs face, or the nature of addiction itself. In essence, what the government is supporting is a model where a drug user is found, tested, brought to treatment, and cured. All of this occurs in a context where people who use drugs are treated as criminals, stigmatized, and are almost entirely responsible on their own to access treatment.

Ideally, work toward a better understanding of drug use would lead to a more humane approach to supporting those who use drugs. This is summed up by Smye et al:

> Harm reduction must move beyond a narrow concern with the harms directly related to drugs and drug use practices to address the harms associated with the determinants of drug use and drug and health policy. An intersectional lens elucidates the need for harm reduction approaches that reflect an understanding of and commitment to addressing the historical, socio-cultural and political forces that shape responses to mental illness/health, addictions, including harm reduction and methadone maintenance treatment. (Smye et al. 2011: 1)

This is an ideal that has yet to be reached in many states, let alone recognized by the international drug control regime or countries with poor health infrastructure. In this sense, however, Magufuli's work to slow progress was even more dire and can be considered a major reversal of the limited supports previously available.

The crackdown and policies of the Tanzanian government are unfolding in front of international donors and agencies whose ability to reach their goals are impacted by these very policies, and will be even further impacted in the future. The ability of Tanzania to neglect the human rights of KVP while donors continue to provide funding to the Tanzanian government is not just a way of framing support for drug users in a narrow way, but also of the active strategies of obfuscation, obstacle setting, and impositions aimed at reducing services for people who use drugs. The lack of real power or concerted effort among larger NGOs, with international backing, to influence this outcome is evident in the government's ability to focus funding only on methadone and silence advocacy for the comprehensive harm reduction programming needed. During my fieldwork, more activist organizations were simply focused on surviving in the country while major funders remained intent on the bigger picture.

I do not intend to criticize the important efforts of these organizations in linking with local activists and advancing harm reduction. Rather, I am simply challenging the categorizations in which people who use drugs fall according to international donors. Other than a select few NGOs trying to advance harm reduction in itself, international development omits people who use drugs as a group deserving of service in their own right. This is not necessarily out of neglect but rather the continued framing of drug use as a medical issue that can be solved through medical interventions alone in the midst of widespread repression. The international focus of NGOs on reducing HIV, along with the repressive domestic approach to drug use, creates an environment in which the needs of people who use drugs are not met. Denying services, or creating an environment in which the services exist and do not meet the needs of Tanzanians due to a myriad of political directives, is not harm reduction. Furthermore, the focus on health so narrowly defined comes at the expense of interventions that are just as evidence based, such as needle exchanges and drop-in centers which the government has opposed.

COMPETING SYSTEMS OF SUPPORT AND CONTROL

I was told by one researcher at Muhimbili University that it was the donors that were driving the overwhelming focus on HIV, stating, "The issue with comprehensive addictions treatment is donors, donors drive the HIV prevention focus to the point it seems to be the only focus of donors" (Individual interview 12, October 2018, Muhimbili). The idea of donors driving the policy agenda is a common understanding. As noted by Hollender et al., "At the core of this inequality [in shaping the drug reform agenda] is that the North's domination of deliberations and policymaking in order to tilt the outcome. This is perhaps most evident in reviewing UNODC's donors. The top contributors are overwhelmingly states promoting the prohibition agenda" (Hollender et al. 2016: 23).

While these funding inequalities exist, Tanzania is not a passive recipient of a war on drugs agenda. Tanzania is also not a major UNODC donor, yet is still able to promote the prohibition agenda. During my fieldwork, several interviewees told me that funding for greater harm reduction supports was available but the government is not active and open to pursuing these funds, a fact evidenced by neighboring Kenya's ability to locate and leverage these funds. Many local NGOs believed that if the Tanzanian government were an active champion and supporter of tackling HIV for all citizens, regardless of moral virtue, donors would see greater impacts from their investments in HIV/AIDS.

The choices of donors are also complex, however, and are reflective of the limitations in funding compared to the need. Funding for HIV across Africa is not enough, let alone funding available for people who use drugs. I also made clear the disparity in funding for securitization and war-on-drugs style policy versus the funding available for the human rights of people who use drugs. Taking these dynamics together presents a more coherent picture of the structural underpinnings of the war on drugs. From the perspective of the global war on drugs, which is still epistemically and structurally dominant, and the low priority of drug users among governments with the resources to advocate for them, the ability of Magufuli to influence policy dynamics despite a lack of resources makes more sense.

Using the lens of extraversion, it is clearer how the Tanzanian government has inserted itself into this dynamic, breaking down previously built partnerships between willing local activists and sources of international funding and instead pushing against the advancement of better services for people who use drugs. The Tanzanian government framing drug policy as less repressive and showcasing its methadone program also allows greater agency to achieve a war on drugs agenda with little opposition.

Even the United Nations has been unable to influence any progressive policy toward drug users in Tanzania under Magufuli. A UNODC representative told me that the UN did not have active funding to support harm reduction and instead tried to advocate for the rights of drug users when possible. However, after the election of Magufuli advocacy became difficult and the government's more active role in driving policy was clear:

> The decrease in funding for drugs is due to the political environment. The uncertainty at the moment has scared off some donors. Family planning has collapsed and it is too volatile to risk major programs. With the KVP guideline change more people have gone into hiding. The key is finding a political window, in the meantime all that can be done is supporting existing programs even when inadequate, and wait for opportunities to arise to push for greater advocacy. (Individual interview 25, November 2018, Msasani)

In the interim, people who use drugs face limitations and the ability to reverse the policies being put in place is difficult.

During my time in Tanzania, people involved with drug users expressed frustrations with the reversal in policy which was definitely shaped by the raising of expectations prior to Magufuli. The situation was summed up to me in conversation with a local NGO:

> The Global Fund, it's not enough. It's very limited otherwise. We appreciate it is the first time the Global Fund is considering funding NSP [needle and syringe programs]. It's the first time. It has never been the case. This was a lot of advocacy and a lot of work done to convince them. We had that filing initially, the previous government, even at the local level, was very supportive. For Temeke, they had even wanted their own [NSP] center. Think about councilors, local leaders of government they are telling you they want to take ownership of that but since the directive is from above they can't speak anymore. So we were on an incline then we went this way and now we are here. Let me tell you, Kenya, I remember they had the first tour in 2013 [of Tanzania's methadone program and harm reduction services]. I was part of this tour, they came to learn, the same from South Africa. They came and learned from us but now when you look at South Africa and Kenya compared to Tanzania? And we talk about this in our working group meetings, we talk about people who come to learn from us but then what has happened with us? That's my question for you. (Individual interview 24, November 2018, Temeke)

In this interview, I was told that the change in policy from the Tanzanian government made already reticent donors unwilling to take greater risks in a charged political environment by supporting NSP. As noted in this quote, the chilling effect was among the government itself, with lower-level bureaucrats and ministers also afraid to "take ownership" of politically unpopular programs. While donors do have a focus on the general issue of HIV/AIDS, local activists had come up with flexible and creative ways to use HIV/AIDS funds for harm reduction. The quote above also reveals the discursive space in which policy develops—despite the major obstacles and underfunding for harm reduction, activists still push and influence the drug policy sector as well.

The result of the revision process and the priorities of the government are clear. NGOs, while working to advocate for better services, are in a position where the services are needed but limited dollars, a restricted donor presence and policy changes reduce services available to people who use drugs. While the outward appearance, given the continuation of existing programs, is of ongoing support and care, Magufuli limited space for vulnerable Tanzanians and weakened the ability of well-funded organizations such as PEPFAR to reach those who need it. In this sense, the Tanzanian government's policy changes have contributed more to the long-term marginalization of people who use drugs than the initial crackdown.

The effects of the policy revisions, in combination with the crackdown, had both ideological and practical impacts. In practical terms, foreign agencies involved in harm reduction are intimidated, fearing harassment or removal from the country or fearing offending the government which could make work harder as employees could face visa denials or temporary detention. The government is also allowing harm reduction to continue under the guise of methadone, meeting their own goals of getting people off drugs and appeasing foreign agencies and donors.

In ideological terms, which I explore more in the next chapter, the government is re-creating the image of drug users as inimical to development, as criminals and agents of corruption. Framing the population in this way justifies the government's policy goals which they have succeeded in implementing despite the impacts these formal and informal measures have on service provision from foreign agencies. These changes went largely unremarked upon by the international community, highlighting the ability of the Tanzanian government to maneuver within a neglected area of development and policy, and push through an abstinence-based and punitive agenda.

LOCATING AGENCY IN THE TANZANIAN DRUG WAR

The capacity of the Magufuli regime to flagrantly attack the human rights of marginalized communities reveals an important, and under-theorized, instance of African state agency. The drug war in Tanzania challenges assumptions of African state marginalization in the international sphere. My aim is not to dismiss the influence of Western donor countries, but rather clarify that influence and examine its discursive relationship with domestic governments in sub-Saharan Africa. Stephen Brown and Rosalind Raddatz make this clear in their work on democracy in Kenya, stating that "a more complete account of donors' ability to influence domestic policy is thus depends on both structure and agency, including the agency of both donor and recipient governments" (Brown and Raddatz 2014: 46).

The Tanzanian government pursuing this agenda supports an argument for the participation and influence of African countries on the international stage in global policy formation and in shaping their own domestic policy agendas despite the seemingly overwhelming influence of Western powers. Extraversion is an important starting point in understanding the inclusion of African actors at the global level, and how agency is utilized within limited structural space.

The war on drugs continues to be upheld by some Western governments and the Tanzanian government through various strategies, including aid, security, loans, training programs and political support; there is also a grass-roots movement opposing the continuation of this war. Unlike in Western countries, where local activism to support drug users is largely a domestic affair, in Tanzania activists opposing the war on drugs also include a number of actors and a network of NGOs, former users, medical professionals, and harm reduction advocates that are linked through shared goals. This complex field of actors pursuing better services for people who use drugs has created various policy outcomes, programs, and initiatives. As legislation and funding remains weighted toward the war on drugs, however, the supports available for marginalized groups most in need of assistance remain inadequate. As I wrote above, the inclusion of a number of actors does not necessarily overcome the Tanzanian governments' role in policy creation.

Over the course of 2016/2017, the Tanzanian government sidelined major NGOs in its drive to change harm reduction policies while it also undertook a crackdown on all KVP. With the methadone program intact, the idea of harm reduction in the country remained in place, even as legal, economic, and policy restrictions hampered the effectiveness of this service. Donors with competing priorities, can see drug users as served by basic interventions which do not fully meet their needs. While I expand on how narratives supported the drug war in Tanzania, the practical policy and legal interventions highlight how a government can systematically marginalize people who use drugs. In Western countries, there is little foreign interference in how drug policy is formulated. In Tanzania, the situation was more similar than I anticipated, despite the discursive policy formation between local activists, donors, NGOs (local and international), and the Tanzanian government. The war on drugs emerged dominant regardless.

CONCLUSION

Magufuli inherited a growing harm reduction infrastructure but slowed progress and implemented policies opposed to the needs of people who use drugs. As the number of right-wing conservative leaders favoring the traditional approach to drug use gain traction in the United States, Tanzania, the Philippines and elsewhere, a resurgence in poor policy choices will undoubtedly follow. International consensus and policy frameworks do not exist in a vacuum, but are discursively shaped by domestic governments with political agendas and values opposed to people who use drugs. Every time drugs are depicted as evil and threatening in the service of political gain, an old narrative is re-awakened and strengthened, renewing the war on drugs at the international level.

In the Tanzanian government's approach to harm reduction, the epistemic roots of the war on drugs are apparent. The war on drugs and its associated policies of prohibition, punishment, and the targeting of vulnerable individuals is not designed to recognize different cultures, histories, and lives. It is not designed to recognize individuals, other than to assign them full blame for their addiction. Under the cover of individual responsibility, governments reduce available services, condemn people who use drugs and leave them to fend for themselves. This uncaring understanding of drug use remains at the epistemological root of drug policy, including harm reduction interventions which are, at best, not extensive enough to meet the needs of drug users and, at worst, simply new ways to enforce abstinence. Despite decades of activism by former drug users and those who work with them, many of these interventions remain trapped within the ontological belief that and those who use drugs are failures, criminals, and corrupters. This ontology underlies the international consensus which is being actively upheld by the government of Tanzania.

My work in Tanzania confirmed, from my perspective, the ongoing lack of recognition for the rights of people who use drugs. The epistemic underpinning of the war on drugs needs to be interrogated to realize the limitations of current policy measures. The war on drugs in Tanzania is a strong example of how an African state, dependent on aid and with few resources, is able to find space to maneuver and create its own repressive agenda within an international system that continues to de-prioritize issues of drug use. This outcome, and what I observed on the ground, is even more surprising considering that support for HIV/AIDS and for drug users are entirely foreign funded by agencies that should be strongly opposed to Magufuli's agenda to reach their goals.

Chapter 8

The International War on Drugs

The Influence of Tanzania, Narrative Production and Outcomes

In 2021, following the death of John Magufuli, the new President Samia Suluhu Hassan stated, "Drugs have negative impact on the nation as they contribute to the existence of moral erosion and undermine the national workforce. Thus, the society should be fully involved in fighting drugs" (Kapama 2021). The prime minister also reiterated his commitment to the war on drugs stating:

> The government is determined to deal with drug traffickers and ensure this problem becomes history in the country. If we are to recover the industrial economy we must have a healthy workforce to be able to participate in legitimate work to build our nation. Anyone who wants to undermine the national workforce or weaken industrial economy efforts will be dealt with mercilessly. It is important for parents, guardians and community to be close to young people and monitor their movements to prevent them from falling into the trap of drug abuse (Kapama 2021).

Both statements signaled continuation with John Magufuli's drug war and the continued production of narratives around drug use in the country. In keeping with Magufuli's vision, drug users are meant to be perceived in the Tanzanian state as threats to development, a drain on the national workforce and examples of moral failure.

In this chapter I consider these narratives and the evolving international consensus around drug use, to situate Tanzania not as a passive recipient of policies and narratives around drugs, but an active participant in these debates. Here I argue that Tanzania is a part of an evolving consensus, supporting policies that may appear compassionate and new that are, in reality, not a real reversal of the repressive and failed policies of the past. I use examples of Tanzania's presence in international debates on drug policy and contrast with my fieldwork, to show the acceptance of repressive policies at the international level. The international consensus does not prioritize drug users, a fact that Tanzania, and other countries enacting visible and repressive war on drugs policies exploit to achieve their agendas. Ultimately, despite all the progress toward harm reduction, drug use is still frequently framed in a way that allows human-rights abuses and neglect.

In the previous chapter, I noted how the Tanzanian government pursued its priorities and marginalized opposition. This chapter focuses on narrative creation and the ideological results of Tanzanian drug policy. Throughout this book, I have discussed global war-on-drugs ideology as a persistent and adaptable method of repressing people who use drugs. In African countries, the war on drugs is often interpreted in through a reductive lens in which major narratives uphold its continuation. These reductive tropes foisted upon drugs in Africa create the image of drugs as an agent of chaos, where substances are the cause of corruption, health crises, and criminality. As famously depicted by Robert Kaplan in 1994, Africa is the site of "disease, overpopulation, unprovoked crime, scarcity of resources, refugee migrations, the increasing erosion of nation-states and international borders, and the empowerment of private armies, security firms, and international drug cartels" (Kaplan 1994). In this nightmarish environment, drugs are a source of chaos and despair, decontextualized completely from the actual experiences of people who use drugs and the policies that impact them.

The narratives ascribed to drug policy in Africa have changed little from this fantastic vision depicted decades ago. While less sensationalist, the idea of drugs introducing corruption, disease, and violence into African states remains present and the goal of tackling these issues justifies repressive policies that do not meet the needs of drug users. Moving deeper into the idea of extraversion, I highlight the ways in which the Tanzanian government is building narratives and leveraging its position to shape drug policy in the country without losing the existing funds available. Tanzania is putting foreign agencies into a position where their influence on drug policy is considerably weakened, leaving people who use drugs at the mercy of domestic policy. Furthermore, I discuss how Tanzania, still a donor darling, obfuscates the reality of its repression and lack of support for drug users through crafting the narrative of comprehensive harm reduction services being available in the country. The lack of actual investigation or concern for drug users is a reflection of the already weak support available for people who use drugs and their position as a low priority for donors and the international community overall. The collusion of these factors contributes to a lack of real support available to people who use drugs.

I conclude this chapter by reflecting on the current trajectory of the war on drugs and Tanzania's role in it. I argue that Tanzania's seemingly repressive war does not deviate much from international norms and expectations, existing in a context where the quixotic mission to reduce drug supply remains a priority. Internationally, governments are grappling with the challenge of implementing humane policy while continuing to prioritize eliminating drug supply. Practices which are not complementary, such as criminalizing drug use while supporting the human rights of people who use drugs, are packaged as a viable alternative to the war on drugs.

THE NARRATIVE AS PRESENTED?

In this chapter, I highlight three narratives surrounding drug use in Tanzania: drugs as a threat to development; drugs as a criminal problem and cause of corruption; and, drugs as a disease to be eradicated. These narratives, which simplify the lives of people who use drugs, are actively promoted by the Tanzanian government, erasing more nuanced understandings of the actual needs of people who use drugs.

Harm reduction and treatment would be much better suited in reducing the burden of infectious disease and poor health outcomes among people who use drugs on already stressed health systems, thus contributing to development over the longer term. Despite strong activism within Tanzania pushing a harm reduction narrative inclusive of the complexities and realities of drug use, this messaging is lost in part due to donor unwillingness to challenge the Tanzanian government and, the fact that Tanzania is shaping and contributing to more facile narratives that are not being interrogated or deconstructed.

Magufuli's rhetoric re-instilled old fears of drug use as linked to corruption and evil, while Tanzanian government policy paints drug users as personally responsible for their addiction in the face of systemic obstacles. The Tanzanian war on drugs not only frames the issue of drug use in the country but also contributes to narratives around people who use drugs and the policies they deserve. In creating a crisis to justify a war on drug users, the war on drugs becomes relevant and, once again is used as a way to address the problems war-on-drugs policies create.

Despite the increased control and move away from harm reduction, the Tanzanian government is working to shape the narrative, somehow utilizing both very harsh language against drug users in Tanzania while acknowledging the importance of helping people who use drugs on the international stage. At the level of the DCEA and Ministry of Health, officials often claim that Tanzania continues to be a leader in a strong harm reduction strategy. However, this harm reduction strategy has changed in meaning, from moving toward the needs of people who use drugs to becoming a system aimed at ridding society of the evils of drug use.

DRUG USE AS A HEALTH CRISIS

Alongside security concerns, the overriding issue of HIV/AIDS rates among injection drug users has driven a large portion of the public health response in Sub-Saharan Africa (SSA). In many countries such as Tanzania with high rates of HIV/AIDS, and with significant foreign investment in their health budget, donors have supported interventions aimed at reducing HIV transmission among key vulnerable populations (KVP). The largely foreign funded interventions from organizations such as the President's Emergency Plan to Fight HIV/AIDS (PEPFAR) and the Global Fund are significant and, despite the challenges remaining, are remarkable responses to a major public health crisis. PEPFAR alone has spent more than "$70 billion on programmes globally to combat HIV and AIDS, tuberculosis, malaria and other opportunistic infections since 2003" (AVERT 2019).

This important work is driven by the disproportionate burden of HIV in SSA, where 12% of the global population makes up 71% of infections (Kharsany and Karim 2016: 35). Despite a focus on treatment and its now greater accessibility, many individuals still do not know their status, prevention is a challenge and, with gender inequality, young women are still disproportionately impacted. While major investments have been made, heterosexual sex remains the dominant mode of HIV transmission, impacting potentially large numbers of people and leaving little focus for marginalized groups who may be considered deserving of their status (Kharsany and Karim 2016).

In Tanzania, I have reviewed how the Global Fund, USAID, and PEPFAR are all major contributors to combating HIV/AIDS. It is important to note that the small portion of funding for KVP is not driven by the needs of people who use drugs, but rather the narrative of health crisis and potential disease spread through this group. While the prevention of HIV/AIDS is crucial, the purely medical-driven narrative opens up space for the government of Tanzania to attack harm reduction as a comprehensive system recognizing human rights, while maintaining the appearance of providing services to people who use drugs.

In 2016, speaking at the Vienna conference on drugs, the head of the DCEA, Rogers Siyanga stated "Tanzania now provides needles and syringes, opiate substitution therapy and anti-retroviral therapy for people who use drugs. In fact we are providing a comprehensive health package to the people who use drugs" (Siyanga Statement, 59th session of the CND, 2016). He does not mention that needle and syringe exchange is limited to one district or that syringes are in fact illegal in Tanzania. He also doesn't mention that, while he made these remarks, Tanzania was preparing to imprison thousands of people who use drugs and undertake reforms to change the policies designed to help them.

Mr. Siyanga continues, "We have seen community based outreach programmes and peer education as modalities for delivering specific services to key populations. In existing programmers, outreach workers and peer educators facilitate linkages of key populations to drop-in centers . . . [Tanzania will] continue to empower civil societies/non-governmental organizations in the fight against the drug problem [and] ensur[e] adequate investment in harm reduction programmes" (Siyanga Statement, 59th session of the CND, 2016). As should be clear based on the previous chapters, the comprehensive health package is not comprehensive at all. Drop-in centers were closed, NGOs have not been empowered but made to fear retribution should they stray from a narrow understanding of harm reduction and the remaining harm reduction services in Tanzania are not adequately funded at all.

This may not be purely the fault of the DCEA, however, it does offer insight into the way in which the Tanzanian government is working to present a picture of their activities externally while changing the narrative within the country. Many interviewees I spoke to were skeptical of the DCEA's power to guide its own agenda. The senior member of the DCEA I spoke to gave me this impression, as his assessment of harm reduction focused much less on abstinence but rather on human rights and the freedom of people who use drugs to continue to use, simply reducing the harms (Individual interview 16, October 2018, Dar es Salaam City Center). His conception of harm reduction was much more in sync with progressive views that are definitely not reflected on the ground in Tanzania. In this interview the increased oversight was not about DCEA control but rather ensuring services, such as sober houses, were improved and run properly. From the perspective of this interviewee, the lack of funding for harm reduction was due to lack of donor interest which did not include drug treatment and supply reduction, including a reference to British funding for training and supply reduction (Individual interview 16, October 2018, Dar es Salaam City Center).

While this may partially be true, it does not explain why, given government interest in less controversial options that support abstinence, such as the sober house model or preventative education in schools, there is absolutely no support for either of these strategies. As I have shown in this book, while drug users are certainly a lower priority globally, there is funding that can be exploited and used to at least offer some greater supports, as was the case prior to 2016.

The Tanzanian government has not always made its intentions clear, pursuing contradictory narratives to normalize its war on drugs. While John Magufuli railed against drug use, other members of his government created the appearance of normal, continued support for people who use drugs. In obfuscating the reality of services available to drug users, the government seemed to be trying to present to outsiders, a better picture of what was really available to people who use drugs. In 2018, Health Minister Ummy Mwalimu noted the reduction in HIV/AIDS rates saying, "Without the Global Fund and other global health partners, these achievements [reduction in cases of HIV] could not have been attained . . . we commit to ensuring continued efforts to scale up and sustain provision of health services that are good quality, equitable, accessible, affordable, sustainable and gender sensitive" (Global Fund 2018). This statement contradicts the reality, in which services are not as equitable or accessible for certain groups and is part of the narrative which does not display the actual motives of the government. When I asked the head of a sober house if the government was doing enough for people who use drugs, he replied:

> No I don't think so, because the two institutions which are dealing with the recovery process is the authority, or the DCEA and the Ministry of Health. Inside these institutions there are a few technical people for recovery only. The government has put much more effort on drug trafficking, smuggling, production . . . bur for recovery very little. Still drugs are everywhere. (Individual interview 19, October 2018, Kigamboni)

During my fieldwork, many interviewees questioned the power Magufuli to spread his influence and the independence of certain branches of government to pursue other agendas. The independence of the Ministry of Health was also unclear, as Health Minister Ummy Mwalimu was supportive of methadone but also was involved in actively restricting KVP supports. One NGO director told me, "I know Mwalimu, her comments on KVP are made under pressure, I don't think this is her belief" (Individual interview 24, November 2018, Temeke). Mwalimu previously made comments supportive of ensuring equitable access to healthcare and is a champion of combatting tuberculosis, which is more common among people who use drugs, raising questions as to her ability to influence policy. Public statements challenging Magufuli and the CCM's positions are unlikely in the current climate. While bureaucracies operated somewhat independently of the government, the initial Magufulication put public servants on alert, creating an environment of caution and fear. Magufuli created an environment amenable to his conservative agenda, bringing public servants and ministers in line and removing those who opposed him.

The minister of health's statements reflect this environment of fear. Regardless of the minister's personal beliefs, the impacts of the Government of Tanzania's crackdowns on vulnerable people and policy changes toward KVP have gone against equitable healthcare under her watch. Human Rights Watch conducted 35 interviews with lesbian, gay, bisexual, and transgender people in 2019 and had similar findings. In a letter to Ummy Mwalimu, HRW raised concerns that "recent laws and policies have prevented key populations from enjoying the right to the highest attainable standard of health, as guaranteed under international law." The forthcoming report assesses:

> The impact of several policies implemented by the Ministry of Health, Community Development, Gender, Elderly and Children, including the ban on water-based and silica-based lubricants, the prohibition on HIV prevention and outreach led by civil society organizations representing men who have sex with men, and the closure of drop-in centers providing HIV services to key populations. It documents how stigma and discrimination continue to affect men who have sex with men and trans people in government health facilities, inhibiting access to health services. It also documents a series of police raids on civil society workshops and trainings related to health and rights. (Human Rights Watch 2019).

It should not be surprising, considering the evidence I have outlined in this book, that HRW found the Tanzanian government's provision of services to KVP to be a serious concern. While the attention raising by HRW is important, advocacy has not challenged the government in pursuing its agenda or brought about change, at least for people who use drugs.

The Ministry of Health, while attempting to provide some semblance of health services to people who use drugs, such as methadone, is at the same time, severely restricting access to more comprehensive supports. Whether the department has greater capacity to act independently is unclear, the reality and apparent outcomes, however, are that it followed Magufuli's directives closely. During Magufuli's reign, the government of Tanzania converged on the idea of drug users needing supports not due to their rights as citizens, but rather their role as a potentially dangerous vector for the spread of disease.

The DCEA is another example of a department making statements not reflected in reality. The ability of the DCEA to influence policy, a relatively new department with a new mandate, is even more questionable. As I was told at the UNODC, "The DCEA is supportive and learning, but their major issue is funding. There is no government funding and very little capacity for the DCEA to undertake all of the plans—no expertise in data or grant writing for example and a lack of human resources to support this" (Individual interview 25, November 2018, Msasani). The DCEA was primarily created as an enforcement agency, borne out of Magufuli's desire to give greater capacity to the organization to punish drug users and traffickers. While prevention and treatment are included as pillars of the agency, the overall funding is very low, as is their ability to build capacity and better address the needs of people who use drugs (Individual interview 25, November 2018, Msasani).

Sober houses have the vocal support of DCEA but no funding, while the Global Fund provides some support for methadone outreach through DCEA.

Among interviewees working at different sober houses, the complaint was that the DCEA was focused more on interdiction and supply control rather than harm reduction or treatment (Individual interviews 17 and 19, October 2018, Kigamboni). As the head of a local harm reduction agency told me, "Yes the support is there. The problem is we do not qualify for accessing grants and funds. The government has funding for DCEA for operations and I am worried they are busy with other priorities" (Individual interview 24, November 2018, Temeke).

The government has prioritized a war on drugs at the expense of people who use drugs, yet is working at the international and domestic levels to create the illusion of care and a comprehensive drug policy. Indeed, looking at Global Fund financing for Tanzania, upon which a number of organizations depend, the story does appear different. The government is the largest recipient of Global Fund financing as of 2018 in Tanzania, and therefore controls the direction of this funding which, as noted in previous chapters is largely not for people who use drugs. The disparity between the claims of the government, especially when interacting with donors, shows how the government controls a narrative and somehow segregates harm reduction from the loud, anti-harm reduction rhetoric of the president. It is a narrative that fits into the vision of harm reduction as an intervention somehow compatible with the war on drugs. However, as is increasingly clear from what I observed among people who use drugs and from advocacy organizations, this vision is not compatible.

The narrative that emerges from the Tanzanian government's work to curtail harm reduction is that harm reduction can indeed be compatible with increased stigma, incarceration, and harassment of people who use drugs. Tanzania is a part of propping these ideas up, sanitizing harm reduction to make it a one-dimensional piece of an overall war-on-drugs strategy. The Tanzanian government has changed the narrative of harm reduction into a narrative of abstinence. This change aligns neatly with the war on drugs, which erases the larger context of drug use. The epistemology of the war on drugs presents drug use as a disease to be eradicated, a goal which complements prohibition, forced treatment, and abstinence rather than supporting the human rights and needs of people who use drugs. In Tanzania, the government used the narrative of drug use as a health crisis to pursue a war on drugs, rather than leveraging this narrative to support expanded harm reduction supports.

DRUG USE AS A CRIMINAL THREAT

In 2010, a US congressional report noted that "U.S. policy responses to the rise in drug trafficking through Africa remain in the formative stages" (Wyler and Cook 2010: 33). Despite this lack of coherent direction, initial concerns were clear: "How to develop a strategy and find the resources to both stem the rising flow of drug trafficking through Africa—particularly West Africa—in the short term, through such means as effective interdiction operations, and simultaneously address the underlying, long-term law enforcement capacity weaknesses that make the Region vulnerable to drug trafficking" (Wyler and Cook 2010: 33).

Militarily, most African countries are a lower priority than other regions involved in drug trafficking. That said, by 2012, United States Africa Command (USAFRICOM) was providing approximately $20 million in aid to various partner nations in Africa for counter-narcotics activities (Turse 2018). USAFRICOM leads the United States' counter-narcotics efforts on the continent among other support such as anti-terrorism. This support, unlike support given by USAID which usually tries to consider human rights or development implications, includes key partners such as Uganda and Ethiopia, repressive regimes aiding in the fight against terrorism in the Horn of Africa (USAFRICOM 2018).

Again, despite some fears being founded—for instance, Al Qaeda in the Maghreb does use drug revenue to fund some activities—these policies and this funding has shown little in terms of results. Remarkably, a review of USAFRICOM and USCENTCOM spending from 2014 to 2016 revealed major flaws with data collection, monitoring of efforts, and coordination to the extent that neither agency could "determine whether their CN [counter-narcotics] programs effectively used the $496 million . . . in fiscal years 2014 through 2016 to counter illicit trafficking" (US Department of Defense 2017: 11). This admission highlights not only how bad policies are pursued, but how they are not even effectively implemented at great cost. It is a statement that also shows how the fractured consensus of global prohibition, while maybe deteriorating in terms of rhetoric, is still supported by high levels of funding.

The costs of propping up this war in one region seem high. United States counter-narcotics activities in the western hemisphere from 2010 to 2015, however, dwarf this, valued at over $5 billion (United States Government Accountability Office 2017: 10). While East Africa is not necessarily a priority region, the high amounts of funding show that even a nonpriority region is able to access funds for security purposes.

Framing the issue of drugs as a threat is so commonplace that it is easy to forget the actual size and extent of drug-related problems prior to the war on drugs. My research on Tanzania showed a growing problem in use; however, there was no sudden and dramatic increase that would precipitate drastic action. As Michelle Alexander writes in reference to the war on drugs in 1980s USA, "At the time the war on drugs was declared, illegal drug use and abuse was not a pressing concern in most communities" (Alexander 2011: 71). The war on drugs was a creation aimed directly at the African American community and which, in the United States, was backed up by policy resulting in mass incarceration and huge growth in funding for police. Tanzania, in embarking on a similar war on drugs, is likewise backing up its efforts to "create" a crisis, with actual policy which makes the crisis an ongoing reality.

Tanzania and the war on drugs are challenging examples of African agency. While the securitization of development as a policy narrative on the African continent makes up a large body of literature, the war on drugs in Tanzania is far from a priority for both Western donors and scholars. Tanzania is a long-time partner of Western countries with few major securitization concerns what would lead to access to security funding at the same level of countries such as Uganda or Ethiopia. In this context, it can be questioned how policy agendas, seemingly passed down from the West are interpreted and implemented in countries that are paid little attention in securitization efforts. The case of Tanzania and the war on drugs also shows how policy imperatives currently persist despite a lack of Western interest. Instead, due to this lack of interest, repressive ideologies such as the war on drugs are co-opted and advanced by African countries.

Certainly John Magufuli, through his intense rhetoric, worked to center the narrative of drug use in his country as a major issue, a criminal threat that must be dealt with. His rhetoric was an interesting example of how, as Western nations lose interest in actively prosecuting the war on drugs, countries in the global south may be taking up the torch to continue it. While narratives of drugs as a cause of corruption and violence are old, the insertion of the Tanzanian government into the debate upholds a fading idea and frames the issue in the country despite the much greater challenges facing the Tanzanian state. In intimidating and sidelining the few foreign agencies with active harm reduction interests and the larger INGOs with other priorities, the framing goes unchecked and the truth of the realities and challenges faced by drug users in the country are hidden and neglected.

International organizations and activists opposed Magufuli's rhetoric faced challenges, as the government shaped the narrative to support a crisis and organizations had to follow suit to try and raise the issue at home and abroad. To date, no country, no donor or organization has meaningfully come out to challenge the continuation of the war on drugs by John Magufuli. I would echo here Jonathan Fisher and David Anderson who argue in regard to securitization that, "each [Ethiopia, Uganda, Rwanda and Chad] has successfully imposed its own priorities onto the security policies of its western allies, often at the expense of other development aims and goals" (Anderson and Fisher 2015: 150). In Tanzania, the government pursued a war on drugs at the expense of advancing harm reduction for people who use drugs, subsequently impacting access to HIV/AIDS treatment and directly opposing donor priorities and development. The influence of Tanzania in shaping its own agenda is underestimated, as the government has continued to uplift the idea of drugs as an invasive criminal threat, a threat that needs to be dealt with by any means necessary. The war on drugs has no major detractors willing to take a position that condemns the Tanzanian government, operating instead in restricted environments as best they can while the government continues the war on drugs.

DRUG USE AS A THREAT TO DEVELOPMENT

A final narrative that is prevalent in Tanzanian drug policy is that drugs impede economic and social development. Drugs as a threat to development is perhaps the strongest narrative in drug policy and development circles. On its face, it seems logical—drugs lead to corruption and disrupt productive youth, slowing down development goals in the global south. In this section, however, I again deconstruct this narrative and dig deeper to understand how this narrative is simply another way to support the war on drugs and ignores the actual systemic issues and policies that impact development. Tanzania contributes to this belief by fostering the idea that the country is indeed under threat from drugs themselves and need interventions that will eliminate drug supply in order to have a safe and healthy population working toward a better future. In making the elimination of drugs a developmental goal, people who use drugs can be justified targets as enemies of development, harmony, and prosperity.

These fears and the associated policies of prohibition, previously depicted in self-interested terms have now become increasingly cloaked in win-win language for third-world countries and the West. Effectively, the punitive language of the war on drugs has transformed into more compassionate language aimed at caring for the developing world and hoping to support development, which illicit drugs prevent. Deborah Alimi tracks the rise of this narrative over the past decade, noting that policy divergence and the desire to improve drug policy has opened up space for the diffusion of this agenda (Alimi 2019). The idea of drugs impacting development needs to be unpacked, however, as it again tends to ignore the histories and complexities of drug use and trade in Africa. While the mantra of drugs being bad for development is assumed, it decontextualizes the ways in which illicit drugs can have complex interactions within the sociocultural, economic, and political environments in specific countries.

War on drugs discourses are connected to drugs and development through the narrative that tackling drug use is somehow a way of fostering development. The narrative offers little analysis of how development is actually impacted and obscures how combatting drug users is often just another way of bolstering government repressive capacity and security. As Klantschnig, Dimova and Cross argue in their introduction to the special edition on drugs in Africa, "It is perceptions of security, rather than real concerns with development, that still drive drug policy elaboration and implementation in Africa" (Klantschnig et al. 2016: 171). While drug use is often repeatedly mentioned as a threat to security and development, there is no evidence of how or why development is impacted by drugs. Instead of considering the actual impacts of drugs in society, let alone the connection to development, many major states and organizations are highly supportive of this agenda.

As Dimova's work has shown, drugs can have a real impact on society but supply reduction and increased enforcement initiatives often impact "street-level dealers, who often come from marginalized backgrounds" (Klantschnig et al. 2016: 171). Furthermore, those who are severely marginalized and who already face major pressures in finding drugs face dangerous withdrawal, switch use to higher-risk substances or engage in riskier behavior such as needle sharing. From interviews with those who work with PWIDs in Dar es Salaam, the only real impacts are felt among the most marginalized population involved in using drugs.

Fears of drug trafficking in East Africa impacting development were illustrated most clearly in a USAID publication entirely focused on the development response to drug trafficking in Africa published in 2013. This document, aimed at guiding development responses framed drug trafficking as a threat to democracy and development, with the "failure to address this threat" posing the risk of "undermining the U.S Agency for International Development (USAID)'s investments and thwarting US Government objectives on the continent" (USAID 2013: 1). The focus of the US Government in building accountable governance to counteract this major threat has had the opposite effect: building up the repressive state apparatus in many countries to combat drugs and supporting the power of authoritarian states. The USAID report reads more like instructions for an enforcement agency, with a focus on "bolstering political will, fostering accountable governance and developing counter-narcotics capacity" (USAID 2013: 25).

The linkage between drugs and development shows a passing focus on human rights and instead a much greater interest in using aid dollars for security efforts. More recently, a high-level US bureaucrat reiterated this grave picture stating, "If we do not act decisively . . . drugs and illicit enterprise will corrode the rule of law and the gains of globalization" (US State Department 2017: 8). The connection between a globalized war on drugs which has inflated the price of illicit drugs and forced traffickers to develop new routes for trafficking is not remarked upon.

Similarly, Penny Mordaunt, the minister of foreign development for the United Kingdom, following suit with the mingling of drugs and development position of USAID, made high-profile visits to Tanzania. Mordaunt was in Tanzania in support of a 1.3 million pound program to support Tanzanian and Kenyan authorities investigate organized crime with the support of the British Royal Marines (Elgot 2018). Mordaunt suggested this initiative would prove that funding has the effect of helping developing countries, where development is compromised by drugs, but also support an end to organized crime in the UK (Rweyemamu 2018). Mordaunt's suggestion promotes the assumption, again without evidence, that increased security in the Indian Ocean somehow reduces traffic to the UK and supports stability in Tanzania. Claiming to have stopped millions of pounds of heroin being trafficked through the Indian Ocean, Mordaunt noted the double-win, "Combating organized crime and improving security is good for developing nations and directly contributes towards the security and safety of the UK" (Elgot 2018). Mordaunt here echoes USAID policy, raising the specter of drugs as a threat to development.

While seemingly an admirable goal, helping a developing country through supply-side interventions, visits like Mordaunt's are simply a continuation of the war on drugs. A common assumption contained in this "drugs threatening development" narrative is the idea that corruption is due to illicit drug trafficking. The removal of drugs from the equation, however, would not solve issues of corruption. As the most recent World Drug Report (2017) states, "Fewer groups are exclusively dedicated to drug trafficking, while more are operating in other illicit sectors" (UNODC 2017: 9). In countries such as Tanzania, there is an array of opportunities for organized crime. Drugs can be, at different times, a viable way to support other illicit activities, and crackdowns seem to have little impact on the major players involved. At worst, slight disruptions and the need to wait out increased efforts to crackdown result in adaptation by criminal groups and elites.

Underlying the claims of championing development, there seems to be little interest in examining how drug use actually impacts Tanzanians. Common phrases attacking corruption or poverty writ large do not actually help people impacted by drug use and instead betray a highly cynical self-interest aimed at reducing supply in the West under the guise of development work. Importantly, in this context, aid dollars become an extension of enforcement in the pursuit of an intervention that will definitely fail. As Carrier and Klantschnig (2016: 185) argue, "Current drug policy itself has the capacity to ruin livelihoods and impede development, sometimes more so than the drugs themselves . . . in most African states, drug-supply control has clearly been prioritized and it is mainly petty cannabis traders, farmers, and users who 'meet justice' as they are easy targets for law enforcement officers." In 2017 in Tanzania, khat farmers were indeed targeted by the Drug Control and Enforcement Agency which obviously did little to contribute to lessening the supply of this mild stimulant, but rather impacted poor farmers (Motani 2017).

The *Tanzanian Daily News* noted, "Narcotic drugs, which include khat, are a health hazard and indeed, a threat to life" (*Tanzanian Daily News* 2016). This bizarre claim is not based in any evidence. Khat is a mild stimulant with a long history of use in East Africa, and it is very unclear how a raid on its production would aid development. The example of the Tanzanian government touting its successes builds its own legitimacy and also raises questions as to where the narrative of drugs impacting development originates. After all, using Tanzania's limited resources to target poor khat farmers would seem questionable outside of the realm of aiding development.

There is a willingness from foreign governments, specifically the United States, to invest in the militarization and the repressive apparatus of African states to pursue certain agendas, especially anti-terrorism and anti-trafficking efforts. While Tanzania is not as high a priority compared to supports for anti-terrorism in Kenya and Uganda for example, there still are efforts to support anti-trafficking. I did not focus on securitization in this book, but I did find continued references to the perceived support of anti-trafficking efforts in East Africa. The DCEA was largely thought of, by local activists and NGOS, to be an agency focused on anti-trafficking efforts entirely. However, when I talked with the DCEA, the reasons for this focus seemed to be due to foreign interests.

The UK, for example, has contributed to supply reduction efforts in an attempt to both reduce supply of heroin reaching the UK and to support development in Tanzania (Elgot 2018). The head of the Tanzanian drug control agency highlighted collaboration with the UK National Crime Agency as a positive, claiming it is reducing the inflow of heroin into the country (Rweyemamu 2018). The senior official I interviewed at the DCEA, however, claimed that the British government did not want to fund treatment in Tanzania—since maybe 85% of drugs are destined for transit the focus is heavily supply focused. The official told me that the British government only cared about limiting transit to Britain (Individual interview 16, October 2018, Dar es Salaam City Center). This claim belies other narratives, depicting the Tanzanian government as helpless in the face of foreign donors wanting prohibition and anti-trafficking efforts only.

Scholars who have studied the influence of African governments in Western policy debates have often focused on higher-level priorities for donors such as democratization or securitization. These dual interests have been particularly important in Uganda, where Yoweri Museveni was able to curtail donors' influence on democratization (Fisher 2013) and shape donor perspectives on the LRA (2014) and in Kenya, where again democratization failed in the 1990s due to short-term donor interests among other factors (Brown 2001). Some of these influences are at play in Tanzania, albeit on a much smaller scale and in relation to a much less salient policy issue.

The evidence and outcomes of Tanzanian policies will be difficult to measure, likely only becoming visible in the years to come. From my experiences in Tanzania, and the impacts of COVID-19 afterward, which dried up donor funding even further, the situation for people who use drugs does not appear amenable to development. There is little evidence that the Tanzanian government's policies toward drug users are aiding development, even as they raise the specter of drug use impacting development in the country. This narrative falsely places vulnerable Tanzanians as the focus of why development is failing, rather than continued poor policy choices by the government. Under the guise of drugs impacting development, old war-on-drugs practices such as securitization and repression continue allowing countries such as Tanzania to continue removing supports from drug users and targeting poor people, all in the name of development.

DONORS, INFLUENCE, AND THE ROLE OF TANZANIA IN FRAMING DRUG USE

In my review of the international dynamics contributing to drug policy in Tanzania, I highlighted three broad areas in which these interventions could be considered; drugs as a threat to development, drugs as agents of crime, and drugs as a health issue (vector for disease). While all three of these narratives may be considered an imposition of Western policies and epistemologies on Tanzania, it is the government of Tanzania that has actively contributed to shaping drug use in their country into these categories, all of which erase the human rights of people who use drugs. Capturing the framework of harm reduction as progressive and user-focused has been a longtime goal of activists in the country, but achieving the recognition of this idea is a tall task when faced with government opposition and a lack of funding and support. Furthermore, many activists are themselves targets of government crackdowns, removing them from involvement in debates or discussions about the direction of Tanzanian drug policy.

The crackdown, policy changes, and rhetoric surrounding drug use in Tanzania are all complementary tools in shaping narratives and ideas that justify harsh drug policy in Tanzania. As Jonathan Fisher notes, "Donor and African governments change, and are changed by, these structures [of donor/dependency relationships] through interacting with them; they are not—or do not have to be—directed, regulated and determined by donors alone" (Fisher 2013: 541). Utilizing Bayart's assertion that African actors are indeed involved in international policy debates and structures, these actors exercising agency through framing and information management, is an important part of contributing to global policy structures. In the case of Tanzania, the use of domestic tools to create crisis narratives, intimidate local and international organizations and the appeasement of donors at the international stage are important examples of agency being utilized to pursue a specific agenda.

As illustrated above, policies most important to Tanzania, which is not a major hub for securitization funding, relate to the idea of drugs causing the corruption and lack of development in the country. In pursuing state-led development goals, drug users are unproductive and unsupportive of developmental goals. Painting people who use drugs as the cause of corruption and slow development erases the CCM's culpability in these issues. Tanzania also promotes the idea of drug use as a disease to be eradicated to support its anti-harm reduction agenda and build up abstinence-based approaches to drug use.

Tanzania pursuing its own agenda raises questions as to why donors, upon which Tanzania depends, and foreign agencies that are established and fund service provision to KVP, do not have greater influence. In his study on democratization in Uganda, Jonathan Fisher identified three factors limiting donor influence: competing foreign policy priorities, the internal politics of the donor community and beliefs that "they do not possess sufficient influence over a particular regime" (Fisher 2013: 485). These are salient factors in major policy debates; however, the war on drugs in Tanzania remains peripheral to a majority of donors. Major donor countries present in Tanzania, including Norway and Canada, have no programming that includes people who use drugs in their development focus. This is due to a variety of factors, not only people who use drugs abroad being a low priority, but also the framing of drug use as being solved through very limited medical interventions. The Tanzanian government contributes directly to ensuring the lives of people who use drugs are obfuscated and the limited programming, which they do little to support, are highlighted.

As I mentioned previously, the smaller international harm reduction agencies in the country focused more on survival and providing the services allowed rather than irritating the Tanzanian government. Larger funding bodies, such as the Global Fund, are effectively funneled through government agencies and again diverted away from a human-rights based approach. Tanzania, is therefore able to limit donor influence through leveraging competing donor priorities and engaging in an area overlooked by donors. Any donors or organizations that might pay attention to drug use in Tanzania are either appeased by the semblance of treatment for people who use drugs, or intimidated in expressing criticism of repressive drug policy. It is now important to offer treatment and appear to support people who use drugs, even when pursuing discriminatory policies. In Tanzania, being able to do so conveniently erases the realities of the drug war and ensures donors take little notice as they attend to higher priority areas of development policy.

The Tanzanian government's ability to sideline donors and foreign agencies in pursuit of its war on drugs appears to be due to differing foreign policy priorities and a lack of political will to challenge the human-rights abuses being committed by the Magufuli regime. Increased calls for aid independence from Magufuli and a lack of clear policy coherence around the issue of drug policy also create a difficult environment to undertake work with drug users, allowing space for the Tanzanian government to pursue its own agenda.

When applying the theory of extraversion, and further to the arguments of Stephen Brown and Jonathan Fisher, the war on drugs can be transformed into a policy agenda that is not "something the West has done to Africa, but rather a set of policy imperatives that some African governments have actively pursued" (Anderson and Fisher 2015: 132). In this case, Tanzania actively pursues a war on drugs that directly impacts a population being served by major international organizations, showing the limited influence of donors over domestic policy and the power of an African government to frame the issue to outsiders. As Peter Haas writes, "Members of transnational epistemic communities can influence state interests either by directly identifying them for decision makers or by illuminating the salient dimensions of an issue from which the decision makers may then deduce their interests" (Haas 1997: 75). The government promotes abstinence on one hand and repression on the other, subverting the interests of donors with the stated goals of promoting human rights, increasing access to needed services, and supporting KVP.

While I cannot argue that Tanzania is influencing how drugs are dealt with in other countries, the Tanzanian case is an important example of how drug use, and ideas of how it should be dealt with, are framed in an African context and the impacts this framing has on how services are provided in the country by external actors. In this sense, Tanzania is producing narratives that can be applied to African countries, which are also developing and are sources of trafficked heroin. The strategies Magufuli pursued were accepted and given legitimacy by the lack of international attention or concern for people who use drugs. The ideology Magufuli promoted results in the same outcomes as anywhere that practices the war drugs—worse health outcomes, greater marginalization of drug users, and longer-term socioeconomic impacts and costs.

Epistemically, the revitalization of the war on drugs and its accompanying narratives on the African continent ensure its continuation. Agency and structure are mutually constitutive, and the use of framing as a mechanism of agency by the Tanzanian government thus influences the structure, domestically and internationally, of the war on drugs. The war on drugs continues at the international level in a similar way to Tanzania, though less concerted and obvious, with milder language hiding continued repression, stigmatization of drug users and a general lack of support or advocacy, especially for drug users in countries that continue to marginalize and attack them.

The end goals remain the same internationally and in Tanzania, eliminating drug use. People who use drugs must either cure themselves or be punished. Continuing policies in this way makes decriminalization, providing safe spaces to people who use drugs and ensuring the needs of drug users are met, appear as far-fetched fantasies despite the evidence that these practices would go much further in aiding development. New policies that would undo the epistemic assumptions of the war on drugs, such as simply seeing drug users as deserving of services and basic rights, would support a different way forward. However, in reflecting international norms and responses to drug use, Tanzania is actively shaping and ensuring the war on drugs continues. None of the assumptions that are driving the Tanzanian war on drugs are being challenged, putting harm reduction and treatment in the service of abstinence and prohibition, rather than in the service of promoting human rights, recognizing drug use as neither a disease nor a crime, and removing the constructed narratives applied to vulnerable populations in order to serve short-term political ends.

CONCLUSION

Drug policy is being discursively shaped by activists, governments, and NGOs spanning borders. However, the example of Tanzania shows how a government, with limited resources, can take an active role in this discursive space and have influence in limiting services for people who use drugs. Using strategies of intimidation, appeasement and narrative framing, obscuring the reality of drug use in Tanzania, foreign agencies are effectively limited in their advocacy, forced to remain silent and forced to follow the narrow directives of the Tanzanian government.

Countries such as Tanzania should be seen as part of the ongoing development of the war on drugs in its current iteration, in which abstinence and prohibition continue to be normalized as effective ways to deal with people who use drugs. This study is another example of a long line of scholarly works that challenge the continued international system of drug control. This is a system that clearly does not work, yet remains relevant and accepted. As long as an approach that actively targets people who use drugs while providing limited supports is a viable and unchallenged policy option, decades of failed policy for people who use drugs will not be reversed.

The Magufuli government used and advanced narratives, successfully framing the issues of drug use in the country as being meaningfully addressed by methadone, while doing little to advance better services for people who use drugs and imposing greater restrictions on their lives. With the fractured international consensus, the continuation of the war on drugs and the minimal harm reduction efforts being made globally, Tanzania can pursue its war on drugs domestically. In doing so, the government of Tanzania, works within and promotes an international consensus that continues to uphold the war on drugs and misinterpret what harm reduction actually means. The recognition of the human rights and dignity of people who use drugs is not present in Tanzania and, until drug users come to be seen as deserving of support, is not present in international norms and practices.

As I noted at the outset, the war on drugs has material and epistemic roots. In the past two chapters, I outlined both the structural changes put in place by the Tanzanian government to achieve its ends, and the ideological framing that accompanied these structural changes. The Tanzanian government changed policy governing KVP services, re-instilled laws and efforts to crackdown on drug users and achieved little in its drug war other than further marginalizing people who use drugs. It is important to consider the epistemic linkages of these actions, and the international consensus on the war on drugs. In the context of high domestic political will and an international environment in which the war on drugs is still considered viable, the Tanzanian government has publicly continued a war on drugs, advancing its own agenda at the expense of drug users in the country.

Conclusion

Advancing Harm Reduction in Belief and Practice

In February 2021, just over two years since I observed the fear wrought by John Pombe Magufuli, the bulldozer with an iron grip on the country simply . . . disappeared. The Tanzanian government, impressively in the age of immediate information, successfully obfuscated his whereabouts for several weeks before his death was confirmed on March 17, 2021. The news immediately brought to mind questions among scholars and observers of Tanzania what his legacy would be and what his intervention in Tanzanian politics would mean for the future of the country. The renowned Tanzanian scholar Issa Shivji began to put the Magufuli phenomenon in context, noting:

> Ultimately the working people have to depend on themselves rather than wait for a messiah to deliver them. Hopefully, the Magufuli phenomenon would have taught progressive African intellectuals to distinguish between rhetorical anti-imperialism and systemic understanding of the global capitalist-imperialist system; between populist demagogues and popular democrats; between mass political line and mass evangelism; and between a protracted struggle of the working people for liberation and emancipation from below and short-cut measures to development and promises of deliverance from above. (Shivji 2021)

Other scholars such as Dan Paget (2021) and Thabit Jacob (2021) considered what Magufuli actually represented for Tanzania, whether it was an authoritarian turn, populism, or elitist plebeianism and what the future is for the party. My first thought was what would happen to drug policy in Tanzania and the many people I had talked to during my time there.

It is unlikely new President Samia Suluhu Hassan, despite her willingness to reverse some decisions made by Magufuli, such as acknowledging the existence of COVID-19, will emerge as a champion of harm reduction. She has in fact already called for an intensification of the war on drugs, reiterating the narrative of youths being lost to drugs and doubling down on attacking supply (Kamala 2021). Just prior to Magufuli's death, the head of the DCEA also trumpeted this commitment, citing over 37,000 individual arrests as just the beginning of a war that must "be guided by the heartfelt commitment of the Commander in Chief of the Armed forces and his high level of patriotism for his country and its people" (Kapama 2021). This jingoistic sentiment certainly does not bode well for less punitive approaches. Magufuli's legacy for people who use drugs may have been the creation of a war on drugs blueprint for successors to follow. This blueprint, as noted by Issa Shivji (2021) above is a top-down, "short-cut measure" to end supply which disrupts the lives of people who use drugs, limits their social supports and cuts their access to services.

In revisiting my conclusions and the media that had surrounded Magufuli when he was alive, it was clear that the man attracted more attention than the government he formed and the political party he was a part of. Magufuli's death both demystified his power while reaffirming the continuities in Tanzanian politics, namely the authoritarian tendencies and unbroken reign of the CCM. While Magufuli was the face of policies that focused on silencing domestic media and dismantling opposition parties, he did not undertake them alone. The CCM aligned behind Magufuli in attacking people who use drugs, homosexuals, and women. One certain legacy of John Magufuli is that the CCM was all too willing to work toward the destruction of the opposition while supporting human-rights abuses previously considered unacceptable in the donor-dependent country. A slightly authoritarian country, perhaps held in check by a desire to appear more acceptable and appease donors, became a pariah in its approaches to vulnerable populations.

Magufuli was not an anomaly in Tanzanian politics, and the focus on morality and unity, naturally excluding undesirable populations will remain an unfortunate part of Tanzanian politics as well. While many aspects of Magufuli's rule will continue to receive greater attention, I was privileged to spend time trying to understand an often ignored issue and listen to those who are often not listened to. Using these perspectives, I tried to depict not just a one-dimensional policy issue, but illustrate the context and the many disparate threads that underlie the evolution of the drug war in Tanzania. I analyzed in-depth where this war came from, how it is understood, the ways in which it is implemented internationally and domestically, and how it unfolded in the unique context of Tanzania under the Magufuli regime.

When I arrived in Tanzania, only a few news articles had covered the Tanzanian government's war on drugs and fewer still reported on its outcomes or continuation over subsequent years. Scholarly analysis focused mainly on the methadone program, but offered little context other than the operation of the program itself. To better illustrate the realities of drug use in Tanzania, I sought to understand drug policy and the outcomes of the policy changes from those involved on the ground. I had the opportunity to spend time doing outreach, conduct interviews at sober houses, observe harm reduction programs, and see many of the diverse and creative ways in which activists tried to help each other and themselves. I was also able to see how the Magufuli government made policy changes and undertook specific actions to undo the progress that had been made prior to Magufuli's election and how the government continued to work against the interests of activists and people who use drugs.

This conclusion summarizes my findings and brings together domestic Tanzanian politics and the global war on drugs to show the importance of understanding the epistemic and material roots governing drug policy, as well as the context in which it is implemented. First, I review the key findings of this book, before summarizing the contributions it makes to understandings of the war on drugs, drug use in Tanzania, and the international consensus on drug policy. I close by looking at broader implications for future research and reflecting on the importance of changing war-on-drugs ideology and policy to benefit people who use drugs.

THE WAR ON DRUGS, HARM REDUCTION, AND TANZANIA: INTIMIDATION AND APPEASEMENT

After the election of John Magufuli, the Tanzanian government embarked on a puzzling change in policy, moving from a position of relative disinterest in drug use and allowing harm reduction supports to take shape with foreign involvement, to a government greatly interested in every aspect of drug users' lives, from treatment to punishment. The government not only implemented policies targeting drug users, it cracked down on all key vulnerable populations, directly challenging local and international NGOs working with these groups and reducing their ability to reach them and provide needed services.

In literature on African politics and international relations, the assumption persists of "developing states as weak, system ineffectual states that can never, acting alone or in small groups, make a significant impact on the system" (Beswick 2013: 159). I expected, therefore, that a poorer state such as Tanzania would be unable to overturn and challenge the growing international presence working to support KVP in Tanzania. Yet, the government of Tanzania did implement a war on drugs and did change policy that would directly reduce the ability of foreign agencies to do their work and achieve their goals. The policy shift and increased push to target drug users led to increased police harassment, higher drug prices, fear of punishment, economic vulnerability, riskier drug use, and reduced access to services.

Over the course of 2016 and 2017, the government of Tanzania made a concerted effort to change drug policy and crackdown on drug users, with the intention of eliminating drug use and reducing access to services for people who use drugs. While these goals were contrary to the harm reduction approaches that local activists worked to implement over the previous years, which were funded and supported by foreign agencies such as the Global Fund, the Tanzanian government used strategies of intimidation and appeasement to achieve its war on drugs agenda. In an area of policy that is a low priority for international agencies and donors, Tanzania used intimidation and appeasement to maneuver, effectively limiting supports for people who use drugs and attacking them openly with little opposition.

During the crackdown on drug users and the policy revisions, the government of Tanzania did not meaningfully engage foreign agencies, which were left instead on the outside of policy processes, unable to contribute to what turned out to be repressive and ideological policies, targeting the people they serve. At this time, many foreign actors working with drug users feared being ejected from the country if they challenged the government. The individuals that I talked to felt that they needed to remain silent to avoid their work being shut down completely or to avoid their employees or colleagues being targeted by the government, either through facing bureaucratic delays that prevent work from being done, or through increased scrutiny and possible harassment. This fear is perhaps surprising among larger foreign agencies, as the government relies on these organizations to lead and largely fund the domestic response to HIV/AIDS and, without their support, Tanzania would see a major reversal in its fight against the virus.

However, despite the fact that it was unlikely foreign agencies would be completely removed from the country, threats to individual employees, especially local workers, were real. News of the Tanzanian government targeting organizations working with gay men, carrying out deportations and erecting bureaucratic hurdles convinced organizations to follow the Tanzanian government's agenda. Jhpiego for instance, a major international HIV/AIDS organization, stopped distributing lubricants and complied with the abstinence-based government approach despite evidence of lubricants reducing the transmission of HIV/AIDS among men who have sex with men.

While the government targeted this sector in 2016/2017, many organizations told me during my fieldwork in 2018 about the difficulties they still faced working in the country, from getting proper permits and visas to being able to do their jobs without constant scrutiny and excessive reporting requirements. For many organizations, the threat of removal from the country also remained, significantly curtailing their ability to express disagreement with the Tanzanian government or take actions that depart from the government's abstinence-based policies. Facing an established development community whose goal was reaching vulnerable populations to reduce high rates of HIV/AIDS, the Tanzanian government deftly used tactics of intimidation and harassment, without attracting international attention, to silence any potential critics.

As local NGOs are much more vulnerable to government restrictions and repressive action than international ones, the cascading effect on the sector was chilling, disrupting what had been, until that point, a fruitful partnership between well-funded foreign organizations and local NGOs and activists. The sector supporting drug users had weaknesses prior to Magufuli, including the need for more funding and the difficulties of organizing among a vulnerable population, that the Tanzanian government exploited to further silence more progressive activists. Funding was further reduced and organizing made even more difficult due to stigma and police intimidation. The resulting picture that emerged in 2018, was a top-down, one-size-fits-all approach to treating drug use within the context of restrictive laws and abstinence-based ideology.

The government also used another tactic, framing a narrative around the existing methadone treatment to appease any donors or foreign agencies that might have been alarmed by the crackdown. Methadone treatment was not targeted, but left alone and touted as an extensive and comprehensive harm reduction intervention. In 2016, at the Vienna Conference on drugs, the head of the Drug Control and Enforcement Agency of Tanzania, Rogers Siyanga, boasted about Tanzania's drug programming, highlighting drop-in centers, comprehensive health packages, and harm reduction programming for drug users in the country. While these barely existed at that time, within a year they all disappeared. In Tanzania, methadone is accepted as a good first step and pumped up narratives of comprehensive support are accepted at the international level without question. The result is the contradictory state of drug policy in Tanzania, but also in other states around the globe and reflected in the international consensus—limited treatment in the midst of stigma, repression, and punishment.

Methadone treatment remained, and the government left the program in place as a demonstration of its compassionate approach to drug users, as if a dose of an opioid substitute once daily could indeed take the place of counseling, peer support, and comprehensive health services. No major donors protested and foreign agencies in the sector, most of which are focused not just on drug users, but HIV/AIDS reduction generally, shifted their focus away from comprehensive harm reduction for people who use drugs, trusting that treatment remained in place.

As a result, people who use drugs, already facing numerous obstacles in accessing services and treatment, had police take a greater interest in "chasing them," were forced into hiding, were the target of renewed stigma directed against them and had the already limited supports available to them further reduced. While I was skeptical about the power of the Tanzanian state's capacity to fully implement policies given its lack of resources and involvement in the sector, it did implement new drug policies that empowered the police, limited foreign support, and narrowed the scope of drug treatment.

While it may be obvious that cracking down on drug use is not good for people who use drugs, this finding is important. The Tanzanian government's strategy had such obvious and apparent negative outcomes for drug users that were hard to not notice by foreign agencies working in the sector. Despite these agencies witnessing the reduction in supports for people who use drugs, hearing that clients were resorting to riskier drug use and seeing clients get arrested and harassed by police, they were unable to challenge the government or prevent these outcomes.

In hot spots and at local NGO offices, people who use drugs all told me how outreach dried up since the crackdown, how they were forced to go further and pay more for drugs, and how the police bothered them. The Tanzanian government revived anti-drug stigma to justify its policies and worked to break up the collaborative effort between foreign agencies and local activists to support people who use drugs.

In place of advancing harm reduction, the government of Tanzania promoted treatment which appeared to be more focused on enforced abstinence and the eradication of drug use rather than meeting drug users' needs. In this way, Tanzanian drug policy, seen as a whole—from legal, social, and health-based perspectives—is simply a continuation of the war on drugs given legitimacy by the false narrative of treatment and support. Magufuli made life for drug users worse and, even should better services be put in place today, this period hindered the implementation of better services and significantly delayed the development of the comprehensive supports that drug users need.

INTERNATIONAL PERSPECTIVES AND WAR ON DRUGS NARRATIVES: THE ROLE OF TANZANIA

In the early chapters of this book, I described the material and epistemic aspects of the war on drugs. In chapter 8, I explored how traditional war-on-drugs narratives are applied to African states where a supposed focus on development justifies a number of policies that repress people who use drugs. In analyzing the war on drugs in Tanzania, it is clear that the Tanzanian government produced the narratives of drugs hindering development and causing corruption, justifying policies focused on eradicating drugs and drug use through abstinence and punishment. The result of framing narratives in this way is that foreign agencies focused less on supporting drug users, instead following an agenda that does not meet drug users' needs, or meet their own goals in reaching vulnerable populations. Tanzania is contributing to an international consensus in which the war on drugs is justified as long as basic treatment is provided.

While the narrative of "drugs hindering development" is found in policy literature from USAID and is also an accepted assumption in academic literature on drugs in Africa, the narrative during my time in Tanzania emanated from the government itself, not from overzealous donors trying to push their own agenda. Tanzania attracted some foreign support, as I noted earlier from countries such as the UK, to support supply-side measures aimed at targeting traffickers. The Tanzanian government also, in government representatives' speeches and in official policy documents, implied that drug users are corrupt and a threat to the goal of development and a united Tanzania. Under the government of President Hassan, it appears Tanzania will continue to reproduce these narratives, painting drugs as an existential threat to be dealt with through supply-side controls.

I described how the government employed these narratives to demonize drug users and obfuscate its own role in corruption and political mismanagement. Scapegoating drug users for a lack of economic development and poor governance, the Tanzanian government effectively framed drug use as a crisis to be addressed through policy change and through the aggressive enforcement of harsh laws and penalties.

This does not ascribe undue influence to Tanzania in shaping ideas around drug use. However, it does open up space to show how the Tanzania government employs war-on-drugs narratives in a domestic environment to justify repressive policies. Utilizing this narrative, and repeating it in policy and rhetoric, the Tanzanian government is reproducing and re-creating war-on-drugs ideology at the domestic level. While Western countries, with greater resources and interest in limiting drug supply, are often considered the drivers of the war on drugs in literature and at the international level, this book shows how Tanzania is discursively upholding a war-on-drugs ideology as well. Tanzania's war on drugs is an example of African agency in shaping perspectives and policies in the relatively neglected area of global drug policy.

While the United States, in the past, aggressively promoted the war on drugs, especially in Latin America, it is now harder to justify such a harsh approach given its well-documented failures. In countries considered peripheral in academic literature in setting a war-on-drugs agenda such as Tanzania, the government there is in fact actively promoting policies and rhetoric directly upholding the repression of drug users. Tanzania is discursively producing and manipulating a war-on-drugs ideology at the domestic level, promoting ideas of drug users as criminals, requiring abstinence and increasing political control over a vulnerable population. While the Magufuli regime was doing this in the service of domestic political goals, the involvement of foreign actors in the sector and the countries' aid dependence necessitated strategies to influence perceptions and policies to limit any external challenges to the anti-drug agenda.

The crackdown was damaging to drug users' access to services, but perhaps more damaging was the delay and interruptions in the longer-term goal of advancing progressive policies for drug users. The Tanzanian government, at home and abroad, will continue to promote its strong harm reduction program, presenting the idea that drug use can be solved during a crackdown and without comprehensive supports. As governments use rhetoric and policy that reflect the war-on-drugs ideology, the use of this ideology by governments such as Tanzania's, results in the ideology changing and adapting. The government of Tanzania's war on drugs appears more humane in allowing treatment, yet offers no real legal, social, economic, or political changes to the repression governing all other aspects of drug users' lives.

Tanzanian government officials pose for pictures and take credit for other efforts aimed at supporting people who use drugs such as sober houses, actively creating the illusion that comprehensive services are available for drug users. Drug users continue to be a population to be punished and controlled, rather than supported due to this lack of systemic change. Yet, this outcome is acceptable to an international community, which does not speak out against repressive drug policies abroad, instead continuing to legitimize and provide support to regimes that attack drug users.

LOOKING AHEAD

The year 2020 was dominated by COVID-19 response across the globe, in all countries except for Tanzania which, along with North Korea, refused to track or publish its COVID-19 statistics. John Magufuli's response to the crisis was so astounding that in his obituaries he seemed to be primarily remembered as the president who believed COVID-19 could be prayed away. Magufuli must be remembered, however, for much more. More than any Tanzanian president before him, he used populist rhetoric and religious nonsense to erode the human rights of the most vulnerable members of the population. The CCM benefited and followed along with the moralizing mission of the president. While the CCM does not have a great record of serving Tanzanians, it should be highlighted that this party of was very willing to target vulnerable people during the Magufuli era. The gains of this period are evident in the continued repression of the opposition and elections which have turned into a farce of performative democracy.

Moving beyond COVID-19, it will also be important to reckon with the legacies of drug policy in Tanzania during Magufuli's tenure. With donors retreating and states providing less aid to focus on pandemic response, people who use drugs became less and less of a priority, both in domestic and international environments. Sadly, the pandemic has impacted vulnerable people the most, reducing access to supports and exacerbating poverty while making the rich richer.

Moving forward, there is an opportunity to transform how society understands and treats people who use drugs. Rather than remaining stubbornly wed to prohibition and social control like Magufuli was, decriminalization, full harm reduction services and a human-rights based approach to drug use may be possible. While John Magufuli is gone, the forceful interventions he made to disrupt the lives of vulnerable Tanzanians will have a longer impact. Other drug warriors, seeing the political expediency of pursuing the war on drugs, will arise and continue to uphold a set of policies that make little sense in a globalized world. A full reversal of old drug policy requires not just changing practices but changing the entire epistemic construction of the war on drugs.

Unfortunately, there is no real commitment to change. While I focused on the case of Tanzania in this book, it is just one example of a larger, global commitment to punishing people who use drugs. Set in a larger international context, the commitment to prohibition largely remains, with governments unwilling to follow the courageous example of drug activists who have taken it upon themselves to move ahead with practices like providing safe supply of drugs, ignoring inhumane laws and vocally opposing the policies that oppress them. Until drug users themselves shape policy and are given the resources to ensure services meet their needs, drug policy will remain a largely top-down, state-centric attempt to remove people from the body politic. Tanzania should not be singled out as states across the globe, with very few notable exceptions, explicitly or implicitly support the war on drugs.

Further studies on the perspectives of drugs users, especially on the policies that impact them, are needed. This should include understanding drug policies in other African states and how these policies are connected to international and domestic actors. Drug use should not be written about in a vacuum, but with deep contextual analysis to understand how policy is constructed, implemented, and what outcomes emerge when these policies are implemented. Too often drug use is seen as a problem in and of itself, easily eradicated through legal or biomedical interventions. When understood as a phenomenon deeply connected to socioeconomic and political trajectories, drug use can move beyond a false dichotomy of disease or choice.

A radical rethinking of drug policy, in which drug use is not stigmatized and drugs are decriminalized, seems a long way off. A first step in removing the barriers to better services and supports for drug users, is lifting the ideological fog established through decades of prohibition, abstinence, and control. Rather than seeing treatment included as part of a wider approach to drug policy that remains entrenched in social, economic and legal repression, war-on-drugs policy needs to be abandoned and governments that persist in upholding these policies should face repercussions, or at least a similar backlash that they would face if they targeted any other group in society.

Drugs are not the problem; they have been crafted as such by powerful actors such as the government of the United States, the UNODC and, as I have shown in this book, the government of Tanzania. Every time a government constructs drugs as an agent of crisis, corruption and violence, the people who use them face unjust policies that reduce their access to services and their right to be free from state violence and arbitrary detention. The war on drugs is a system of oppression. Similar to other systems of oppression that governments adapt and frame for political gain, the war on drugs is being constantly redesigned by states and international institutions in the service of an impossible goal.

In its current iteration, drug policies in most countries across the globe appear more humane than in the past. However, the purpose remains the same for governments such as Tanzania's: forcing vulnerable people to bear the blame for much more complex socioeconomic and societal failings, such as corruption or a lack of development. Future studies need to continue to challenge these policies, question why and how they are implemented and advocate for a future where drug policy is inclusive of the needs, beliefs, and aspirations of people who use drugs.

References

INTERVIEWS

Interview 1 – Mainline Tanzania. Location and Date – Interviewed Remotely, September 2018.

Interview 2 – MEFADA. Location and Date – MEFADA Office, Kinondoni, October 2018.

Interview 3 – LEAHN. Location and Date – Interviewed Remotely, August 2018.

Interview 4 – Tanzanian Network of People Who Use Drugs (TANPUD). Location and Date – Mikocheni, September 2018.

Interview 5 – Kigamboni Sober House. Location and Date – Kigamboni Sober House, Kigamboni, October 2018.

Interview 6 – TACOSODE. Location and Date – Mikocheni, August 2018.

Interview 7, 8, 9 – ICAP. Location and Date – ICAP Office, Mikocheni, September 2018.

Interview 10, 11 – TACOSODE. Location and Date – TACOSODE Office, Mikocheni, August 2018.

Interview 12 – MUHAS. Location and Date – MUHAS Office, October 2018.

Interview 13 – Centre for Disease Control (CDC). Location and Date – CDC Office, Dar es Salaam, September 2018.

Interview 14 – Legal and Human Rights Centre (LHRC). Location and Date – LHRC Office, Mikocheni, October 2018.

Interview 15 – Muhimbili University. Location and Date – MUHAS Office, Muhimbili Campus, October 2018.

Interview 16 – Drug Control and Enforcement Agency (DCEA). Location and Date – DCEA Office, Dar es Salaam, October 2018.

Interview 17 – Kigamboni Sober House. Location and Date – Kigamboni Sober House, Kigamboni, October 2018.

Interview 18 – MRC Kigamboni Sober House. Location and Date – MRC Kigamboni Sober House, Kigamboni, October 2018.

Interview 19 – MRC Kigamboni Sober House. Location and Date – MRC Kigamboni Sober House, Kigamboni, October 2018.
Interview 20 – Medecins du Monde. Location and Date – MDM Office, Temeke, October 2018.
Interview 21 – Temeke Methadone Clinic. Location and Date – Temeke Hospital, October 2018.
Interview 22 – Temeke Methadone Clinic. Location and Date – Temeke Hospital, October 2018.
Interview 23, 24 – MUKIKUTE. Location and Date – MUKIKUTE Office, Temeke, October 2018.
Interview 25 – UNODC Tanzania Office. Location and Date – UN Office, UN Headquarters, Msasani, November 2018.

HOT SPOTS

Interview 26–29, PEDDEREF Sober House, October 2018.
Interview 31–33 and Participant Observation, Kigamboni Ferry Hotspot, October 2018.
Interview 34–38 and Participant Observation MRC Kigamboni Sober House, October 2018.
Interview 39–43 and Participant Observation, MRC Kigamboni Sober House, October 2018.
Interview 44, MEFADA Office, October 2018.
Interview 45–49 and Participant Observation, Mwananyamala Hotspot, October 2018.
Interview 50, 51 Manyanya Hotspot, Kinondoni, October 2018.
Interview 52–54 Mwenge Hotspot, October 2018.
Interview 55–56 MEFADA Office, November 2018.
Interviews 57–61 and Participant Observation, Mwenge Hotspot, November 2018.
Interviews 62–67 and Participant Observation, Temeke Hotspot, November 2018.
Interview 68 – Mainline Tanzania, Remotely Interviewed From Edmonton, November 2019.

REFERENCES

Abdool, Reychad. 2016. "Policy Change Towards Implementing Harm Reduction in Sub-Saharan Africa." *International Journal of Drug Policy*, 30, pp. 140–142.
Acker, Caroline Jean. 2010. "How Crack Found a Niche in the American Ghetto: The Historical Epidemiology of Drug-Related Harm." *BioSocieties*, 5(1), pp. 70–88.
Acuda, Wilson, Othieno, Caleb, Obondo, Anne, and Crome, Ilana. 2011. "The Epidemiology of Addiction in Sub-Saharan Africa: A Synthesis of Reports, Reviews, and Original Articles." *The American Journal on Addictions*, 20, pp. 87–99.

Affinnih, Yahya. 2002. "Revisiting Sub-Saharan African Countries' Drug Problems: Health, Social, Economic Costs, and Drug Control Policy." *Substance Use and Misuse*, 37(3), pp. 265–290.

African Union. 2016. "Common African Position (CAP) for the UN General Assembly Special Session on the World Drug Problem, 19–21 April 2016" Publication of the African Union.

African Union – AU Plan of Action on Drug Control (2013–2017).

African Union – Common African Position (CAP) for the UN General Assembly Special Session on the World Drug Problem, April 19–21, 2016.

Ahearne, Rob. 2017. "Tanzania at 56: Echoes of the Best and Worst of Nyerere Under Magufuli." *The Conversation.* Published Online December 13, 2017. theconversation.com/tanzania-at-56-echoes-of-the-best-and-worst-of-nyerere-under-magufuli-88812.

Ahmed, Mohamed, and Ocharo, Brian. 2015. "Insufficient Funds Hurting War on Drugs, Says Nacada." *Daily Nation Online*. September 4, 2015. http://www.nation.co.ke/news/Insufficient-funds-hurting-war-on-drugs-Nacada/1056-2858020-12avmlv/index.html.

Akindipe, Taiwo, Abiodun, Lolade, Adebajo, Sylvie, Lawal, Rahman, and Rataemane, Solomon. 2014. "From Addiction to Infection: Managing Drug Abuse in the Context of HIV/AIDS in Africa." *African Journal of Reproductive Health*, 18(3), pp. 47–54.

Akumu, Patience. 2018. "A Tainted Imperial Legacy That Fuels the Oppression of Gay People in Africa." *The Guardian.* Published Online November 4, 2018. https://www.theguardian.com/commentisfree/2018/nov/04/tainted-imperial-legacy-that-fuels-oppression-of-gay-people-in-africa.

Akyeampong, Emmanuel. 2005. "Diaspora and Drug Trafficking in West Africa: A Case Study of Ghana." *African Affairs*, 104(416), pp. 429–447.

Alexander, Bruce. 2012. "Addiction: The Urgent Need for a Paradigm Shift." *Substance Use & Misuse*, 47, pp. 1475–1482.

Alexander, Michelle. 2011. *The New Jim Crow: Mass Incarceration in the Age of Colorblindness.* New York: The New Press.

Alimi, Deborah. 2019. "An Agenda in the Making: The Linking of Drugs and Development Discourses." *Journal of Illicit Economies and Development*, 1(1), pp. 37–51.

Al Jazeera News. 2019. "Landslide Win for Tanzania Ruling Party in Boycotted Local Polls." *Al Jazeera News Online.* Published November 25, 2019. https://www.aljazeera.com/news/2019/11/landslide-win-tanzania-ruling-party-boycotted-local-polls-191126052300259.html.

All Africa Online. 2017. "Tanzania: Magufuli Adds Weight to War on Drugs." *All Africa Online*, February 7, 2017. http://allafrica.com/stories/201702070044.html.

Allen, Chris. 1999. "Africa and the Drugs Trade." *Review of African Political Economy*, 26(79), pp. 5–11.

Anderson, David, Beckerleg, Susan, Hailu, Degol, and Klein, Axel. 2007. *The Khat Controversy: Stimulating the Debate on Drugs.* Oxford: Berg Publishers.

Anderson, David, and Carrier, Neil. 2009. "Khat in Colonial Kenya: A History of Prohibition and Control." *The Journal of African History*, 50(3), pp. 377–397.

Andreasson, Stefan. 2013. "Elusive Agency: Africa's Persistently Peripheral Role in International Relations." In Brown, William, and Harman, Sophie, eds. *African Agency in International Politics.* London: Routledge Publishing, pp. 143–158.

Ane, Maria-Goretti. 2016. "Africa: The Road After the UNGASS Fracas: Are Things Falling Apart for Africa?" *allafrica.* Published Online May 25, 2016.

Anyimadu, Adjoa. 2016. "Politics and Development in Tanzania: Shifting the Status Quo." Chatham House Research Paper, Africa Programme, March 2016.

Apolinairi, Tairo. 2017. "4,000 Arrested in the Tanzania War on Drugs." *The East African*, July 12, 2017. http://www.theeastafrican.co.ke/news/4000-arrested-in-Tanzania-war-on-drugs-/2558-4011662-e6l87f/index.html.

AVERT. 2017. "HIV/AIDS in Tanzania." Updated August 22, 2018. https://www.avert.org/professionals/hiv-around-world/sub-saharan-africa/tanzania.

Ayers, Alison, ed. 2008. *Gramsci, Political Economy, and International Relations Theory: Modern Princes and Naked Emperors.* New York: Palgrave Macmillan.

Balaji, Divya, Mlunde, L. B., Tran, O. C., Lambdin, B., Mbwambo, J., Nyandindi, C., Matiko, E., Copenhaver, M., and Bruce, R. D. 2016. "First Report of Gender Based Violence as a Deterrent to Methadone Access Among Females Who Use Heroin in Dar es Salaam, Tanzania." *AIDS Behaviour*, 21, pp. 2093–2100.

Barrett, Damon. 2010. "Security, Development and Human Rights: Normative, Legal and Policy Challenges for the International Drug Control System." *International Journal of Drug Policy*, 21, pp. 140–144.

Bayart, Jean-Francois. 2000. "Africa in the World: A History of Extraversion." *African Affairs*, 99, pp. 217–267.

BBC News. 2018a. "John Magufuli: Tanzania Prefers 'Condition-Free' Chinese Aid." *BBC News Online.* Published Online November 27, 2018. https://www.bbc.com/news/world-europe-46364342.

BBC News. 2018b. "Tanzania 'Suspends' Family Planning Advertisements." *BBC News Online.* Published Online September 21, 2018. https://www.bbc.com/news/live/world-africa-45546165.

Beaumont, Peter. 2018. "Fears Grow That Trump's Threat to US Foreign Aid is Putting Lives at Risk." *The Guardian.* Published Online February 11, 2018. https://www.theguardian.com/us-news/2018/feb/11/fears-grow-trump-threat-us-foreign-aid-putting-live-at-risk.

Becker, Felicitas. 2013. "Remembering Nyerere: Political Rhetoric and Dissent in Contemporary Tanzania." *African Affairs*, 112, pp. 238–261.

Becker, Felicitas. 2019. *The Politics of Poverty: Policy-Making and Development in Rural Tanzania.* Cambridge: Cambridge University Press.

Beckerleg, Susan. 1995. "'Brown Sugar' or Friday Prayers: Youth Choices and Community Building in Coastal Kenya." *African Affairs*, 94(374), pp. 23–28.

Beckerleg, Susan, Telfer, Maggie, and Lewando Hunt, Gillian. 2005. "The Rise of Injecting Drug Use in East Africa: A Case Study From Kenya." *Harm Reduction Journal*, 2(12), pp. 1–9.

Belair, Joanny. 2018. "Land Investments in Tanzania: Assessing the Role of State Brokers." *Journal of Modern African Studies*, 56(3), pp. 371–394.

Bergman, Marcelo. 2010. "Narco-politique et narco-économie en Amérique latine." *Problèmes d'Amérique latine*, 2(76), pp. 25–41.

Berman, Bruce. 1998. "Ethnicity, Patronage and the African State: The Politics of Uncivil Nationalism." *African Affairs*, 97(388), pp. 305–341.

Bernstein, Henry. 1999. "Ghana's Drug Economy: Some Preliminary Data." *Review of African Political Economy*, 26(79), pp. 13–32.

Beswick, Danielle. 2013. "From Weak State to Savvy International Player? Rwanda's Multi-Level Strategy for Maximising Agency." In Brown, William, and Harman, Sophie, eds. *African Agency in International Politics*. London: Routledge Publishing, pp. 158–175.

Bewley-Taylor, David. 2018. "Canada, Cannabis Legalization and Uncertainty Around the United Nations Drug Control Conventions." *Addiction*, 113, pp. 1226–1227.

Bjerk, Paul. 2016. "Enter the Bulldozer." *Africa is a Country, Blog Post*. Published Online October 14, 2016. https://africasacountry.com/2016/10/enter-the-bulldozer.

Bohela, Tulanana, and Nwaka, Frederick. 2019. "One Year to Go for Tanzania's President Magufuli and the Reviews Are Mixed." *DW News*. Published Online April 11, 2019. https://www.dw.com/en/one-year-to-go-for-tanzanias-president-magufuli-and-the-reviews-are-mixed/a-51107885

Boister, Neil. 2016. "Waltzing on the Vienna Consensus on Drug Control? Tensions in the International System for the Control of Drugs." *Leiden Journal of International Law*, 29, pp. 389–409.

Boone, Catherine. 1998. "State Building in the African Countryside: Structure and Politics at the Grassroots." *The Journal of Development Studies*, 34(4), pp. 1–31.

Boswell, Frederica, and Warner, Gregory. 2015. "It's Been a Hard 12-Step Road for Zanzibar's Heroin Addicts." *NPR News*. Published Online January 27, 2015. https://www.npr.org/sections/goatsandsoda/2015/01/27/381625994/its-been-a-hard-road-to-12-step-for-zanzibars-heroin-addicts.

Bourgois, Philippe. 2003. "Crack and the Political Economy of Suffering." *Addiction & Research Theory*, 11(1), pp. 31–37.

Bourgois, Philippe, and Ciccarone, Daniel. 2016. "Injecting Drugs in Tight Spaces: HIV, Cocaine and Collinearity in the Downtown Eastside, Vancouver, Canada." *International Journal of Drug Policy*, 33, pp. 36–43.

Bowring, Anna L., Luhmann, N., Pont, S., Debaulieu, C., Derozier, S., Asouab, F., Toufik, A., Van Gemert, C., Dietze, P., and Stoove, M. 2013. "An Urgent Need to Scale Up Injecting Drug Harm Reduction Services in Tanzania: Prevalence of Blood-Borne Viruses Among Drug Users in Temeke District, Dar es Salaam, 2011." *International Journal of Drug Policy*, 24, pp. 78–81.

Bridge, James, Hunter, Benjamin, Atun, Ritaf, and Lazarus, Jeffrey. 2012. "Global Fund Investments in Harm Reduction From 2002 to 2009." *International Journal of Drug Policy*, 23, pp. 279–285.

Brook, Heather, and Stringer, Rebecca. 2005. "Users, Using, Used: A Beginner's Guide to Deconstructing Drugs Discourse." *International Journal of Drug Policy*, 16, pp. 316–325.

Brown, Stephen. 2001. "Authoritarian Leaders and Multiparty Elections in Africa: How Foreign Donors Help to Keep Kenya's Daniel Arap Moi in Power." *Third World Quarterly*, 22(5), pp. 725–739.

Brown, Stephen, and Raddatz, Rosalind. 2014. "Dire Consequences or Empty Threats? Western Pressure for Peace, Justice and Democracy in Kenya." *Journal of Eastern African Studies*, 8(1), pp. 43–62.

Brown, William. 2013. "Sovereignty Matters: Africa, Donors and the Aid Relationship." *African Affairs*, 112(447), pp. 262–282.

Brown, William, and Harman, Sophie, eds. 2013a. *African Agency in International Politics.* London: Routledge Publishing.

Brown, William, and Harman, Sophie. 2013b. "African Agency in International Politics." In Brown, William, and Harman, Sophie, eds. *African Agency in International Politics.* London: Routledge Publishing, pp. 1–17.

Bruce, Douglas, Lambdin, B., Chang, O., Masao, F., Mbwambo, J., Mteza, I., Nyandindi, C., Zamudio-Haas, S., Buma, D., Dunbar, M. S., and Kilonzo, G. 2014. "Lessons From Tanzania on the Integration of HIV and Tuberculosis Treatments into Methadone Assisted Treatment." *International Journal of Drug Policy*, 25, pp. 22–25.

Buxton, Julia. 2006. *The Political Economy of Narcotics: Production, Consumption & Global Markets.* London: Zed Books.

Canadian Drug Policy Coalition. 2015. "Drug Policy and Harm Reduction." A Briefing Report of the Canadian Drug Policy Coalition, Canadian HIV/AIDS Legal Network Policy Series.

Carrier, Neil. 2005. "The Need for Speed: Contrasting Timeframes in the Social Life of Kenyan Miraa." *Africa*, 75, pp. 539–558.

Carrier, Neil. 2006. "Bundles of Choice: Variety and the Creation and Manipulation of Kenyan Khat's Value." *Ethnos: Journal of Anthropology*, 71(3), pp. 415–437.

Centre for Disease Control and Prevention. 2018. "CDC in Tanzania." *CDC Online.* www.cdc.gov/globalhealth/countries/tanzania.

Chabal, Patrick, and Daloz, Jean-Francois. 1999. *Africa Works: Disorder as a Political Instrument.* Oxford: James Currey.

Cheadle, Bruce. 2015. "Anti-Drug ad blitz Cost Government $7 Million, Documents Show." *CBC News.* Posted January 27, 2015. http://www.cbc.ca/news/politics/anti-drug-ad-blitz-cost-government-7-million-documents-show-1.2933830.

Citizen Editorial. 2018a. "Seek Common Ground With the World Bank." *The Citizen.* Published Online November 2, 2018. https://www.thecitizen.co.tz/oped/EDITORIAL--Seek-common-ground-with-the-World-Bank/1840568-4834070-147w6dwz/index.html.

Citizen Editorial. 2018b. "Seek Ways to Mend Ties With Donor Community." *The Citizen.* Published Online November 18, 2018. https://www.thecitizen.co.tz/oped/1840568-4857030-cijpmlz/index.html.

Citizen Reporters. 2017a. "New Anti-Drug Boss Receives MPs' Backing." *The Citizen Online*, February 11, 2017. http://mobile.thecitizen.co.tz/news/New-anti-drugs-boss-receives-MPs--backing/2304482-3808838-format-xhtml-13wm1ikz/index.html.

Citizen Reporters. 2017b. "Tanzania: Thousands Nabbed in Anti-Drugs Campaign, Says PM." *The Citizen*. Published Online April 6, 2017. https://allafrica.com/stories/201704070042.html.

Citizen Reporters. 2018. "Tanzania Government Clarifies 'Gay Crackdown' Report." *The Citizen*. Published Online November 4, 2018. https://www.thecitizen.co.tz/news/Tanzania-Government-clarifies--gay-crackdown--report/1840340-4836670-ls5j46z/index.html.

Collins, John. 2017. "Losing UNGASS? Lessons From Civil Society, Past and Present." *Drugs and Alcohol Today*, 17(2), pp. 88–97.

Collins, John. 2018. "Rethinking Flexibilities in the International Drug Control System – Potential, Precedents and Models for Reforms." *International Journal of Drug Policy*, 60, pp. 107–114.

Collord, Michaela. 2019. "Drawing the Wrong Lessons From Magufuli's Rule in Tanzania." *Africa is a Country. Blog Post*. Published Online May 6, 2019. https://africasacountry.com/2019/05/drawing-the-wrong-lessons-from-the-magufuli-experience-in-tanzania.

Commonwealth Secretariat. 2010. *Report of the Commonwealth Observer Group: Tanzania General Elections*. New York: Commonwealth Secretariat.

Cook, Catherine, and Davies, Charlotte. 2018. "The Lost Decade: Neglect for Harm Reduction Funding and the Health Crisis Among People Who Use Drugs." *Harm Reduction International Association*.

Corva, Dominic. 2008. "Neoliberal Globalization and the War on Drugs: Transnationalizing Illiberal Governance in the Americas." *Political Geography*, 27, pp. 176–193.

Cox, Robert. 1981. "Social Forces, States and World Orders: Beyond International Relations Theory." *Millennium – Journal of International Studies*, 10(2), pp. 126–155.

Cox, Robert W. 1983. "Gramsci, Hegemony and International Relations: An Essay in Method." *Millenium: Journal of International Studies*, 12(2), pp. 162–175.

Crick, Elizabeth. 2012. "Drugs as an Existential Threat: An Analysis of the International Securitization of Drugs." *International Journal of Drug Policy*, 23, pp. 407–414.

Cummings, Andre Douglas Pond. 2012. "'All Eyez on Me": America's War on Drugs and the Prison-Industrial Complex." *The Journal of Gender, Race & Justice*, 15, pp. 417–448.

Dahir, Abdi Latif. 2019. "The Case Against an Investigative Journalist Shows Tanzania's Magufuli Widening a Media Crackdown." *Quartz Africa*. Published Online September 17, 2019. https://qz.com/africa/1710510/tanzania-journalist-erick-kabendera-arrest-as-magufuli-eyes-media/.

Dausen, Nuzulack. 2018. "World Bank Re-Engages Tanzania on Scrapped Education Plan." *Reuters Online*. Published November 2, 2018. https://af.reuters.com/article/topNews/idAFKCN1NN07T-OZATP.

Davey, Melissa. 2016. "Drug Expert Says Australia's Presence at UN Summit a Waste of Money." *The Guardian*. Published April 8, 2016. https://www.theguardian.com/society/2016/apr/08/drug-expert-says-australias-presence-at-un-summit-a-waste-of-money.

Dayo, Amenna. 2019. "President Magufuli's Party Wins 99% of Seats in Tanzania's Local Elections." *The African Exponent.* Published Online November 26, 2019. https://www.africanexponent.com/post/4586-tanzania-president-john-magufulis-party-wins-99-of-local-seats.

Degenhardt, Louisa, and Hall, Wayne. 2012. "Extent of Illicit Drug Use and Dependence, and Their Contribution to the Global Burden of Disease." *The Lancet*, 379, pp. 55–70.

Dimova, Margarita. 2014. "A New Agenda for Policing: Understanding the Heroin Trade in East Africa." *Africa Centre for Strategic Studies.* Published Online December 31, 2014.

Dimova, Margarita. 2016. "'The First Dragon to Slay': Unpacking Kenya's War on Drugs." *Review of African Political Economy*, 43(148), pp. 227–242.

Diyammi, Mark Paul, and Japhet, Stanley. 2018. "Illicit Drug Trafficking and Its Negative Impacts on Youth in Kinondoni and Temeke Districts (Tanzania)." *International Journal of Research in Social Sciences*, 8(8), pp. 7–27.

Domasa, Sylivester. 2018. "Tanzania: Demand for Drugs Soars Across Tanzania." *All Africa.* Published Online March 27, 2018. http://allafrica.com/stories/201803270668.html1/.

Economic and Social Council, United Nations. 2017a. "Consolidated Budget for the Biennium 2018–2019 for the United Nations Office on Drugs and Crime: Report of the Executive Director." E/CN.7/2017/12 – E/CN.15/2017/14, October 13, 2017.

Economic and Social Council, United Nations. 2017b. "Responding to the Prevalence of HIV/AIDS and Other Blood-Borne Diseases Among Drug Users: Report of the Executive Director." E/CN.7/2018/8, December 21, 2017.

Economic and Social Council, United Nations. 2018a. "Activities of the United Nations Office on Drugs and Crime: Report to the Executive Director." E/CN.7/2018/2 – E/CN.15/2018/2, January 9, 2018.

Economic and Social Council, United Nations. 2018b. "Reports by Intergovernmental Organizations on Drug Control Activities: Report of the Secretariat." E/CN.7/2018/CRP.6, March 7, 2018.

Elgot, Jessica. 2018. "UK Aid Minister Hails 'Double Win' of Heroin Crackdown in Tanzania: Combating Drug Trade Benefits Developing Nations and UK, Says Penny Mordaunt." *The Guardian*, August 19, 2018. https://www.theguardian.com/world/2018/aug/19/uk-aid-minister-hails-double-win-of-heroin-crackdown-in-tanzania.

Elias, Peter. 2018. "Eyakuze's Citizenship Probe in New Twist." *The Citizen.* Published Tuesday October 16, 2018. http://www.thecitizen.co.tz/News/-Eyakuze-s-citizenship-probe-in-new-twist/1840340-4807858-v6ben1/index.html.

European Monitoring Centre for Drugs and Drug Addiction. 2014. *Regional Strategies Across the World: A Comparative Analysis of Intergovernmental Policies and Approaches.* EMCDDA Papers Luxembourg: Publications Office of the European Union.

European Union Official Statement – H.E Ambassador Roeland van de Geer recalled to Brussels for Consultations. http://eueuropaeeas.fpfis.slb.ec.europa.eu:8084/

delegations/tanzania/53272/he-ambassador-roeland-van-de-geer-recalled-brussels-consultations_en.

Evered, Kyle. 2011. "'Poppies are Democracy!' A Critical Geopolitics of Opium Eradication and Reintroduction in Turkey." *The Geographical Review*, 101(3), pp. 299–315.

Fernandez, Humberto, and Libby, Therissa. 2011. *Heroin: Its History, Pharmacology, and Treatment*, 2nd ed. Centre City: Hazelden.

Fisher, Jonathan. 2013a. "Image Management' and African Agency: Ugandan Regional Diplomacy and Donor Relations Under Museveni." In Brown, William, and Harman, Sophie, eds. *African Agency in International Politics*. London: Routledge Publishing, pp. 97–114.

Fisher, Jonathan. 2013b. "Structure, Agency and Africa in the International System: Donor Diplomacy and Regional Security Policy in East Africa Since the 1990s." *Conflict, Security and Development*, 13(5), pp. 537–567.

Fisher, Jonathan. 2013c. "The Limits – and Limiters – of External Influence: Donors, the Ugandan Electoral Commission and the 2011 Elections." *Journal of Eastern African Studies*, 7(3), pp. 471–491.

Fisher, Jonathan. 2014. "Framing Kony: Uganda's War, Obama's Advisers and the Nature of 'Influence' in Western Foreign Policy Making." *Third World Quarterly*, 35(4), pp. 686–704.

Fisher, Jonathan, and Anderson, David. 2015. "Authoritarianism and the Securitization of Development in Africa." *International Affairs*, 91(1), pp. 131–151.

Fouere, Marie-Aude. 2014. "Julius Nyerere, Ujamaa and Political Morality in Contemporary Tanzania." *African Studies Review*, 57(1), pp. 1–24.

Fritze, John, and Shesgreen, Deirdre. 2018. "Trump Implores World Leaders at United Nations to Confront 'Scourge' of Drug Addiction." *USA Today*. Published Online September 24, 2018. https://www.usatoday.com/story/news/politics/2018/09/24/donald-trump-united-nations-must-confront-confront-scourge-drugs/1408197002/.

Furukawa, Mitsuaki. 2016. "Management of the International Development Aid System: The Case of Tanzania." *Development Policy Review*, 36, pp. 0270–0284.

Gberie, Lansana. 2016. "Crime, Violence and Politics: Drug Trafficking and Counternarcotics Policies in Mali and Guinea." *Centre for 21st Century Security and Intelligence*.

Gezon, Lisa. 2012. "Drug Crops and Food Security: The Effects of Khat on Lives and Livelihoods in Northern Madagascar." *Culture, Agriculture, Food and Environment*, 34, pp. 124–135.

Gichuni, Grace, and Orinde, Hillary. 2018. "Unsafe Place? World Bank Cancels Missions to Tanzania." *Standard Media*. Published Online November 9, 2018. https://www.standardmedia.co.ke/article/2001302127/unsafe-place-world-bank-cancels-missions-to-tanzania 7/.

Gilder, Regan. 2016. "The Political Crisis in Zanzibar." *Center for Strategic and International Studies*. Published Online March 18, 2016. https://www.csis.org/analysis/political-crisis-zanzibar.

Girei, Emanuela. 2015. "NGOs, Management and Development: Harnessing Counter-Hegemonic Possibilities." *Organization Studies*, 37(2), pp. 193–212.

Githaiga, Hellen. 2017. "Tanzanian Teen Mothers Will Not Be Allowed Back to School." *The East African.* Published Online June 22, 2017. http://www.theeastafrican.co.ke/news/ea/Teen-pregnancies-Tanzania-no-school-Magufuli/4552908-3982870-12w6f52z/index.html.

Glenza, Jessica. 2016. "Russia's 'Cold Turkey' Approach Highlights Global Divide Over Drug Treatment at UN." *The Guardian.* Published Online April 20, 2016. https://www.theguardian.com/world/2016/apr/20/ungass-russia-drug-treatment-heroin-methadone.

Global Commission on Drug Policy. 2011. "The Global Commission on Drug Policy." *War on Drugs.* http://www.globalcommissionondrugs.org/wp-content/themes/gcdp_v1/pdf/Global_Commission_Report_English.pdf.

Global Fund. 2018a. "Global Fund Grants to Tanzania (Mainland) Follow-Up Audit." *The Global Fund to fight AIDS, Tuberculosis and Malaria.* Published March 21, 2018.

Global Fund. 2018b. "Tanzania and Global Fund Sign New Grants to Accelerate End of Epidemics." *The Global Fund to Fight AIDS, Tuberculosis and Malaria.*https://www.theglobalfund.org/en/news/2018-01-30-tanzania-and-global-fund-sign-new-grants-to-accelerate-end-of-epidemics/.

Global Fund. 2019. "HIV/AIDS Results Profile: Tanzania (United Republic) September 2019." *The Global Fund to Fight AIDS, Tuberculosis and Malaria Online Database.*

Global HIV Prevention Coalition. 2017. "United Republic of Tanzania – Country Position Paper." *Global HIV Prevention Coalition Report.*

Gowan, Teresa, Whetstone, Sarah, and Andic, Tanja. 2012. "Addiction, Agency, and the Politics of Self-Control: Doing Harm Reduction in a Heroin Users' Group." *Social Science and Medicine*, 74, pp. 1251–1260.

Greenall, Matthew, Kunii, O., Thomson, K., Bangert, R., and Nathan, O. 2017. "Reaching Vulnerable Populations: Lessons From the Global Fund to Fight AIDS, Tuberculosis and Malaria." *Bulletin of the World Health Organization.* Published January 2018. http://www.who.int/bulletin/volumes/95/2/16-179192/en/.

Guise, Andy, Dimova, Margarita, Ndimbii, James, Clark, Phil, and Rhodes, Tim. 2015. "A Qualitative Analysis of Transitions to Heroin Injection in Kenya: Implications for HIV Prevention and Harm Reduction." *Harm Reduction Journal*, 12(27), pp. 1–9.

Haas, Peter. 2015. *Epistemic Communities, Constructivism and International Environmental Politics.* New York: Routledge.

Harm Reduction International. 2012. "Partners in Crime: International Funding for Drug Control and Gross Violations of Human Rights." *Harm Reduction International.*

Harm Reduction International. 2014. "The Global State of Harm Reduction 2014." *Harm Reduction International.*

Harm Reduction International. 2018a. "The Global State of Harm Reduction 2018." *Harm Reduction International.*

Harm Reduction International. 2018b. "The Funding Crisis for Harm Reduction: Donor Retreat, Government Neglect and the Way Forward." *Harm Reduction International.*

Haysom, Simone, Gastrow, Peter, and Shaw, Mark. 2018. "The Heroin Coast: A Political Economy Along the Eastern African Seaboard." A Research Paper, ENACT. Published by the European Union, June 2018.

Herschinger, Eva. 2011. *Constructing Global Enemies: Hegemony and Identity in International Discourses on Terrorism and Drug Prohibition.* New York: Routledge.

Hibou, Beatrice. 1998. "Retrait ou redéploiement de l'État?" *Critique Internationale*, 1, pp. 151–168.

Hinton, Elizabeth. 2016. *From the War on Poverty to the War on Crime: The Making of Mass Incarceration in America.* Cambridge: Harvard University Press.

Hobson, Christopher. 2014. "Privatising the War on Drugs." *Third World Quarterly*, 35(8), pp. 1441–1456.

Hollender, Rebecca, and Whitaker, Emma. 2016. "Prescription for Failure: Examining the Drug Policy and Development Nexus, Shaping the UNGASS 2016 Discussion." The New School's Milano School of International Affairs, Management and Urban Policy and Observatory on Latin America, With Support From the Open Society Foundation.

Howell, Simon, and Atta-Asamoah, Andrews. 2014. "West Africa and the Transnational Trade in Illegal Drugs: Physical Properties, Policing and Power." *African Review*, 7(1), pp. 1–14.

Human Development Index Yearly Report 2018.

Human Rights Watch. 2019. "If We Don't Get Services We Die – Annex II: Human Rights Watch Letter to Health Minister Ummy Mwalimu, December 24, 2019." *Human Rights Watch Reports.*

Hunter, Emma. 2008. "Revisiting Ujamaa: Political Legitimacy and the Construction of Community in Post-Colonial Tanzania." *Journal of East African Studies*, 2(3), pp. 471–485.

Hunter, Emma. 2013. "Dutiful Subjects, Patriotic Citizens and the Concept of 'Good Citizenship' in Twentieth-Century Tanzania." *The Historical Journal*, 56, pp. 257–277.

Hyde, Lily. 2016. "Achievements and Challenges in Introducing a Harm Reduction Programme in Kenya: A Case Study." *Alliance for Public Health: Community Action on Harm Reduction.* Published April 2016.

Hyden, Goran. 1993. "Structural Adjustment as a Policy Process: The Case of Tanzania." *World Development*, 21(9), pp. 1395–1404.

Hyden, Goran. 2017. "President Magufuli and the Development State Model." *The Citizen.* Published July 25, 2017. https://www.thecitizen.co.tz/magazine/political-reforms/President-Magufuli-and-the-development-state-model/1843776-3959320-format-xhtml-el7rgi/index.html.

Inspector General U.S. Department of Defense. 2017. "U.S. Central and U.S. Africa Commands' Oversight of Counternarcotics Activities." Report No. DODIG-2018-059, December 26, 2017.

International Drug Policy Consortium. 2016. "The United Nations General Assembly Special Session (UNGASS) on the World Drug Problem, Report of Proceedings." Published Online by IDPC, September 2016.

International Drug Policy Consortium. 2018. "Trump to Host UN Meeting on Drug Policy: Veneer of Consensus Masks Deep Disagreement on Global Drug Policy." *IDPC Blog*. Published Online September 21, 2018. https://idpc.net/blog/2018/09/trump-to-host-un-meeting-on-drug-policy-veneer-of-consensus-masks-deep-disagreement-on-global-drug-policy.

Jacob, Thabit. 2021. "In Magfuli's Shadow: The Stark Choices Facing Tanzania's New President." *The Conversation*. Published Online March 23, 2021. https://theconversation.com/in-magufulis-shadow-the-stark-choices-facing-tanzanias-new-president-157602.

James, Bernard. 2016. "Tanzania's Global Drug Kingpin is Unmasked." *The Citizen*. Published March 3, 2016. http://mobile.thecitizen.co.tz/news/Tanzania-s-global-drug-kingpin-is-unmasked/2304482-3112224-format-xhtml-wxxyb1z/index.html.

Jelsma, Martin. 2003. "Drugs in the UN System: The Unwritten History of the 1998 United Nations General Assembly Special Session on Drugs." *International Journal of Drug Policy*, 14, pp. 181–195.

Jelsma, Martin. 2011. "The Development of International Drug Control: Lessons Learned and Strategic Challenges for the Future." Working Paper, First Meeting of the Global Commission on Drug Policy, Geneva. http://www.globalcommissionondrugs.org/wp-content/themes/gcdp_v1/pdf/Global_Com_Martin_Jelsma.pdf.

Jelsma, Martin, and Bewley-Taylor, David. 2011. "Fifty Years of the 1961 Single Convention on Narcotic Drugs: A Reinterpretation." *Transnational Institute, Series on Legislative Reform of Drug Policies,* 12. Published March 2011.

Jennings, Michael. 2002. "'Almost an Oxfam in Itself': Oxfam, Ujamaa and Development in Tanzania." *African Affairs*, 101(405), pp. 509–530.

Jennings, Michael. 2015. "The Precariousness of the Franchise State: Voluntary Sector Health Services and International NGOs in Tanzania, 1960s – Mid-1980s." *Social Sciences and Medicine*, 141, pp. 1–8.

Jensen, Anne Kidmose. 2016. "Inside Dar es Salaam City's Heroin Veins." *The Citizen*. Published Online February 21, 2016. http://www.thecitizen.co.tz/magazine/soundliving/Inside-Dar-es-Salaam-city-s-heroin-veins/1843780-3086672-13jf.

Jerving, Sarah. 2019. "Repressive Laws in Tanzania Stifle the Work of NGOs." *DevEx Onlines*. Published October 28, 2019. https://www.devex.com/news/repressive-laws-in-tanzania-stifle-the-work-of-ngos-95913.

Jojarth, Christine. 2009. *Crime, War and Global Trafficking: Designing International Cooperation*. Cambridge: Cambridge University Press.

Jordan, David C. 1999. *Drug Politics: Dirty Money and Democracies*. Oklahoma City: University of Oklahoma Press.

Kabendera, Erick, and Mirondo, Rosemary. 2015. "Tanzania in Plans to Amend Budget, Exclude Donor Funding." *The East African*. Published Online February 28, 2015. https://www.theeastafrican.co.ke/news/ea/Tanzania-in-plans-to-amend-budget--exclude-donor-funding/4552908-2638200-sra9fxz/index.html.

Kamagi, Deogratius. 2018. "Majaliwa Trumps Success in Drug War in Tanzania." *The Citizen*. Published September 17, 2018. http://www.thecitizen.co.tz/News/Majaliwa-trumps-success-in-drug-war-in-Tanzania-/1840340-4763920-qugffbz/index.html.

Kapama, Faustine. 2017. "Tanzania: Convicted Shkuba Says His Extradition is 'Rape of the Law'." *Tanzania Daily News*. Published May 4, 2017. https://allafrica.com/stories/201705040333.html.

Kapama, Faustine. 2021. "Tanzania: Enhanced Anti-Drug War Silences Barons, Peddlers." *Tanzania Daily News*. Published January 28, 2021. https://allafrica.com/stories/202101280057.html.

Kaplan, Robert. 1994. "The Coming Anarchy." *The Atlantic Monthly*. Published February 1994.

Kelsall, Tim. 2002. "Shop Windows and Smoke-Filled Rooms: Governance and the Re-Politicisation of Tanzania." *The Journal of Modern African Studies*, 40(4), pp. 597–619.

Kelsall, Tim. 2003. "Governance, Democracy and Recent Political Struggles in Mainland Tanzania." *Commonwealth & Comparative Politics*, 41(2), pp. 55–82.

Kelsall, Tim. 2007. "The Presidential and Parliamentary Elections in Tanzania, October and December 2005." *Electoral Studies*, 26, pp. 507–533.

Khan, Adnan. 2015. "From One War to Another: Why So Many Think That Barack Obama's New War Against Drugs is Bound to Fail." *Maclean's*, 128(46), p. 28.

Kharsany, Ayesha, and Karim, Quarraisha. 2016. "HIV Infection and AIDS in Sub-Saharan Africa: Current Status, Challenges and Opportunities." *The Open AIDS Journal*, 10, pp. 34–48.

Kilmister, Andrew, and Browning, Gary. 2006. *Critical and Post-Critical Political Economy*. New York: Palgrave Macmillan.

Kimani, Geofrey. 2018. "Couple Linked With Same Sex Marriage Released on Bail." *The Citizen*. Published Online December 29, 2018. https://www.thecitizen.co.tz/News/1840340-4230136-3tsw80z/index.html.

Kimboy, Frank. 2019. "Tanzania: 'Foreigners' Sabotage Our Efforts – Magufuli." *The Citizen*. Published Online December 13, 2019. https://allafrica.com/stories/201912130972.html.

Kirby, Jen. 2018. "Tanzania's Anti-Gay Crackdown is Sending People into Hiding." *Vox*. Published Online November 5, 2018. https://www.vox.com/2018/11/5/18057112/tanzania-anti-gay-crackdown-makonda.

Klantschnig, Gernot, and Carrier, Neil. 2012. *The War on Drugs in Africa*. London: Zed Books.

Klantschnig, Gernot, Carrier, Neil, and Ambler, Charles. 2014. *Drugs in Africa*. New York: Palgrave Macmillan.

Klantschnig, Gernot, Dimova, Margarita, and Cross, Hannah. 2016. "Africa and the Drugs Trade Revisited." *Review of African Political Economy*, 43(148), pp. 167–173.

Kottasova, Ivana. 2018. "Tanzania Loses $300 Million World Bank Loan Amid Crackdown Concerns." *CNN Business*. Published Online November 13, 2018. https://www.cnn.com/2018/11/13/africa/tanzania-world-bank-loan-intl/index.html.

Kruk, Margaret, and Mbaruku, Godfrey. 2015. "Public Health Successes and Frail Health Systems in Tanzania." *The Lancet*, 3, pp. 348–349.

Kurth, A. E., Cherutich, P., Conover, R., Chhun, N., Bruce, R. D., and Lambdin, B. H. 2018. "The Opioid Epidemic in Africa and Its Impact." *Current Addictions Report*, 5, pp. 428–453.

Labate, Beatriz Caiuby, Cavnar, Clancy, and Rodrigues, Thiago, eds. 2016. *Drug Policies and the Politics of Drugs in the Americas.* Switzerland: Springer Publishing International.

Lambdin, B. H., Masao, F., Chang, O., Kaduri, P., Mbwambo, J., Magimba, A., Sabuni, N., and Bruce, R. D. 2014. "Methadone Treatment for HIV Prevention – Feasibility, Retention and Predictors of Attrition in Dar es Salaam, Tanzania: A Retrospective Cohort Study." *Clinical Infectious Diseases*, 59(5), pp. 735–742.

Lambdin, Barrot, Mbwambo, Jessie, Josiah, Robert, and Bruce, Robert. 2015. "Service Integration: Opportunities to Expand Access to Antiretroviral Therapy for People Who Inject Drugs in Tanzania." *Journal of the International AIDS Society*, 18(19936), pp. 1–3.

LaMonaca, K., Dumchev, K., Dvoriak, S., Azbel, L., Morozova, O., and Altice, F. L. 2019. "HIV, Drug Injection, and Harm Reduction Trends in Eastern Europe and Central Asia: Implications for International and Domestic Policy." *Current Psychiatry Reports*, 21(47), pp. 1–11.

Lee, Bryant, and Tarimo, Kuki. 2018. "Analysis of the Government of Tanzania's Budget Allocation to the Health Sector for Fiscal Year 2017/18." *Health Policy Plus a Publication of USAID*, January 2018. http://www.healthpolicyplus.com/pubs.cfm?get=7144.

Legal and Human Rights Centre and Zanzibar Legal Services Centre. 2017. "Unknown Assailants' a Threat to Human Rights: Tanzania Human Rights Report – 2017." Published by the Legal and Human Rights Centre, Dar es Salaam.

Lissu, Tundu. 2019. "Human Rights Continue to Worsen in Tanzania as Magufuli Cracks Down on Critics." *The Daily Maverick*. Published Online May 20, 2019. https://www.dailymaverick.co.za/article/2019-05-20-human-rights-continue-to-worsen-in-tanzania-as-magufuli-cracks-down-on-critics/.

Maclean, Ruth and Agencies. 2019. "Arrest of Tanzanian Journalist Heightens Fears Over Press Safety: President Accused of Media Crackdown After Police Detain Erick Kabendera." *The Guardian.* Published Online July 30, 2019. https://www.theguardian.com/world/2019/jul/30/arrest-of-tanzanian-journalist-sparks-fears-over-press-safety.

MacQueen, Ken. 2015. "Harper's Pot Stance Versus Science: A New Report Counters Many of the PM's Campaign Trail Claims About Marijuana Policy." *Maclean's.* Published August 12, 2015. http://www.macleans.ca/news/canada/harpers-pot-stance-versus-science/.

Maher, Lisa, and Dertadian, George. 2017. "Qualitative Research." *Addiction*, 113, pp. 167–172.

Mainline. 2017. "Annual Report 2016 – 25 Years of Harm Reduction." *Mainline Foundation.* Published May 2017.

Mainline. "Tanzania – Initial Consultation Report." Unpublished.

Makoye, Kizito. 2014. "Donors Freeze Aid to Tanzania." *DW*. Published Online October 10, 2016. https://www.dw.com/en/donors-freeze-aid-to-tanzania/a-17999275.

Malanga, Alex. 2018. "Tanzania Concerned as FDI Inflows Dwindle for Three Years." *The Citizen*. Published Online July 12, 2018. https://www.thecitizen.co.tz/magazine/Concern-as-FDI-inflows-dwindle-for-three-years/1840564-4659638-tr4ya2z/index.html.

Manda, Constantine. 2017. 'It's Not Just a Rapper's Arrest That Should Raise Alarms About Authoritarianism in Tanzania." *The Washington Post, Online*. Published March 29, 2017. https://www.washingtonpost.com/news/monkey-cage/wp/2017/03/29/its-not-just-a-rappers-arrest-that-should-raise-alarms-about-authoritarianism-in-tanzania/?utm_term=.f216b787095d.

Marez, Curtis. 2004. *Drug Wars: The Political Economy of Narcotics*. Minneapolis: University of Minnesota Press.

May, Channing. 2017. "Transnational Crime and the Developing World." *Global Financial Integrity Report*, March 2017.

Mbashiru, Katare. 2015. "Tanzania Tables Tough New Law to Curb Drug Trafficking." *Africa Review*. Published Online Wednesday March 25, 2015. http://www.africareview.com/news/Tanzania-tables-tough-new-law-to-curb-drug-trafficking/979180-2664842-m39fdz/index.html.

Mbiritu, Njihia. 2015. "News: The Missing Middle: Harm Reduction in East Africa." *Global Fund Observer Newsletter*, Issue 265, May 6, 2015.

McCurdy, Sheryl. 2007. "Harm Reduction in Tanzania: An Urgent Need for Multisectoral Intervention." *International Journal of Drug Policy*, 18, pp. 155–159.

McCurdy, Sheryl, and Kaduri, Pamela. 2016. "The Political Economy of Heroin and Crack Cocaine in Tanzania." *Review of African Political Economy*, 43(148), pp. 312–319.

McCurdy, Sheryl, Lambdin, B. H., Bruce, R. D., Chang, O., Nyandindi, C., Sabuni, N., Zamudio-Haas, S., Masao, F., Ivo, Y., Msami, A., and Ubuguy, O. 2013. "Identifying Programmatic Gaps: Inequities in Harm Reduction Service Utilization Among Male and Female Drug Users in Dar es Salaam, Tanzania." *PLoS One*, 8(6), pp. 1–7.

McCurdy, Sheryl, Ross, Michael W., Williams, Mark L., Kilonzo, Gad P., and Leshabari, Melkizedek T. 2006. "HIV/AIDS and Injection Drug Use in the Neighborhoods of Dar es Salaam, Tanzania." *Drug and Alcohol Dependence*, 82(1), pp. S23–S27.

McCurdy, Sheryl, Ross, Michael W., Williams, Mark L., Kilonzo, Gad P., and Leshabari, Melkizedek T. 2009. "Flashblood: Blood Sharing Among Female Injecting Drug Users in Tanzania." *Addiction*, 105, pp. 1062–1070.

McLean, Katherine. 2011. "The Biopolitics of Needle Exchange in the United States." *Critical Public Health*, 21(1), pp. 71–79.

McLean, Susie. 2012. "Challenges for Harm Reduction: Funding for the International Scale Up of Services." *International HIV/AIDS Alliance*. Presentation May 7, 2012.

McNeill, Casey. 2017. ""Playing the Away Game": AFRICOM in the Sahara-Sahel." *Political Geography*, 58, pp. 46–55.

Metaal, Pien. 2012. "Drug Policy in the Americas – A New Set of Latin American Policy Proposals." *Drugs and Alcohol Today*, 12(3), pp. 141–145.

Mhango, Nkwazi. 2018. "Bottom Line: The World Needs to Be Clear and Sincere On Gay Rights." *The Citizen.* Published Online November 21, 2018. https://www.thecitizen.co.tz/magazine/politicalreforms/1843776-4862142-g2xud9/index.html.

Mkony, Albert. 2016. "#WhatwouldNyereredo?" *Africa is a Country*, *Blog Post.* https://africasacountry.com/2016/10/whatwouldnyereredo/.

Mohammed, Omar. 2018. "Under Pressure From Western Donors, Tanzanian Leader Prefers Chinese Aid." *Reuters Online.* Published Online November 27, 2018. https://www.reuters.com/article/us-tanzania-china-aid/under-pressure-from-western-donors-tanzanian-leader-prefers-chinese-aid-idUSKCN1NW1SB.

Mohammed, Omar, and Fick, Maggie. 2018. "In Tanzania, a Bulldozer President Tests Donors." *Reuters Online.* Published Online November 22, 2018. https://www.reuters.com/article/us-tanzania-politics/in-tanzania-a-bulldozer-president-tests-donors-idUSKCN1NS08R.

Motani, Mira. 2017. "Tanzanian Leaders Pledge Crackdown on Drug Trade Then Raid Village Farms and Imprison Low-Level Offenders." *Talking Drugs.* Published Online July 19, 2017. http://www.talkingdrugs.org/tanzania-drug-imprisonment-low-level-crackdown.

Mpondo, Bonaventura, Gunda, Daniel, and Kilonzo, Semvua. 2017. "HIV Epidemic in Tanzania: The Possible Role of the Key Populations." *AIDS Research and Treatment*, 2017, pp. 1–7.

Msekwa, Pius. 2019. "Tanzania: Magufuli's Four Legendary Successful Years." *Tanzania Daily News.* Published Online November 21, 2019. https://allafrica.com/stories/201911210716.html.

Mukiza, Darius. 2019. "In Defence of President John Magufuli: 'Tanzania is a Beacon of Democracy'." *The Daily Maverick.* Published Online May 28, 2019. https://www.dailymaverick.co.za/article/2019-05-28-in-defence-of-president-john-magufuli-tanzania-is-a-beacon-of-democracy/.

Murage, George. 2016. "MPs Want Legislation Merged to Win the War on Drug Abuse." *The Star.* Published Online May 17, 2016. http://www.the-star.co.ke/news/2016/05/17/mps-want-legislation-merged-to-win-the-war-on-drug-abuse_c1351124.

Musiyo, Victor. 2017. "Tanzania: Top Names Listed in Drug Trafficking Racket." *Africa News.* Published February 2, 2017. http://www.africanews.com/2017/02/11/tanzania-top-names-listed-in-drug-trafficking-racket/.

Mwangode, Henry. 2018. "Tanzania's Anti-Drugs Push Having Positive Impact, Says New Report." *The Guardian Tanzania.* Published July 3, 2018. https://www.ippmedia.com/en/news/tanzania%E2%80%99s-anti-drugs-push-having-positive-impact-says-new-report.

Ng'wanakilala, Fumbuka. 2017a. "Gates Foundation to Spend Over $300 Million in Tanzania in 2017." *Reuters.* Published Online August 13, 2017. https://www.reuters.com/article/us-tanzania-health-idUSKCN1AT0IF.

Ng'wanakilala, Fumbuka. 2017b. "Tanzania Extradites Three Alleged Drug Traffickers to U.S." *Reuters.* Published Online May 3, 2017. https://www.reuters

.com/article/uk-tanzania-drugs/tanzania-extradites-three-alleged-drug-traffickers-to-u-s-idUKKBN17Z0RZ.

Ng'wanakilala, Fumbuka. 2019. "President Urges Tanzania's Women to 'Set Ovaries Free,' Have More Babies to Boost Economy." *Reuters Online*. Published July 10, 2019. https://www.reuters.com/article/us-tanzania-politics/president-urges-tanzanias-women-to-set-ovaries-free-have-more-babies-to-boost-economy-idUSKCN1U51AZ.

Ngware, Suleiman. 2005. "Final Report, Strategic Studies on Corruption: Corruption in Local Authorities in Tanzania." Institute of Development Studies, University of Dar es Salaam.

Nichols, Michelle, and Mason, Jeff. 2018. "Some 129 Countries Sign Up to Trump's Pledge at U.N. to Fight Drugs." *Reuters Online*. Published Online September 24, 2018. https://www.reuters.com/article/us-usa-un-trump/some-129-countries-sign-up-to-trumps-pledge-at-u-n-to-fight-drugs-idUSKCN1M41LH.

Nieburg, Phillip, and Carty, Lisa. 2011. "HIV Prevention Among Injection Drug Users in Kenya and Tanzania: New Opportunities for Progress." Centre for Strategic and International Studies.

Nixon, Richard. 1971. "Special Message to the Congress on Drug Abuse Prevention and Control." Online by Gerhard Peters and John T. Woolley, The American Presidency Project. http://www.presidency.ucsb.edu/ws/?pid=3048.

Nolen, Stephanie. 2018. "Canada Signs on to U.S.-Led Renewal of War on Drugs." *The Globe and Mail*. Published Online September 25, 2018. https://www.theglobeandmail.com/world/article-canada-signs-on-to-us-led-renewal-of-war-on-drugs/.

Norbrook, Nicholas. 2019. "Is Magufuli's Economic Nationalism Working?' *The Africa Report*. Published Online May 9, 2019. https://www.theafricareport.com/12725/is-magufulis-economic-nationalism-working/.

Nord, Roger, Dunn, David, Sobolev, Yuri, Hajdenberg, Alejandro, Hobdari, Niko, Maziad, Samar and Roudet, Stephane. 2009. "Tanzania: The Story of an African Transition." The International Monetary Fund, IMF Multimedia Services.

Norwegian Agency for Development Cooperation. 2011. "Joint Evaluation of Support to Anti-Corruption Efforts: Tanzania Country Report." *Norad Report 6/2011 – Study*.

Nyambura-Mwaura, Helen. 2019. "Tanzania Blocks IMF Report Release as Economic Growth Slows." *Bloomberg*. Published Online April 18, 2019. https://www.bloomberg.com/news/articles/2019-04-18/tanzania-blocks-international-monetary-fund-report-publication.

Oakford, Samuel. 2016. "How Russia Became the New Global Leader in the War on Drugs." *Vice News*. Published Online April 18, 2016. https://www.vice.com/en_us/article/bjk3b4/how-russia-became-the-new-global-leader-in-the-war-on-drugs-ungass.

OECD Data – Aid to Africa, 2000–2016.

O'Gorman, Melanie. 2012. "Why the CCM Won't Lose: The Roots of Single-Party Dominance in Tanzania." *Journal of Contemporary African Studies*, 30(2), pp. 313–333.

Okoth, Brian. 2015. "Tanzanian Singer Ray C Tears Painfully After Being Denied Drug Which Treats Heroin Addiction." *Entertainment News*.https://www.sde.co.ke/article/2000165519/tanzanian-singer-ray-c-tears-painfully-after-being-denied-drug-which-treats-heroin-addiction.

Otu, Smart E. 2011. "A Nation at Crossroads: Debating South Africa's War on Drug Policy." *Nordic Studies on Alcohol and Drugs*, 28(4), pp. 379–388.

Paget, Dan. 2017a. "John Magufuli Has Changed Tanzania in Just Two Years as President." *Quartz*, Academic One File. http://link.galegroup.com/apps/doc/A513761628/AONE?u=otta77973&sid=AONE&xid=8d8269bd. Accessed May 17, 2018.

Paget, Dan. 2017b. "Tanzania: Shrinking Space and Opposition Protest." *Journal of Democracy*, 28(3), pp. 153–167.

Paget, Dan. 2020. "Again, Making Tanzania Great; Magufuli's Restorationist Developmental Nationalism." *Democratization*, 27(7), pp. 1240–1260.

Paget, Dan. 2021. "Mistaken for Populism: Magufuli, Ambiguity and Elitist Plebeianism in Tanzania." *Journal of Political Ideologies*, 26(2), pp. 1–21.

Paoli, Letizia, Greenfield, Victoria A., and Reuter, Peter. 2009. *The World Heroin Market: Can Supply Be Cut?* New York: Oxford University Press Inc.

Paoli, Leitzia, Greenfield, Victoria A., and Reuter, Peter. 2012. "Change is Possible: The History of the International Drug Control Regime and Implications for Future Policymaking." *Substance Use & Misuse*, 47(8–9), pp. 923–935.

Patten, Daniel. 2017. "The Mass Incarceration of Nations and the Global War on Drugs: Comparing the United States' Domestic and Foreign Drug Policies." *Social Justice*, 43(1), pp. 85–94.

Pedersen, Jarle, Klepp, Ingun, and Mauly, Suleiman. 2019. "Drug Addiction and Recovery in Tanzania." Volda University Research Proposal. https://www.hivolda.no/forsking/forskingsgrupper-0/drug-addiction-and-recovery-tanzania.

Pembleton, Matthew. 2016. "Imagining a Global Sovereignty: U.S. Counternarcotic Operations in Istanbul During the Early Cold War and the Origins of the Foreign "War on Drugs." *Journal of Cold War Studies*, 18(2), pp. 28–63.

PEPFAR. 2017a. "PEPFAR Tanzania Implementing Partner COP 2017 Out-Brief." *The United States President's Emergency Plan for AIDS Relief*. Presentation May 18, 2017.

PEPFAR. 2017b. "Tanzania Country Operational Plan COP 2017: Strategic Direction Summary." *The United States President's Emergency Plan for AIDS Relief*. Published March 2, 2017.

PEPFAR. 2018a. "PEPFAR 2018 Country Operational Plan Guidance for Standard Process Countries." *The United States President's Emergency Plan for AIDS Relief*.

PEPFAR. 2018b. "Tanzania Country Operational Plan COP 2018: Strategic Direction Summary." *The United States President's Emergency Plan for AIDS Relief*. Published April 17, 2018.

PEPFAR. 2019. "Tanzania Country Operational Plan COP 2019: Strategic Direction Summary." *The United States President's Emergency Plan for AIDS Relief*. Published May 10, 2019.

Phelan, Maria, Nougier, Marie, and Bridge, Jamie. 2013. "HIV Prevention Among People Who Use Drugs in East Africa." *International Drug Policy Consortium, Briefing Paper*, pp. 1–11.

Plokhii, Olesia. 2014. "Canada Opposes 'Harm Reduction' in UN Drug Talks, NGO Alleges." *iPolitics*. Published Monday, February 3, 2014. http://ipolitics.ca/2014/02/03/canada-opposes-harm-reduction-in-un-drug-talks-ngo-alleges/.

Policy Forum. 2010. "Dependency on Foreign Aid, How the Situation Could Be Saved: An Analysis of Tanzania's Budget 2010/2011." *Policy Forum, Policy Brief* 3:10.

Policy Forum. 2014. "Tanzania Governance Review 2014: The Year of 'Escrow'." *Policy Forum*.

Pommerolle, Marie-Emmanuelle. 2010. "The Extraversion of Protest: Conditions, History, and Use of the 'International' in Africa." *Review of African Political Economy*, 37(125), pp. 263–279.

Rahman, Kaunain. 2019. "Overview of Corruption and Anti-Corruption in Tanzania." *Transparency International Anti-Corruption Helpdesk.* A Publication of Transparency International. Published Online September 30, 2019.

Ratcliffe, Rebecca. 2018. "'No Need for Birth Control': Tanzanian President's Views Cause Outrage." *The Guardian.* Published September 11, 2018. https://www.theguardian.com/global-development/2018/sep/11/no-need-for-birth-control-tanzanian-presidents-views-cause-outrage.

Ratliff, Eric, Kaduri, Pamela, Masao, Frank, Mbwambo, Jessie, and McCurdy, Sheryl. 2016. "Harm Reduction as a Complex Adaptive System: A Dynamic Framework for Analyzing Tanzanian Policies Concerning Heroin Use." *International Journal of Drug Policy*, 30, pp. 7–16.

Rawson, Richard, Woody, George, Kresina, Thomas, and Gust, Steven. 2014. "The Globalization of Addiction Research: Capacity-Building Mechanisms and Selected Examples." *Harvard Review of Psychiatry*, 23(2), pp. 147–156.

Regilme, Salvador Santino. 2020. "Visions of Peace Amidst a Human Rights Crisis: War on Drugs in Colombia and the Philippines." *Journal of Global Security Studies*, 10, pp. 1–19.

Reid, Savanna R. 2009. "Injection Drug Use, Unsafe Medical Injections, and HIV in Africa: A Systematic Review." *Harm Reduction Journal*, 6(24), pp. 1–11.

Reiss, Suzanna. 2010. "Beyond Supply and Demand: Obama's Drug Wars in Latin America." *NACLA Report on the Americas*, pp. 27–38.

Reuters Online. 2017a. "Tanzanian President Tells Security Forces to Target Drug Traffickers." *Reuters Online News Service.* Published February 6, 2017. http://www.reuters.com/article/us-tanzania-drugs-idUSKBN15L1QU?il=0.

Reuters Online. 2017b. "U.S. Pledges $526 Million Aid in 2017 to Tanzania to Fight AIDS." Published May 18, 2017. https://www.reuters.com/article/us-tanzania-aid-usa/u-s-pledges-526-million-aid-in-2017-to-tanzania-to-fight-aids-idUSKCN18E1EL.

Reuters Online. 2018. "Popular Tanzanian Musician Arrested in Latest Internet Crackdown." *Reurters.* Published Online April 19, 2018. https://www.standardmedia.co.ke/business/article/2001277481/internet-censorship-in-tanzania.

Rhodes, Tim. 2018. "The Becoming of Methadone in Kenya: How an Intervention's Implementation Constitutes Recovery Potential." *Social Science & Medicine*, 201, pp. 71–79.

Rhodes, Tim, and Abdool, Reychad. 2016. "Editorial: Drug Harms and Drug Policies in Sub-Saharan Africa: Implementation Science and HIV Epidemics." *International Journal of Drug Policy*, 30, pp. 1–6.

Rhodes, Tim, Rance, Jake, Fraser, Suzanne, and Treloar, Carla. 2017. "The Intimate Relationship as a Site of Social Protection: Partnerships Between People Who Inject Drugs." *Social Science & Medicine*, 180, pp. 125–134.

Rhodes, Tim, Stevens, Alex, Ritter, Alison, and Decorte, Tom. 2016. "Editorial: Advancing the Science, Methods and Practices of Drug Policy Research." *International Journal of Drug Policy*, 31, pp. 1–3.

Richardson, Kataisee. 2018. "Tanzania's TB/HIV Funding Request to the Global Fund Yields Three Grants." *Aidspan: Independent Observer of the Global Fund.* Published Online March 6, 2018. www.aidspan.org/gfo_article/tanzanias-tbhiv-funding-request-global-fund-yields-three-grants.

Roberts, Bryan, and Chen, Yu. 2013. "Drugs, Violence and the State." *Annual Review of Sociology,* 39, pp. 105–125.

Rose, Sarah, and Madan Kellar, Janeen. 2019. "With Budget Cuts Looming Again, Can PEPFAR Keep the Gas on Its Acceleration Strategy?" *The Center for Global Development.* Published Online March 19, 2019.

Rotberg, Robert. 2016. "The War on Drugs Is Fuelling Islamist Terrorism." *Newsweek Online*. Published February 17, 2016. http://www.newsweek.com/war-drugs-fueling-islamist-terrorism-427716.

Russian-African Anti-Drug Dialogue – The Banjul Declaration, Banjul, The Gambia July 23, 2015.

Rweyemamu, Aisia. 2018. "Tanzania Discovers New Drug Trafficking Route From Asia." *The Guardian Tanzania.* Published August 25, 2018. https://www.ippmedia.com/en/news/tanzania-discovers-new-drug-trafficking-route-asia.

Rweyemamu, Filbert. 2018. "Tanzania: Mahiga – EU Ambassador Not Expelled, But Recalled." *All Africa.* Published Online November 4, 2018. https://allafrica.com/stories/201811060087.html.

Said, Khalifa. 2018. "Gay Crackdown Fiasco in Tanzania Leaves Dar es Salaam RC Makonda Exposed." *The Citizen.* Published Online November 6, 2018. https://www.thecitizen.co.tz/news/Gay-crackdown-fiasco-in-Tanzania-leaves-Dar-es-Salaam-/1840340-4839046-13pb1y3/index.html.

Saleem, Haneefa, Mushi, D., Hassan, S., Bruce, R. D., Cooke, A., Mbwambo, J., and Lambdin, B. H. 2016. "'Can't You Initiate Me Here?': Challenges to Timely Initiation on Antiretroviral Therapy Among Methadone Clients in Dar es Salaam, Tanzania." *International Journal of Drug Policy*, 30, pp. 59–65.

Sandefur, Justin. 2018. "Tanzania Outlaws Fact-Checking, Seeks World Bank Aid to Create New Facts." *Center for Global Development.* Published Online September 28, 2018. https://www.cgdev.org/blog/tanzania-outlaws-fact-checking-seeks-world-bank-aid-create-new-facts.

Schneider, Leander. 2014. "Liberating Development? Rule and Liberation in Post-Independence Tanzania." *Journal of Contemporary African Studies*, 32(3), pp. 319–330.

Security Assistance Monitor. 2017. "U.S. Foreign Military Training Reached Records in 2015." *Center for International Policy, Report 2017.*

Seddon, Toby. 2008. "Drugs, the Informal Economy and Globalization." *International Journal of Social Economics*, 35(10), pp. 717–728.

Seddon, Toby. 2010. *A History of Drugs: Drugs and Freedom in the Liberal Age.* New York: Routledge Publishing.

Shaban, Abdur Rahman Alfa Shaban. 2017. "Even If My Wife Does Narcotics, Arrest Her – Tanzanian President Orders." *Africa News.* Published Online July 2, 2017. https://www.africanews.com/2017/02/07/even-if-my-wife-does-narcotics-arrest-her-tanzanian-president-orders//.

Shekighenda, Lydia. 2016. "Government Urges End to Donor Dependence as MCC Cancels Aid." *The Guardian.* Published March 30, 2016. https://www.awaazmagazine.com/volume-13-issue-1/other-articles/item/781-government-urges-end-to-donor-dependence-as-mcc-cancels-aid.

Shiundu, Linda. 2018. "Magufuli Moves Hearts With Humble Past, Claims He Had No Suit or Rings for His Wedding." *TUKO.* Published Online November 6, 2018. https://www.tuko.co.ke/290697-magufuli-moves-hearts-humble-claims-suit-rings-wedding.html#290697.

Shivji, Issa. 2021. "Tanzania: The Dialectics of Maguphilia and Maguphobia." *The Elephant.* Published June 11, 2021. https://www.theelephant.info/long-reads/2021/06/11/tanzania-the-dialectics-of-maguphilia-and-maguphobia/.

Sieff, Kevin. 2016. "Tanzania Suspends U.S.-Funded AIDS Programs in a New Crackdown on Gays." *The Washington Post.* Published November 23, 2016. https://www.theeastafrican.co.ke/news/ea/Tanzania-not-to-publish-gays/4552908-3830782-12516gm/index.html.

Singer, Merrill. 2008a. *Drugging the Poor: Legal and Illegal Drugs and Social Inequality.* Illinois: Waveland Press Inc.

Singer, Merrill. 2008b. "Drugs and Development: The Global Impact of Drug Use and Trafficking on Social and Economic Development." *International Journal of Drug Policy*, 19, pp. 467–478.

Singer, Merrill. 2012. "Anthropology and Addiction: An Historical Review." *Addiction*, 107, pp. 1747–1755.

Singer, Merrill, and Page, Bryan J. 2014. *The Social Value of Drug Addicts: Uses of the Useless.* New York: Routledge Publishing.

Sixpence, Leyson. 2017. "Tanzania: Who is Yusuf Manji?" *The Citizen.* Published February 23, 2017. https://allafrica.com/stories/201702230510.html.

Smye, Victoria, Browne, Annette, Varcoe, Colleen, and Josewski, Viviane. 2011. "Harm Reduction, Methadone Maintenance Treatment and the Root Causes of Health and Social Inequities: An Intersectional Lens in the Canadian Context." *Harm Reduction Journal*, 8(17), pp. 1–12.

States News Service. 2019. "11 Sentenced in Transnational Heroin Trafficking Ring." *States News Service.* Published Online August 9, 2019. Gale Academic Onefile.

https://link.gale.com/apps/doc/A596026268/AONE?u=otta77973&sid=AONE&xid=c97b888a.

Stevens, Alex. 2011. *Drugs, Crime and Public Health: The Political Economy of Drug Policy*. New York: Routledge Publishing.

Strang, John, Babor, Thomas, Caulkins, Jonathan, Fischer, Benedikt, Foxcroft, David, and Humphreys, Keith. 2012. "Drug Policy and the Public Good: Evidence for Effective Interventions." *The Lancet*, 379, pp. 71–81.

Syvertsen, Jennifer, Ohaga, Spala, Agot, Kawango, Dimova, Margarita, Guise, Andy, Rhodes, Tim, and Wagner, Karla. 2016. "An Ethnographic Exploration of Drug Markets in Kisumu, Kenya." *International Journal of Drug Policy*, 30, pp. 82–90.

Tanzania Daily News. 2016. "Tanzania: Khat Chewers Court Both Prosecution, Health Risks." *Tanzania Daily News, Dar es Salaam*. Published June 13, 2016. https://allafrica.com/stories/201606130159.html.

Tanzania Daily News. 2018. "Tanzania: We Should Join Forces in the Anti-Drugs Battle." *Tanzania Daily News, Dar es Salaam*. Published September 19, 2018. https://allafrica.com/stories/201809190658.html.

The Africa Group. 2015. "The Africa Group Contribution for the UNGASS Outcome Document." Board Tasked by the Commission on Narcotic Drugs With Preparations for UNGASS 2016, A.288/15.

The Daily Nation. 2016. "Zanzibar President Declared Winner as Election Boycotted." *Daily Nation*. Published March 22, 2016. https://www.nation.co.ke/news/africa/Zanzibar-president-declared-winner-as-election-boycotted/1066-3128156-eyvnpg/index.html.

The Daily Nation. 2018. "World Bank, EU Cut Tanzania Aid After Rights Crackdown." *The Daily Nation*. Published Online December 30, 2018. https://www.nation.co.ke/news/africa/Donors-cut-aid-to-Tanzania-after-rights-crackdown/1066-4914998-boepn6/index.html.

The Daily News. 2017. "Let's Join Hands, Frown at and Act Against Homosexuality, Prostitution." *The Daily News*. Published Online September 17, 2017. https://dailynews.co.tz/news/let-s-join-hands-frown-at-and-act-against-homosexuality-prostitution.aspx.

The Daily News. 2018a. "State to Help Treat Drug Addicts." *The Daily News*. Published Online May 24, 2017. https://www.dailynews.co.tz/news/state-at-help-treat-drug-addicts.aspx.

The Daily News. 2018b. "Tanzania: We Should Join Forces in the Anti-Drugs Battle." *The Daily News*. Published Online September 19, 2018. https://allafrica.com/stories/201809190658.html.

The East African. 2018. "Tanzania Government Denounces Makonda's Anti-Gay Clampdown." *The East African*. Published Online November 5, 2018. https://www.theeastafrican.co.ke/news/ea/Tanzania-government-denounces-Makonda-anti-gay-clampdown/4552908-4837714-m0w84v/index.html.

The Economist. 2018a. "Falling into Dictatorship; Tanzania." p. 46 Academic OneFile. http://link.galegroup.com/apps/doc/A531093040/AONE?u=otta77973&sid=AONE&xid=47db46e0. Accessed May 17, 2018.

The Economist. 2018b. "John Magufuli is Fostering a Climate of Fear in Tanzania." *The Economist.* Published Online November 6, 2018. https://www.economist.com/middle-east-and-africa/2018/11/06/john-magufuli-is-fostering-a-climate-of-fear-in-tanzania.

The Economist. 2019. "Heroin Highways: Drugs in Africa." p. 38 Academic OneFile. http://link.galegroup.com/apps/doc/A571863465/AONE?u=otta77973&sid=AONE&xid=d8bf1ba2.

The Famagusta Gazette. 2017. "Magufuli Opens All-Out War on Drugs in Tanzania." *Famagusta Gazette Online Archives.* Published Online February 13, 2017. http://famagusta-gazette.com/magufuli-opens-allout-war-on-drugs-in-tanzania-p38533-69.htm.

The President's Emergency Fund for AIDS (PEPFAR) and the Centres for Disease Control and Prevention (CDC). 2018. "Tanzania HIV Impact Survey (THIS): A Population Based HIV Impact Assessment 2016–2017." PEPFAR Population Based HIV Impact Assessment (PHIA). Published December 2018.

The United Republic of Tanzania. Chapter 95, 1996 The Drugs and Prevention of Illicit Traffic in Drugs Act.

The United Republic of Tanzania. The Drug Control and Enforcement Act, 2015.

The United Republic of Tanzania Ministry of Health, Community Development, Gender, Elderly and Children. 2017a. "Statement by the Minister for Health, Community Development, Gender, Elderly and Children Hon. Ummy Mwalimu (MP) Regarding HIV and AIDS Service Delivery to Key and Vulnerable Population Groups and Its Implementation: 16th February, 2017."

The United Republic of Tanzania Ministry of Health, Community Development, Gender, Elderly and Children. 2017b. "National Guidelines for the Management of HIV and AIDS, Sixth Edition October 2017." Published 2017.

The United Republic of Tanzania Ministry of Health, Community Development, Gender, Elderly and Children. 2017c. "The National Health Policy 2017." Sixth Draft Version, Tuesday October 24, 2017.

The United Republic of Tanzania Ministry of Health and Social Welfare, Tanzania Mainland. 2014. "National Guideline for Comprehensive Package of HIV Interventions for Key Populations September 2014." A Publication of the Ministry of Health and Social Welfare and the National AIDS Control Programme (NACP).

Throup, David. 2016. "The Political Crisis in Zanzibar." *Commentary – The Center for Strategic and International Studies (CSIS).* Published Online March 18, 2016. https://www.csis.org/analysis/political-crisis-zanzibar.

Tiberio, J., Laurent, Y. I., Ndayongeje, J., Msami, A., Welty, S., Ngonyani, A., Mwankemwa, S., Makumbuli, M., McFarland, W., and Morris, M. D. 2018. "Context and Characteristics of Illicit Drug Use in Coastal and Interior Tanzania." *International Journal of Drug Policy*, 51, pp. 20–26.

Tripp, Aili Mari. 2012. "Working Paper No. 2012/37: Donor Assistance and Political Reform in Tanzania." United Nations University.

Turse, Nick. 2018. "Drug Wars, Missing Money and a Phantom $500 Million." *Salon.* Published Online February 10, 2018. https://www.salon.com/2018/02/10/drug-wars-missing-money-and-a-phantom-500-million_partner/.

United Nations. 1961. "Single Convention on Narcotic Drugs, 1961 (As Amended by the 1972 Protocol Amending the Single Convention on Narcotic Drugs, 1961." A Publication of the United Nations.

United Nations. 1971. "Convention on Psychotropic Substances, 1971." A Publication of the United Nations.

United Nations. 1988. "Convention Against Illicit Traffic in Narcotic Drugs and Psychotropic Substances." *International Legal Materials*, 28(2), pp. 493–526.

United Nations Children's Fund (UNICEF). 2018a. "Health Budget Brief 2018: Tanzania." A Publication of UNICEF.

United Nations Children's Fund (UNICEF). 2018b. "HIV and AIDS Budget Brief 2018: Tanzania." A Publication of UNICEF.

United Nations Development Programme. 2016. *Human Development Report 2016: Human Development for Everyone.* New York: United Nations Development Programme.

United Nations Development Programme. 2018. "Human Development Report 2018: Human Development for Everyone." Prepared by the United Nations Development Programme, 2018.

United Nations General Assembly Special Session. 2016. *Our Joint Commitment to Effectively Addressing and Countering the World Drug Problem, A/RES/S-30/1*, April 19, 2016. undocs.org/A/RES/S-30/1.

United Nations Office on Drugs and Crime. 2011. *Estimating Illicit Financial Flows Resulting From Drug Trafficking and Other Transnational Organized Crimes – Research Report.* Vienna: UNODC.

United Nations Office on Drugs and Crime. 2016. *The Afghan Opiate Trade and Africa – A Baseline Assessment.* Vienna: UNODC.

United States Africa Command. 2018. "2018 Posture Statement." US AFRICOM 2018.

United States Bureau of International Narcotics and Law Enforcement Affairs. 2019. "Tanzania Summary – United States Department of State." https://www.state.gov/bureau-of-international-narcotics-and-law-enforcement-affairs-work-by-country/tanzania-summary/.

United States Department of Justice. 2015. "Drugs of Abuse, 2015 Edition: A DEA Resource Guide." A Publication of the United States Drug Enforcement Administration.

United States Department of State. 2014. "International Narcotics Control Strategy Report – Kenya 2014." A Publication of United States Department of State – Bureau for International Narcotics and Law Enforcement Affairs. https://www.state.gov/j/inl/rls/nrcrpt/2015/vol1/238969.htm.

United States Department of State. 2015a. "International Narcotics Control Strategy Report – Tanzania 2015." A Publication of United States Department of State – Bureau for International Narcotics and Law Enforcement Affairs. https://www.state.gov/j/inl/rls/nrcrpt/2015/vol1/239016.htm.

United States Department of State. 2015b. "Money Laundering and Financial Crimes Country Database." A Publication of the United States Department of State – Bureau for International Narcotics and Law Enforcement Affairs, June 2015.

United States Department of State. 2016. "Diplomacy in Action: Tanzania Bureau of International Narcotics and Law Enforcement Affairs." Part of the International Narcotics Control Strategy Report. http://www.state.gov/j/inl/rls/nrcrpt/2016/index.htm.

United States Department of State. 2017. "Diplomacy in Action: Trans-Africa Security: Combatting Illicit Trafficking and Organized Crime in Africa." Publication of the United States Department of State – Bureau for International Narcotics and Law Enforcement Affairs, May 12, 2017.

United States Embassy in Tanzania. 2018. "United States Renews Support to the Tanzanian People to Combat HIV/AIDS." https://tz.usembassy.gov/united-states-renews-support-tanzanian-people-combat-hivaids/.

United States Government Accountability Office. 2017. "Counternarcotics – Overview of U.S. Efforts in the Western Hemisphere." Report to the Ranking Member, Committee on Foreign Affairs, House of Representatives, GAO-18-10, October 2017.

USAID. 2013. "The Development Response to Drug Trafficking in Africa: A Programming Guide." Report Prepared by the United States Agency for International Development by Brooke Stearns Lawson, April 2013.

USAID. 2016. "Health Financing Profile: Tanzania, May 2016." Report Prepared by the United States Agency for International Development, 2016.

USAID. 2018. "Fiscal Year 2018 USAID Development and Humanitarian Assistance Budget." Report Prepared by the United States Agency for International Development, 2018.

Valenzuela, Cesar Martinez. 2012. "The "War on Drugs" and the "New Strategy": Identity Constructions of the United States, U.S. Drug Users and Mexico." *Mexican Law Review*, 5(2), pp. 245–275.

Valleriani, Jenna, and MacPherson, Donald. 2015. "Why Canada is No Longer a Leader in Global Drug Policy." *The Globe and Mail Online.* Published February 27, 2015. http://www.theglobeandmail.com/opinion/why-canada-is-no-longer-a-leader-in-global-drug-policy/article23225460/.

Wainana, Binyavanga. 2005. "How to Write About Africa." *Granta*, 92. Re-Published Online May 2, 2019.

Waititu, Ernest. 2018. "Tanzania and Global Fund Sign New Grants to Accelerate End of Epidemics." News and Stories, The Global Fund, January 30, 2018. https://www.theglobalfund.org/en/news/2018-01-30-tanzania-and-global-fund-sign-new-grants-to-accelerate-end-of-epidemics/.

Wako, Amina. 2019. "Tanzanian Opposition Leader Zitto Kabwe Arrested, Banned From Foreign Travel." *Nairobi News*, June 13, 2019. https://allafrica.com/stories/201906130158.html.

Warioba, Joseph. 1997. "Corruption and the State: The Warioba Report." *Soundings*, 7, pp. 198–208.

Wendt, Alexander. 1995. "Constructing International Politics." *International Security*, 20(1), pp. 71–81.

Wendt, Alexander. 2000. "On the Via Media: A Response to Critics." *Review of International Studies*, 26, pp. 165–180.

Wexler, Alexandra. 2018. "Tanzania's President Got Off to a Strong Start, Then Turned into a Strongman." *The Wall Street Journal*. Published Online June 6, 2018. https://www.wsj.com/articles/tanzanias-president-got-off-to-a-strong-start-then-turned-into-a-strongman-1528277400.

White, Daniel Linn. 2018. "International Drug Reform: Medicalized Harm Reduction, Cannabis and the Global Legislative Reality." *Journal of Drug Policy Analysis*, 11(2), pp. 1–7.

Wild, Joshua. 2013. "Epic Failure: The Uncomfortable Truth About the United States' Role in the Failure of the Global War on Drugs and How It Is Going to Fix It." *Suffolk Transnational Law Review*, 36(2), pp. 423–446.

Williams, Stewart, and Warf, Barney. 2016. "Drugs, Law, People, Place and the State: Ongoing Regulation, Resistance and Change." *Space and Polity*, 20(1), pp. 1–9.

Wilson, Tom, and Mohammed, Omar. 2017. "Surprise, You Owe Tanzania $300 Million and 50% of What Your Gold Mine Makes." *Financial Post*. Published Online October 20, 2017. http://business.financialpost.com/commodities/barrick-brokered-tanzania-pact-leaves-acacia-mining-in-the-dark.

Windle, James. 2013. "How the East Influenced Drug Prohibition." *The International History Review*, 35(5), pp. 1185–1199.

Windle, James. 2015. "A Slow March From Social Evil to Harm Reduction: Drugs and Drug Policy in Vietnam." *Journal of Drug Policy Analysis*, 20150011.

Wodak, Alex. 2014. "The Abject Failure of Drug Prohibition." *Australian & New Zealand Journal of Criminology*, 47(2), pp. 190–201.

Wodak, Alex. 2018. "From Failed Global Drug Prohibition to Regulating the Drug Market." *Addiction*, 113, pp. 1225–1226.

Wodak, Alex, Sarkar, Swarup, and Mesquita, Fabio. 2004. "The Globalization of Drug Injecting: Editorial." *Addiction*, 99, pp. 799–801.

World Bank Group. 2015. "Tanzania Mainland Poverty Assessment." *The World Bank*.

World Health Organization. 2013. "New Treatment Gives Hope to East Africa's Drug Users." *Bulletin of the World Health Organization*, 91, pp. 89–90.

World Health Organization. 2016a. *Definitions of Key Terms – Consolidated Guidelines on HIV Prevention, Diagnosis, Treatment and Care for Key Populations*. Geneva: World Health Organization.

World Health Organization. 2016b. "HIV Prevention, Diagnosis, Treatment and Care for Key Populations – Consolidated Guidelines." *World Health Organization Policy Brief*.

Wuyts, Marc, Mushi, Desmond, and Kida, Tausi. 2017. "Aid Dependency in Financing the Space for Social Provisioning in Tanzania: A Macroeconomic Perspective." THDR 2017: Background Paper No. 5, ESRF Discussion Paper 73.

Wyler, Liana Sun, and Cook, Nicolas. 2010. "Illegal Drug Trade in Africa: Trends and U.S. Policy." *CRS Report for Congress*, pp. 1–56.

Xinhua News Service. 2016. "Tanzania's Newly Appointed Minister Declares War Against Drug Traffickers." *Xinhua News Online*. Published June 14, 2016. http://news.xinhuanet.com/english/2016-06/14/c_135433705.htm.

Xinhua News Service. 2017. "Tanzania Strengthens Anti-Drugs Body." *Xinhua News Service*. Published Online November 18, 2017. http://www.xinhuanet.com/english/2017-11/18/c_136761178.htm.

Xinhua News Service. 2018a. "Tanzania PM Warns Against Surging Drug Uses in NW Regions." *Xinhua News Online*. Published Online February 22, 2018. http://www.xinhuanet.com/english/2018-02/22/c_136989674.htm.

Xinhua News Service. 2018b. "Tanzania Urges African Countries to Fight Against Illicit Drugs Trafficking." *Xinhua News Online*. Published September 18, 2018. http://www.china.org.cn/world/Off_the_Wire/2018-09/18/content_63557165.htm.

Xinhua News Service. 2019. "Tanzanian President Vows to Carry On With Founding Father's Legacy." *Xinhua News Online*. Published Online October 15, 2018. www.xinhuanet.com/english/2018-10/15/c_137532768.htm.

Xulin, Tan, Annabel, Kapiga, Saidi, Khoshnood, Kaveh, and Bruce, Douglas R. 2015. "Epidemiology of Drug Use and HIV-Related Risk Behaviors Among People Who Inject Drugs in Mwanza, Tanzania." *PLoS One*, 10(12), pp. 1–15.

Yee, Amy. 2019. "The Darker Side of Paradise: Heroin Addiction in Zanzibar." *The Lancet*, 394, pp. 721–722.

Yussuf, Issa. 2016. "Tanzania: Need to Intensify War on Drug Abuse." *AllAfrica Online*. Published June 22, 2016. http://allafrica.com/stories/201606220634.html.

Yusuph, Kambuga, and Negret, Ion. 2016. "Adolescents and Drug Abuse in Tanzania: History and Evolution." *Advances in Research*, 7(2), pp. 1–10.

Zondi, Siphamandla. 2013. "Common Positions as African Agency in International Negotiations." In Brown, William, and Harman, Sophie, eds. *African Agency in International Politics*. London: Routledge Publishing, pp. 19–34.

Index

About the Author

Dane Degenstein has a PhD in political science from the University of Ottawa and an MSc in African studies from the University of Oxford. He has lived and worked across East Africa and has presented and written on Tanzanian politics and drug policy. This is his first book. Dane currently lives with his family in Edmonton, Alberta.

www.ingramcontent.com/pod-product-compliance
Ingram Content Group UK Ltd.
Pitfield, Milton Keynes, MK11 3LW, UK
UKHW041837031026
15587UKWH00002B/843

9 781793 654199